The Flight of the Wild Gander

Contents

Illustrations

ACKNOWLEDGMENTS FOR ILLUSTRATIONS

1. From Robert J. and Linda S. Braidwood, Edna Tulane, and Ann L. Perkins, "New Chalcolithic Material of Samarran Type and Its Implications," *Journal of Near Eastern Studies*, Vol. III, No. 1, 1944.

2. From Emma Lila Fundaburk and Mary Douglass Fundaburk Foreman, *Sun Circles and Human Hands* (Luverne, Alabama: Emma Lila Fundaburk, 1957), Plates 26 and 23.

3. After Leo Frobenius, *Monumenta Terrarum* (Frankfurt am Main: Forschungsinstitut für Kulturmorphologie, 1929), p. 309.

4. After Frobenius, *op. cit.*, p. 323.

5. After l'Abbé H. Breuil, *Four Hundred Centuries of Cave Art* (Montignac: Centre d'Études et de Documentation Préhistoriques, no date), Figure 130.

6. After Breuil, *op. cit.*, Figures 114–115. (In the datings I am following André Leroi-Gourhan, *Les Religions de la préhistoire* (Paris: Presses Universitaires de France, 1964), pp. 87–88.

7. From James Mellaart, *Çatal Hüyük: A Neolithic Town in Anatolia*, (New York: McGraw-Hill Book Company, 1967), Figure 52.

8. From Mellaart, *op. cit.*, Figure 37.

9. From Mellaart, *op. cit.*, Figures 14, 15.

10. After M. E. L. Mallowan and J. Cruikshank Rose, "Excavations at Tall Arpachiyah," *Iraq* (British School of Archaeology in Iraq), Vol. II, Part I, 1935.

11. After Franz Hančar, "Zum Problem der Venusstatuetten in eurasiatischen Jungpaläolithicum," *Prähistorische Zeitschrift* XXX–XXXI Band, 1939–1940, 1/2 Heft, Figures VII, VIII, pp. 127, 129.

12. Collection of Henry H. Getty. After Alice Getty, *The Gods of Northern Buddhism* (London: Oxford University Press, 1914), Plate XVIII a.

13. National Museum, New Delhi. After Sir John Marshall (ed.), *Mohenjo-daro and the Indus Civilization* (London: Arthur Probsthain, 1931).

14. Berlin Museum. From William Hayes Ward, *The Seal Cylinders of Western Asia* (Washington, D.C.: The Carnegie Institution of Washington, 1910), Figure 302.

15. Museum of The Hague. From Ward, *op. cit.*, Figure 389.

16. British Museum. From Ward, *op. cit.*, Figure 388.

Sketches for Figures 2, 5, 6, and 13 are by John L. Mackey.
Sketches for Figures 10 and 12 are by Al Burkhardt.

The Flight of the Wild Gander

Introduction

The writing of the following chapters occupied, or rather punctuated, a period of twenty-four years, during the whole course of which I was circling, and from many quarters striving to interpret, the mystery of mythology; to lift the veil, so to say, of that Goddess of the ancient temple of Saïs who could say with truth, and can say today, and will say to the end of time, οὐδεὶς ἐμὸν πέπλον ἀνεῖλε, "no one has lifted my veil."

The first chapter, "The Fairy Tale," was published in 1944 as a Commentary to the Pantheon edition of *Grimm's Fairy Tales*, and is intended here to introduce the whole problem of the fascination, sources, preservation, and interpretation of those dreamlike images and narratives that reappear in more impressive dress in the holy scriptures both of the Orient and of the Occident, as well as in our higher secular arts. In the second chapter, "Bios and Mythos," which deals with the pedagogical (actually biological) function and necessity both of mythology and of the rites through which its images are displayed and psychologically assimilated, I have set forth my basic thesis—that myths are a function of nature as well as of culture, and as necessary to the balanced maturation of the human psyche as is nourishment to the body; while in the following chapter, "Primitive Man as Metaphysician," I have revived a formula, first proposed by Kant, for the release of the archetypal symbolic images of mythic thought from their various local matrices of culturally conditioned references and "meaning," so that, viewed apart from the uses to which they have been applied in the social provinces of human life, they may be recognized in themselves as *natural* phenomena, opening backward to mystery—like trees, like hills, or like mountain streams—antecedent (like the wood of trees) to the "meanings" that have been given them and the uses to which they have been put.

What is the "meaning" of a tree? of a butterfly? of the birth of a child? or of the universe? What is the "meaning" of the song of a rushing stream? Such wonders simply *are*. They are antecedent to meaning, though "meanings" may be read into them. They are, as the Buddhists say, *tathāgata*, "thus come," the Buddha himself being known as the Tathagata, "The One Thus Come"; and all things, we are told, are "Buddha things." So, likewise, are the images of myth, which open like flowers to the conscious mind's amazement and may then be searched to the root for "meaning," as well as arranged to serve practical ends.

That dream and vision have been, everywhere and forever, the chief creative and shaping powers of myth is generally recognized today by the leading students of mythic lore; and the fairy tale is of the same species. "In the best interpreted dreams," wrote Freud, "we often have to leave one passage in obscurity because we observe during the interpretation that we have here a tangle of dream-thoughts which cannot be unravelled, and which furnishes no fresh contribution to the dream-content. This, then, is the keystone of the dream, the point at which it ascends into the unknown. For the dream-thoughts which we encounter during the interpretation commonly have no termination, but run in all directions into the netlike entanglement of our intellecual world. It is from some denser part of this fabric that the dream-wish then arises, like the mushroom from its mycelium." [1] *

C. G. Jung discoursed in the same vein: "A dream, like every element in the psychic structure, is a resultant of the total psyche. Hence we may expect to find in dreams everything that has ever been of significance in the life of human-

---

* Numbered reference notes begin on page 227.

ity. Just as human life is not limited to this or that fundamental instinct, but builds itself up from a multiplicity of instincts, needs, desires, and physical and psychic conditions, etc., so the dream cannot be explained by this or that element in it, however beguilingly simple such an explanation may appear to be. We can be certain that it is incorrect, because no simple theory of instinct will ever be capable of grasping the human psyche, that mighty and mysterious thing, nor, consequently, its exponent, the dream. In order to do anything like justice to dreams, we need an interpretive equipment that must be laboriously fitted together from all branches of the humane sciences." [2]

Jung developed the idea of the *compensatory* and *projecting, guiding* function of dream, and the same can be told of myth. "As a rule," he remarked, "the unconscious content contrasts strikingly with the conscious material, particularly when the conscious attitude tends too exclusively in a direction that would threaten the vital needs of the individual. The more one-sided his conscious attitude is, and the further it deviates from the optimum, the greater becomes the possibility that vivid dreams with a strongly contrasting but purposive content will appear as an expression of the self-regulation of the psyche." He further compared this compensatory action of the psyche to that of the body throwing off disease. "Just as the body reacts purposively to injuries or infections or any abnormal conditions, so the psychic functions react to unnatural or dangerous disturbances with purposive defence-mechanisms." [3] And to that extent and end, of course, the dream, the vision or nightmare, must be said indeed to have "meaning": such a "meaning" as that of a sneeze, the festering of an infected wound, or a fever.

The teachings of a prophet will have a "meaning" of this kind for a whole society: to set and retain it on its path of health. However, the guiding mythic symbols—the notions of divinity, rites of praise or of atonement, festivals of accord, etc.—inspired or renewed by such teachings will have a salutary effect only so long as the circumstance prevails, or threatens to prevail, to which the teachings were addressed. A shift, for example, from a hunting to a pastoral age, or from pastoral to industrial, and the myths also will change—unless artificially retained, in which case they will themselves have become the agents of a disease to the cure of which new visions will arise, new prophecies, new prophets, and new gods.

The common tendency today to read the word "myth" as meaning "untruth" is almost certainly a symptom of the incredibility and consequent inefficacy of our own outdated mythic teachings, both of the Old Testament and of the New: the Fall of Adam and Eve, Tablets of the Law, Fires of Hell, Second Coming of the Savior, etc.; and not only of those archaic religious Testaments, but also of the various, more modern, secular "Utopiates" (let us call them) that are being offered today in their place. Living myths are not mistaken notions, and they do not spring from books. They are not to be judged as true or false but as effective or ineffective, maturative or pathogenic. They are rather like enzymes, products of the body in which they work; or in homogeneous social groups, products of a body social. They are not invented but occur, and are recognized by seers, and poets, to be then cultivated and employed as catalysts of spiritual (i.e., psychological) well-being. And so, finally, neither a stale and overdue nor a contrived, plastic mythology will serve; neither priest nor sociologist takes the place of the poet-seer—which, however, is what we all are in our dreams, though when we wake we may again render only prose. "Just as those not knowing the place," we read in the Chandogya Upanishad, "might walk time and again over a hidden treasure of gold without discovering it, so do all creatures here go, day by day, into that world of unconditioned being-consciousness-and-bliss without discovering it, because held astray by false thoughts." [4]

Not the promise of any given myth or the claims of any inherited god but the living source of all myths and of all the gods and their worlds is what today is holy and to be sought; and in the following pages I have sought for it—while aware

nevertheless of the irony of such questing, inherent in the aim
itself. For, as declared in the Kena Upanishad:

> There the eye goes not;
> Speech goes not, nor the mind.
> We know not, we understand not
> How one might teach it.
>
> To whom It is unknown, to him It is known;
> The one knowing, knows It not:
> Understood not by those that understand,
> It is understood by those understanding not.[5]

And in Lao-tzu's *Tao Te Ching;*

> Those who know do not speak;
> Those who speak do not know.[6]

Chapters II and III, then, of this present work, treat,
as said, of mythology as a production of nature, serving, on
one hand, the biological function of fostering a wholesome
maturation of the psyche, and, on the other hand, the metaphysical, or mystagogic function of a Buddha-thing, "thus
come," *tathāgata*, opening backward to mystery. Both chapters were composed and published in honor of distinguished
friends to whose works my own are deeply indebted: "Bios
and Mythos" in 1951, for the festival volume *Psychoanalysis
and Culture*, celebrating the sixtieth birthday of Géza
Róheim; and the following chapter, "Primitive Man as Metaphysician," for the volume *Culture and History*, which appeared in 1960, in memory of the truly pioneer anthropologist Paul Radin (1883–1959).

Chapter IV, however, "Mythogenesis"—which is a largely
revised redaction of my paper read in Ascona, Switzerland,
at the annual Eranos Meeting of 1959—turns from the
natural, biological, to the cultural, historical aspect of the rise,
flowering, and decline of a mythology, treating of a single
American Indian legend and the circumstances of its origin, as
well as the personal experiences of the visionary, the old medicine man through whose memory it has been preserved.

Chapter V, "The Symbol without Meaning," was also presented first in Ascona, at the Eranos Meeting of 1957; it culminates the present series of explorations in what I have termed the "mythological dimension." To take into account certain recent findings in the archaeological field, I have had to revise the second section of Part I of this chapter; otherwise, however, the piece remains as written, when it served me as a preliminary sketch for the structuring of my four-volume history of mythological forms, *The Masks of God*.

And then, finally, in the last of the present chapters, "The Secularization of the Sacred" (which appeared in the first of what is expected to be an annual series of symposiums, *The Religious Situation: 1968*), my theme is of the present moment in its crisis of confrontation between Europe, with its heritage of respect for individual creativity, and the massive anonymities of a now mechanized, traditionally despotic Asia.

[I]

The Fairy Tale

[1]

The Work of the Brothers Grimm

Frau Katherina Viehmann (1755–1815) was about fifty-five when the young Grimm brothers discovered her. She had married in 1777 a tailor of Niederzwehren, a village near Kassel, and was now a mother and a grandmother. "This woman," Wilhelm Grimm wrote in his preface to the first edition of their second volume (1815), ". . . has a strong and pleasant face and a clear, sharp look in her eyes; in her youth she must have been beautiful. She retains fast in mind these old sagas—which talent, as she says, is not granted to everyone; for there be many that cannot keep in their heads anything at all. She recounts her stories thoughtfully, accurately, with uncommon vividness and evident delight—first quite easily, but then, if required, over again, slowly, so that with a bit of practice it is possible to take down her dictation, word for word. Much was recorded in this way, and its fidelity is unmistakable. Anyone believing that traditional materials are easily falsified and carelessly preserved, and hence cannot survive over a long period, should hear how close she always keeps to her story and how zealous she is for its accuracy; never does she alter any part in repetition, and she corrects a mistake herself, immediately she notices it. Among people who follow the old life-ways without change, attachment to inherited patterns is stronger than we, impatient for variety, can realize." * 1

* Some four years after the brothers had come to know her, she abruptly fell into poverty and sickness, and in another few months had died.

It was from such people that Jacob and Wilhelm collected, through a period of years, the materials for their book: simple folk of the farms and villages round about, and in the spinning rooms and beer halls of Kassel. Many stories were received, too, from friends. In the notes it is set down frequently, "From Dortchen Wild in Kassel," or "From Dortchen, in the garden house." Dorothea Wild—later Wilhelm's wife—supplied over a dozen of the stories. Together with her five sisters, she had been grounded in fairy lore by an old nurse, *die alte Marie.** [2] Another family were the Hassenpflugs, who had arrived with a store of tales from Hanau; † [3] still another, the von Haxthausens, who resided in Westphalia. [4] The brothers grubbed for materials also in medieval German manuscripts, and in the Folk Books and collections from the time of Luther.

The special distinction of the work of Jacob and Wilhelm Grimm (1785–1863 and 1786–1859) was its scholarly regard for the sources. Earlier collectors had felt free to manipulate folk materials; the Grimms were concerned to let the speech of the people break directly into print. Among the Romantics of the generation just preceding, folk poetry had been venerated profoundly. Novalis had pronounced the folk tale the primary and highest poetical creation of man. Schiller had written extravagantly:

> *Tiefere Bedeutung*
> *Liegt in dem Märchen meiner Kinderjahre*
> *Als in der Wahrheit, die das Leben lehrt.*‡

Sir Walter Scott had collected and studied the balladry of the Scottish border. Wordsworth had sung of the Reaper. Yet no one before the Grimms had really acquiesced in the irregulari-

---

* The Wilds were six daughters and one son, the Grimms five sons and one daughter.

† Ludwig Hassenpflug married Lotte Grimm.

‡ Deeper meaning lies in the fairy tale of my childhood than in the truth that is taught by life (*Die Piccolomini*, III. 4).

ties, the boorishness, the simplicity, of the folk tale. Anthologists had arranged, restored, and tempered; poets had built new masterpieces out of the rich raw material. But an essentially ethnographical approach no one had so much as conceived.

The remarkable fact is that the Grimm brothers never *developed* their idea; they began with it full blown, as young students hardly out of law school. Jacob, browsing in the library of their favorite professor, the jurist Friedrich Karl von Savigny, had chanced on a selection of the German Minnesingers, and almost immediately their life careers had stood before them. Two friends, Clemens Brentano and Ludwig Achim von Arnim, who in 1805 had published, in the Romantic manner, the first volume of a collection of folk songs, *Des Knaben Wunderhorn,* gave the brothers valuable encouragement. Jacob and Wilhelm assisted with the later volumes of the *Wunderhorn* and began collecting from their friends. But at the same time, they were seeking out, deciphering, and beginning to edit manuscripts from the Middle Ages. The book of fairy tales represented only a fraction of their immediate project. It would be comparable, in a way, to the popular exhibition hall of an ethnological museum: in the offices upstairs researches would be going forward which the larger public would hardly wish or know how to follow.

The program proceeded against odds. In 1806 the armies of Napoleon overran Kassel. "Those days," wrote Wilhelm, "of the collapse of all hitherto existing establishments will remain forever before my eyes. . . . The ardor with which the studies in Old German were pursued helped overcome the spiritual depression. . . . Undoubtedly the world situation and the necessity to draw into the peacefulness of scholarship contributed to the reawakening of the long forgotten literature; but not only did we seek something of consolation in the past, our hope, naturally, was that this course of ours should contribute somewhat to the return of a better day." While "foreign persons, foreign manners, and a foreign, loudly spoken language" promenaded the thoroughfares, "and poor people staggered along the streets, being led away to death," the brothers stuck to their work tables, to resurrect the present through the past.

Jacob in 1805 had visited the libraries of Paris; his ability to speak French now helped him to a small clerkship in the War Office. Two of his brothers were in the field with the hussars. Just after his mother's death, in 1808, he was appointed auditor to the state council and superintendent of the private library of Jérôme Bonaparte, the puppet king of Westphalia. Thus he was freed from economic worry, but had considerable to do. Volume One of the *Nursery and Household Tales* appeared the winter of Napoleon's retreat from Moscow (1812); two years later, in the midst of the work on Volume Two, Jacob was suddenly dispatched to Paris to demand restitution of his city's library, which had been carried away by the French. Then in 1816, after attending the Congress of Vienna as secretary of legation, he was again dispatched, to reclaim another treasure of books. He found the predicament not a little awkward. The librarian, a certain Monsieur Langlès, seeing him studying manuscripts in the *Bibliothèque*, protested with indignation: "*Nous ne devons plus souffrir ce Monsieur Grimm, qui vient tous les jours travailler ici et qui nous enlève pourtant nos manuscrits.*"

Wilhelm was never as vigorous and positive as Jacob, but he was more gay and gentle. During the years of the collection he suffered from a severe heart disorder, which for days riveted him to his room. The two were together all their lives. As children they had slept in the same bed and worked at the same table; as students they had had two beds and tables in the same room. Even after Wilhelm's marriage to Dortchen Wild, in 1825, Uncle Jacob shared the house, "and in such harmony and community that one might almost imagine the children were common property." [5] Thus it is difficult to say, with respect to their work, where Jacob ended and Wilhelm began.

The engraved portraits of the brothers reveal two very

good-looking youths, clear-eyed, with delicately modeled features. Wilhelm's forehead is the larger, his chin the sharper; his eyes look out from arched, slightly nettled brows. With firmer jaw Jacob watches, and a sturdier, more relaxed poise. His hair is a shade darker, less curled and tousled. Their mouths, well shaped, are identical. Both are shown with the soft, flaring, highly stocked collars and the wind-blown hairtrim of the period. They are alert, sharp-nosed, sensitive-nostriled, and immediately interest the eye.

In the labor on the fairy tales Jacob supplied, apparently, the greater initiative, the stricter demands for scholarly precision, and a tireless zeal for collecting. Wilhelm toiled over the tales with sympathetic devotion, and with exquisite judgment in the patient task of selecting, piecing together, and arranging. As late as 1809, they had considered the advisability of turning over the manuscripts to Brentano. But Jacob mistrusted their friend's habit of reworking traditional materials —shooting them full of personal fantasy, cutting, amplifying, recombining brilliantly, and always flavoring to the contemporary palate. He complained of the mishandling of the texts of the *Wunderhorn*. The poet, however, thought the scholar a little dull, and exhibited no interest whatsoever in the ideal of the chaste historical record. Achim von Arnim, on the other hand, aided and advised. Though he strove to persuade Jacob to relent a little, here and there, he did not reject the brothers when they insisted on their program. It was he who found a printer for the collection, Georg Andreas Reimer, in Berlin.

Volume One came out at Christmastime, with a dedication to Bettina, the wife of Achim von Arnim, for her little son, Johannes Freimund. In Vienna the book was banned as a work of superstition; but elsewhere, in spite of the political tension of the times, it was eagerly received. Clemens Brentano declared that he found the unimproved materials slovenly and often very boring; others complained of the impropriety of certain of the tales; newspaper reviews were few and cold. Nevertheless, the book enjoyed immediate success, and prospered. The Brothers Grimm had produced, in an unpredicted way, the masterpiece which the whole Romantic movement in Germany had been intending.

Von Arnim wrote to Wilhelm with quiet satisfaction, "You have collected propitiously, and have sometimes right propitiously helped; which, of course, you don't let Jacob know. . . ." Not all the tales had come from such talented heads as that of the story-wife of Niederzwehren. Some had been rather garbled. Many had been relayed by friends and had lost flavor. A few had been found in fragments, and these had had to be matched. But Wilhelm had kept note of his adjustments; and their end had been, not to embellish, but to bring out the lines of the story which the inferior informant had obscured. Furthermore, throughout the later editions, which appeared from year to year, the work of the careful, loving, improving hand could be increasingly discerned. Wilhelm's method, as contrasted with the procedures of the Romantics, was inspired by his increasing familiarity with the popular modes of speech. He noted carefully the words that the people preferred to use and their typical manners of descriptive narrative, and then, very carefully going over the story-texts, as taken from this or that raconteur, he chiseled away the more abstract, literary, or colorless turns and fitted in such characteristic, rich phrases as he had gathered from the highways and the byways. Jacob at first demurred. But it was clear that the stories were gaining immensely by the patient devotion of the younger brother; and since Jacob, anyhow, was becoming involved in his grammatical studies, he gradually released to Wilhelm the whole responsibility. Even the first edition of Volume Two was largely in the hands of Wilhelm; thereafter the work was completely his.

Volume Two appeared in January 1815, the brothers having received assistance from all sides. "The two of us gathered the first volume alone," Wilhelm wrote to a friend, "quite by ourselves and hence very slowly, over a period of six years; now things are going much better and more rapidly" The second edition was issued in 1819, improved and considerably enlarged, and with an introduction by Wilhelm, "On the Na-

ture of Folk Tales." Then, in 1822, appeared a third
volume—a work of commentary, compiled partly from the
notes of the earlier editions, but containing additional matter,
as well as a thoroughgoing comparative-historical study.[6]
The brothers published a selection of fifty favorites in 1825,
and in 1837 released a third edition of the two-volume original, again amplified and improved. Still further betterments
were to be noted in the editions of 1840, 1843, 1850, 1857.
Translations in Danish, Swedish, and French came almost
immediately; presently in Dutch, English, Italian, Spanish,
Czech, Polish, Russian, Bulgarian, Hungarian, Finnish, Esthonian, Hebrew, Armenian, and Esperanto. Tales derived
from the Grimm collection itself, directly or indirectly, have
since been recorded among the natives of Africa, Mexico, and
the South Seas.

[2]

The Types of Story

The first effect of the work was a transformation throughout
the world of the scholarly attitude toward the productions of
the folk. A new humility before the informant becomes
everywhere perceptible after the date 1812. Exactitude, not
beautification, becomes thereafter the first requirement,
"touching up" the unforgivable sin. Furthermore, the number
and competence of the collectors greatly and rapidly increased. Field-workers armed with pad and pencil marched
forth to every corner of the earth. Solid volumes today stand
ranged along the shelf from Switzerland, Frisia, Holland,
Denmark, Sweden, Norway, Iceland, and the Faroes, England, Scotland, Wales, Ireland, France, Italy, Corsica, Malta,
Portugal, and Spain; the Basques, the Rhaeto-Romanic moun-
taineers, the modern Greeks, Rumanians, Albanians, Slovenes,
Serb-Croatians, Bulgarians, Macedonians, Czechs, Slovaks,
Serbs, and Poles; Great, White, and Little Russians; Lithuani-
ans, Latvians, Finns, Lapps, and Esthonians; Cheremiss,
Mordvinians, Votyaks, and Syryenians; Gipsies and Hungari-

ans; Turks, Kasan-Tatars, Chuvash, and Bashkirs; Kalmuks, Buryats, Voguls, and Ostyaks; Yakuts, Siberian Tatars, the peoples of the Caucasus, the populations of India and Iran, Mesopotamia, Syria, the Arabian desert, Tibet, Turkestan, Java and Sumatra, Borneo, the Celebes, the Philippines, Burma, Siam, Annam, China, Korea and Japan, Australia, Melanesia, Micronesia, Polynesia, the continent of Africa, South, Middle, and North America. Still-unpublished archives accumulate in provincial, national, and international institutes. Where there was a lack, there is now such abundance that the problem is how to deal with it, how to get the mind around it, and what to think.

In this ocean of story, a number of kinds of narrative are encompassed. Many of the collections of the so-called primitive materials include *myths*—that is to say, religious recitations conceived as symbolic of the play of eternity in time. These are rehearsed, not for diversion, but for the spiritual welfare of the individual or community. *Legends* also appear; —i.e., reviews of a traditional history (or of episodes from such a history) so rendered as to permit mythological symbolism to inform human event and circumstance. Whereas myths present in pictorial form cosmogonic and ontological intuitions, legends refer to the more immediate life and setting of the given society.* Something of the religious power of myth may be regarded as effective in legend, in which case the native narrator must be careful concerning the circumstances of his recitation, lest the power break astray. Myths and legends

---

* In German criticism the terms *Sage* and *Legende* are commonly distinguished. *Sage* designates any little, local story, associated with this or that specific hill or grove, pond or river. By a people inhabiting a spirit-haunted and memory-haunted landscape, the *Sage* is conceived to be a recitation of fact. The *Sage* may be developed into the *Kunstsage*, or "Literary saga." *Legende*, on the other hand, denotes the religious tale associated with some specific shrine or relic. It is a later and more elaborate form than the *Sage*. The "Children's Legends" of the Grimm collection bring fairy-tale motifs to play around elements of Christian belief. But the term "legend," as used above, is more general. It includes both *Sage* and *Legende*, and also the materials of Chronicle and Epic.

may furnish entertainment incidentally, but they are essentially tutorial.

Tales, on the other hand, are frankly pastime: fireside tales, winternights' tales, nursery tales, coffee-house tales, sailor yarns, pilgrimage and caravan tales to pass the endless nights and days. The most ancient written records and the most primitive tribal circles attest alike to man's hunger for the good story. And every kind of thing has served. Myths and legends of an earlier period, now discredited or no longer understood, their former power broken (yet still potent to charm), have supplied much of the raw material for what now passes simply as *animal tale, fairy tale,* and *heroic or romantic adventure.* The giants and gnomes of the Germans, the "little people" of the Irish, the dragons, knights, and ladies of Arthurian Romance, were once the gods and demons of the Green Isle and the European continent. Similarly, the divinities of the primitive Arabians appear as Jinn in the story-world of Islam. Tales of such origin are regarded with differing degrees of seriousness by the various people who recount them; and they can be received by the sundry members of the audience, severally, with superstitious awe, nostalgia for the days of belief, ironic amusement, or simple delight in the marvels of imagination and intricacies of plot. But no matter what the atmosphere of belief, the stories, in so far as they now are "tales," are composed primarily for amusement. They are reshaped in terms of dramatic contrast, narrative suspense, repetition,* and resolution.

Certain characteristic opening and closing formulas set apart from the common world the timeless, placeless realm of faërie: "Once upon a time"; "In the days of good King Arthur"; "A thousand years ago tomorrow"; "Long, long ago, when Brahmadatta was the ruler of Benares"—"And so they lived happily ever after"; "That's all"; "A mouse did run, the story is done"; "So there they remain, happy and

---

* Throughout the Old World, repetition is commonly in threes; in aboriginal America, in fours.

contented, while we stand barefoot as packasses and lick our teeth"; "Bo bow bended, my story's ended; if you don't like it, you may mend it." A handsome conclusion is attributed to the Zanzibar Swahili: "If the story was beautiful, the beauty belongs to us all; if it was bad, the fault is mine only, who told it." [7]

Prose is the normal vehicle of story, but at critical points little rhymes commonly appear:

> Looking-glass, Looking-glass, on the wall,
> Who in this land is the fairest of all?

> Turn back, turn back, young maiden dear,
> 'Tis a murderer's house you enter here.

> Peace, peace, my dear little giants,
> I have had a thought of ye,
> Something I have brought for ye.

> Little duck, little duck, dost thou see,
> Hänsel and Gretel are waiting for thee?
> There's never a plank, or bridge in sight.
> Take us across on thy back so white.

In Arabian tales, and less commonly in European, the prose of the text slips momentarily into rhyme: "Thereupon sat a lady bright of blee, with brow beaming brilliantly, the dream of philosophy, whose eyes were fraught with Babel's gramarye and her eyebrows were arched for archery"; "They all lived happy and died happy, and never drank out of a dry cappy"; "Now I had an army of a thousand thousand bridles, men of warrior mien with forearms strong and keen, armed with spears and mail-coats sheen and swords that gleam."

In the lovely French medieval chante-fable, *Aucassin et Nicolette*, verse passages regularly alternate with prose. In the *bardic lays* that served to entertain the heroes in the mead-hall, in the long *epics* woven in later times, and in the *ballads* of the folk, narrative goes into verse entirely. The spell of rhythm and rhyme is the spell of "once upon a time." *

"And as the cup went round merrily, quoth the Porter to the Kalandars: 'And you, O brother mine, have ye no story or rare adventure to amuse us withal?' " The empty hour is as gladly filled with a good personal adventure as with a fragment of traditional wonder. Hence, the world of actual life as caught in *anecdote*, paced and timed to fix and justify attention, has contributed to the great category of the tale. The anecdote may range from the ostensibly truthful, or only slightly exaggerated, to the frankly unbelievable. In the latter range it mingles readily with sheer *invention:* the joke, merry tale, and ghost adventure. Again, it can unite with the mythological stuff of traditional romance, and thus acquire some of the traits of legend.

A distinct and relatively recently developed category is the *fable*. The best examples are the Greek and medieval collections attributed to "Aesop," and the Oriental of the Brahmins, Buddhists, and Jains. The fable is didactic. It is not, like myth, a revelation of transcendental mysteries, but a clever illustration of a political or ethical point. Fables are witty, and not to be believed but understood.†

Under the single heading *Märchen*, the Germans popularly comprehend the whole range of the *folk tale*. The Brothers Grimm, therefore, included in their collection folk stories of every available variety. Scholars since their day have analyzed the assortment and classified the tales according to type. For one listing of this kind, based on the standard index of story-

* The literary folk tale can be rendered in either verse or prose. In eighteenth-century Germany, Johann Musäus (1735–1787) composed in prose, Christoph Wieland (1735–1813) in verse. The huge Hindu collection of the *Kathāsaritsāgara*, "Ocean of the Streams of Story" (c. 1063–1081), is entirely in verse; the Arabian *Thousand Nights and One Night* (eleventh to fifteenth centuries) is in prose.

† Some of the Jatakas, or tales of the early lives of the Buddha, are fables that half pretend to be little legends. Buddhist and Jain fables teach religious lore; Aesop and the Brahminical *Panchatantra* teach the wisdom of life.

types prepared by the Finnish folklorist Antti Aarne,[8] see the Appendix, below, p. 41.

[3]

The History of the Tales

The patterns of the folk tale are much the same throughout the world. This circumstance has given rise to a long and intricate learned discussion.[9] By and large, it is now fairly agreed that the general continuity, and an occasional correspondence in detail, can be referred to the psychological unity of the human species, but that over this ground a profuse and continuous passing along of tales from mouth to ear—and by book—has been taking place, not for centuries only but for millenniums, and over immense reaches of the globe. Hence the folklore of each area must be studied for its peculiar history. Every story—every motif, in fact—has had its adventurous career.

The Grimm brothers regarded European folklore as the detritus of Old Germanic belief: the myths of ancient time had disintegrated, first into heroic legend and romance, last into these charming treasures of the nursery. But in 1859, the year of Wilhelm's death, a Sanskrit scholar, Theodor Benfey, demonstrated that a great portion of the lore of Europe had come, through Arabic, Hebrew, and Latin translations, directly from India—and this as late as the thirteenth century A.D.[10] Since Benfey's time, the evidence for a late, polygenetic development of the folk tale of Christian Europe has become abundant and detailed.

The scholars of the English anthropological school at the close of the nineteenth century (E. B. Tylor, Andrew Lang, E. S. Hartland, and others), believed that the irrational elements of fairy lore were grounded in savage superstition. Totemism, cannibalism, taboo, and the external soul they discovered on every page. But today it is clear that such irrationalities are as familiar to modern European dream-life as to society on the Congo, and so we are no longer disposed to run a tale back to the paleolithic caves simply because the heroine marries a gazelle or eats her mother. Yet in a few of the stories of the Grimm collection actual vestiges of primitive ways can be identified with reasonable assurance; * and in perhaps half a dozen others signs persist from the barbaric period of the Migrations.†

A crisis in the history of the European folk tradition becomes apparent about the tenth century A.D. A quantity of Late Classical matter was being imported from the Mediterranean by the itinerant entertainers, minstrels, and pranksters who came swarming from the sunny south to infest the pilgrim routes and present themselves at castle doors.‡ And not only minstrels but missionaries too were at work. The fierce warrior ideals of earlier story were submitting to a new piety and sentimental didactic: Slandered Virtue is triumphant, Patience is rewarded, Love endures.

There seems, however, to have prevailed a comparative poverty of invention until the twelfth century, when the matter of India and the matter of Ireland found their ways to the fields of Europe. This was the period of the Crusades and the rise of Arthurian romance, the former opening Europe wide to the civilization of the Orient, the latter conjuring from the realm of Celtic faërie a wild wonderworld of princesses enchanted in sleep, castles solitary in the forest adventurous,

---

* For examples, see the Appendix, infra, pp. 37–42.

† Magic formulae betraying features of the early Germanic verse-style stand to this day in the Grimm collection:

> Rapúnzel, Rapúnzel,
> Lass dein Haár herúnter. (Number 12)

> Éntchen, Éntchen,
> Da steht Grétel und Háensel
> Kein Stég und keíne Brúecke
> Nimm úns auf deínen weíssen Rúecken. (Number 15)

‡ How much Hellenistic and Roman material had infected the German tribal mythologies during earlier centuries, before and after the fall of Rome, remains a question; it is certain that much of the Balder and Woden imagery is not "primitive Aryan." (Cf. Franz Rolf Schröder, Germanentum und Hellenismus [Heidelberg: Carl Winter's Universitätsbuchhandlung, 1924]; Altgermanische Kulturprobleme [Berlin and Leipzig: Walter de Gruyter & Co., 1929].)

dragons steaming in rimy caverns, Merlin-magic, Morgan le Fay, cackling hags transmuted by a kiss into the damsel of the world. Europe inherited nearly everything of its fairyland from the imagination of the Celt.*

Shortly after this time came the Hindu *Panchatantra*. The work had been translated from Sanskrit into Persian in the sixth century A.D., from Persian into Arabic in the eighth, and from Arabic into Hebrew around the middle of the thirteenth. About 1270, John of Capua turned the Hebrew into Latin, and from this Latin version the book passed into German and Italian. A Spanish translation had been made from the Arabic in 1251; an English was later drawn from the Italian. Individual stories became popular in Europe, and were then rapidly assimilated. "Out of the literary works," wrote Benfey, "the tales went to the people, and from the people they returned, transformed, to literary collections, then back they went to the people again, etc., and it was principally through this cooperative action that they achieved national and individual spirit—that quality of national validity and individual unity which contributes to not a few of them their high poetical worth." [11] †

A wonderful period opened in the thirteenth century. With the passing of the gallant days of the great Crusades, the aristocratic taste for verse romance declined, and the lusty prose of the late medieval towns moved into its own. Prose compendiums of traditional lore began appearing, filled with every kind of gathered anecdote and history of wonder— vast, immeasurable compilations, which the modern scholar has hardly explored. A tumbling, broad, inexhaustible flood of

* The youth of Siegfried, Brynhild's sleep, the sword in the tree, and the broken sword, are motifs adopted from the Celtic tradition. The Icelandic Sagas and Eddas were powerfully influenced by the bards of Ireland. In the classification in the Appendix, the tales under heading IV, *Chivalrous work of the Middle Ages,* represent this body of matter as it was reworked under the influence of twelfth-century romance.

† On the basis of a garbled story from the East, the Buddha was canonized by the medieval Church as Saints Barlaam and Josaphat, Abbots; Feastday, November 27. Following the work of the nineteenth-century folklorists, these names were expunged from the calendar.

popular merry tales; misadventures; hero, saint, and devil legends; animal fables, mock heroics, slapstick jokes, riddles, pious allegories, and popular ballads burst abruptly into manuscript and carried everything before it. Compounded with themes from the cloister and the castle, mixed with elements from the Bible and from the heathenesse of the Orient, as well as the deep pre-Christian past, the wonderful hurlyburly broke into the stonework of the cathedrals, grinned from the stained glass, twisted and curled in humorous grotesque in and out of the letters of illuminated manuscripts, appeared in tapestries, on saddles and weapons, on trinket-caskets, mirrors, and combs.[12] This was the first major flourishing in Europe of a literature of the people. From right and left the materials came, to left and right they were flung forth again, sealed with the sign of the late Gothic, so that no matter what the origin, they were now the re-creation of the European folk.

Much of this matter found its way into the literary works of the late Middle Ages, the Reformation, and the Renaissance (Boccaccio, Chaucer, Hans Sachs, *Les Cent Nouvelles Nouvelles*, etc.), and then back, reshaped, to the people. The period of abundance continued to the time of the Thirty Years' War (1618–1648).

Finally, in France, at the court of Louis XIV, a vogue commenced for the delicate refashioning of fairy tales and fables —inspired in part by a new French translation of a later Persian rendering of the *Panchatantra* and in part by Antoine Galland's rendition of the Arabian *Thousand Nights and One Night*. The pastime yielded a plentiful harvest of freshly wrought, delicate pieces (La Fontaine, Perrault, the forty-one volumes of the *Cabinet des Fées*). Many were taken over by the people and crossed the Rhine.

Thus, by the time the Grimm brothers arrived to begin their collection, much material had overlain the remote mythology of the early tribes. Tales from the four quarters, inventions from every level of society and all stages of Western history were commingled. Nevertheless, as they observed, a homogeneity of style and character pervades the total inheritance. A continuous process of re-creation, a kind of spiritual metabolism, has so broken the original structures in assimilating them to the living civilization, that only the most meticulous and skillful observation, analysis, and comparative research can discover their provenience and earlier state. The Grimm brothers regarded this rich composition as a living unit and sought to probe its past; the modern scientist, on the other hand, searches the unit for its elements, then ferrets these to their remote sources. From the contemporary work we receive a more complex impression of the processes of culture than was possible in the period of the Grimms.

Let us turn, therefore, to the problem of the individual tale —the migratory element that enters our system and becomes adapted to our style of existence. What is *its* history? What can happen to it during the course of its career?

Passing from Orient to Occident, surviving the revolutions of history and the long attrition of time, traversing the familiar bounds of language and belief—the favorite now of a Saracen king, now of a hard warrior, now of a Capuchin monk, now of old Marie—the tale undergoes kaleidoscopical mutations. The first problem of research is to identify, fix, and characterize the key-complex, the formal principle of the story's entity, that without which the story would not be. As the story then is followed throughout its peregrination, it is observed to assimilate to itself the materials offered from land to land. It changes, like a chameleon; puts on the colors of its background; lives and shapes itself to the requirements of the moment. "Such a tale," writes an American authority, "is at the same time a definite entity and an abstraction. It is an entity in the particular form in which it happens to be recorded at any moment; it is an abstraction in the sense that no two versions ever exactly agree and that consequently the tale lives only in endless mutations." [13]

In the life-course of any given version of a tale, a number of typical accidents may occur. A detail may be forgotten. A foreign trait may become naturalized, an obsolete modernized.

A general term (animal) may become specialized (mouse), or, vice versa, a special term generalized. The order of events may be rearranged. The personages may become confused, or the acts confused, or in some other way the traits of the story may cross-influence each other. Persons and things may become multiplied (particularly by the numbers three, five, and seven). Many animals may replace one (polyzoism). Animals may assume human shape (anthropomorphism), or vice versa. Animals may become demons, or vice versa. The narrator can appear as hero (egomorphism). Furthermore, the story may be amplified with new materials. Such materials are generally derived from other folk tales. The expansion may take place at any point, but the beginning and end are the most likely to be amplified. Several tales can be joined into one. Finally, the inventiveness of an individal narrator may lead to intentional variations—for better or for worse.[14]

The serious study of popular story began, in Europe, with the Romantics. With the Grimm brothers the science came of age. With the foundation in Helsingfors, in 1907, of the Finnish society of the "Folklore Fellows," the now colossal subject was coordinated for systematic research over the entire world. The technique of the geographical-historical method, perfected by the associates of this pivotal group,* enables the modern scholar to retrace the invisible path of the spoken tale practically to the doorstep of the inventor—over the bounds of states, languages, continents, even across oceans and around the globe. The work has required the cooperation of the scholars of the five continents; the international distribution of the materials has demanded an international research. Yet the work started in the usual way of folklore studies, as a labor of local patriotic pride.

About the middle of the nineteenth century, a strong na-

---

* The technique was perfected by the Finnish School, but was independently developed by scholars in several quarters; for example, in America by Franz Boas, in Denmark by Axel Olrik, in France by Gaston Paris and E. Cosquin, in Germany by Johannes Bolte, William Herz, Ernst Kuhn, and Theodor Zachatiae, in Russia by L. Kolmachevski.

tionalist movement had begun to mature in Finland. Buffeted for five hundred years between Sweden and Russia, the little nation had been annexed in 1809 by Czar Alexander I. Since the close of the eighteenth century, Swedish had been the official academic language. A group of young patriots now began to agitate for the restoration of the native spirit and the native tongue.

Elias Lönnrot (1802–1884), a country physician and student of Finnish philology, collected ballads and folk tales among the people. His work was a northern echo of the labors of the Brothers Grimm. Having gathered a considerable body of folk poetry around the legendary heroes, Väinämöinen, Ilmarinen, Lemminkainen, and Kullervo, he composed these in coordinated sequence and cast them in a uniform verse. Thus, in 1835, he published the first edition of what has since become known as the folk-epic of Finland, the *Kalevala*, "The Land of Heroes." *

Julius Krohn (1835–1888), the first student at the university to presume to present his graduate thesis in Finnish, devoted himself to the study of the folk tradition, and in particular to the materials gathered by Lönnrot in the *Kalevala*. He discovered that among the ballads and popular stories of the Swedes, Russians, Germans, Tatars, etc., many of the motifs of Lönnrot's epic reappeared, but in variant combinations. The *Kalevala*, therefore, could not be studied all of a piece; its elements had to be traced down separately. With this discovery he took the first step toward the development of the Finnish geographical-historical method.

Julius Krohn next found that not all the Finnish examples of a given theme could be compared trait for trait with the foreign versions; only what seemed to him to be the oldest of the Finnish forms closely resembled those of the neighboring

---

* A second edition, improved and enlarged, appeared in 1849. Translated into German (1852), it came under the eyes of Henry Wadsworth Longfellow, who was inspired to attempt a similar deed in the same meter for the American Indian; result: "The Song of Hiawatha."

lands. He concluded that the materials of the native epic had entered Finland from without and had undergone within the country gradual modification.

Furthermore and finally, Julius Krohn perceived that each of the native modifications seemed to be limited in its geographical distribution. He took care, therefore, to keep precise note of the geographical sources as well as chronological relationships of his materials. In this way he was enabled to study the transformation of the motifs of a tale in its passage from mouth to mouth over the land and through the years. "First I sift and arrange the different variants according to chronology and topography," he wrote to the Hungarian philologist P. Hunfalvy in 1884; "because I have discovered that only in this way is it possible to distinguish the original elements from the later additions." [15]

With respect to the *Kalevala*, Julius Krohn concluded that neither was it a very old legend nor were its materials originally Finnish. The narrative elements had arrived on the waves of a culture tide that had streamed over Europe through the centuries. Stemming from the gardens of the East and the fertile valleys of Antiquity, they had crossed southern Europe—largely by word of mouth—then turned eastward again to the regions of the Slavs and Tatars, whence they had passed to the peoples of the north.[16] And as each folk had received, it had developed, reinterpreted, and amplified, and then handed along the inheritance to the neighbor.

Thus in Finland, as in Germany, what had begun as the study of a national tradition developed inevitably into the review of an international tradition. And the scholarship that had started in patriotic fervor opened immediately into a worldwide collaboration. The son of Julius Krohn, Kaarle Krohn, applied the geographical method developed by his father to the special problem of the folk tale,[17] and it was he who in 1907, in collaboration with German and Scandinavian scholars, founded the research society that since his time has coordinated the work of many regions.

To illustrate the way in which the research has been carried on:

An index of folk-tale types was issued in 1911 by Antti Aarne.[18] (The types distinguished in this basic study are those indicated in the appendix, below, p. 41, for the varieties of story in the Grimm collection.) Each class was subdivided, and under each head appeared a directory of examples. Coordinated to Aarne's index then were published a series of special catalogues for a number of folk traditions: Finnish, Esthonian, Finnish-Swedish, Flemish, Norwegian, Lapp, Livonian, Rumanian, Hungarian, Icelandic, Spanish, and Prussian. For each culture all the available tales from the various published and unpublished archives were classified according to the principles of Aarne's index. Thus an order was beginning to be brought into fluid chaos.*

Another type of work undertaken was that of the monograph. A monograph is a special study devoted to the tracing of a single tale through its twists and turns, disappearances and reappearances, over the globe and through the corridors of time. The technique for the preparation of such a work has been described as follows:

1) The scholar undertaking to write a monograph on any folk narrative (folk tale, saga, legend, anecdote), must know all the extant versions ("variants") of this narrative, whether printed or unprinted, and no matter what the language in which they appear.

2) He must compare all these versions, carefully, trait by trait, and without any previously formed opinion.

3) During the investigation, he must always keep in mind the place and time of the rendering of each of the variants.[19]

* Antti Aarne's work has been translated, brought up to date, and greatly enlarged by his distinguished American collaborator, Dr. Stith Thompson of Indiana University, in *The Types of the Folktale*, Folklore Fellows Communications (Helsinki, second edition, 1964), No. 184. A second work, of even greater use and range, is Dr. Thompson's monumental *Motif-Index of Folk Literature* in six volumes (Copenhagen and Bloomington, Ind., 1955–1958).

The homeland of any given folk tale can generally be judged to be the region in which the richest harvest of variants appears; furthermore, where the structure of the tale is most consistent, and where customs and beliefs may serve to illuminate the meaning of the tale. The farther a folk tale wanders from its home, the greater the damage to its configurations.[20]

The researches of the Finnish folklore school were supported and extended by an originally independent enterprise in Germany. In 1898 Professor Herman Grimm, the son of Wilhelm, turned over to Johannes Bolte (1858–1937) the unpublished materials of his father and his uncle, with the hope that a new edition might be prepared of the *Commentaries to the Nursery and Household Tales*. These commentaries had first appeared as appendices to the volumes of 1812 and 1815, then as a special volume in 1822, and finally in a third edition, 1856. Professor Bolte collated, trait by trait, with all the tales and variants gathered by the Grimms everything that could be drawn from the modern archives. He enlisted in the enterprise Professor Georg Polívka of Prague, who assisted in the analysis of the Slavic analogues. During the course of the next thirty-four years the opus grew to five closely printed volumes. The original work of the Grimms, which had opened a rich century of folk studies, collection, and interpretation, was brought by this labor to stand securely in the mid-point of the modern field; so that the *Nursery and Household Tales* are today, as they were the moment they left the press, the beginning and the middle, if nowise the end, of the study of the literature of the people.

The classification of the stories according to the above-described stages of development, which appears below, p. 42, has been adapted from that supplied by Friedrich von der Leyen to his edition of the *Nursery and Household Tales* (Jena, 1912). It is a very useful listing and will enable the reader to explore in his own good way the history and stratifications of the inexhaustible text.

[4]
The Question of Meaning

The Grimm brothers, Max Müller, Andrew Lang, and others, have pointed out that folk tales are "monstrous, irrational and unnatural," both as to the elements of which they are composed and as to the plots that unify these elements. Since a tale may have a different origin from its elements, two questions propose themselves: What is the origin and meaning of the motifs? What is the origin and meaning of the tales?

[a] THE MOTIFS

Many of the incidents of the merry tales, jokes, yarns, tall stories, and anecdotes are simply comical and clever inventions spun from life. These offer no problem.

The "monstrous, irrational and unnatural" incidents, however, are of a kind with those of myth; indeed, they are frequently derived from myth. They must be explained as myth is explained. But then, how is myth explained?

The reply varies according to the authority.

Euhemerus, a Greek writer of the fourth century B.C., noting that Alexander the Great, shortly after his death, was already appearing in legend as a demigod, propounded the view that the gods are only great mortals, deified. Snorri Sturleson (1179–1241), in the preface to his *Prose Edda*, explained in the same way the pagan divinities of the Norse. This theory, called "Euhemerism," has its advocates to this day.

Among the Indo-Germanic philologists in the period of the ascendancy of Max Müller, it was believed that myths were originally sentimental descriptions of nature. Man half consciously read the tragedy of his own life in the birth of the sun, its "kissing of the dew to death," its culmination, descent, and disappearance into the arms of night. Because of the fact that Indo-European nouns are either masculine or feminine, the descriptions tended to personify their objects. And because of the fact that the language was evolving, the original references of the personifying nouns were presently forgotten, so that the words were finally taken to be personal names.[21] For example, such a metaphorical name for the sun as Kephalos, the "Head" (of light), presently lost its meaning and was thought to refer to a human youth; and correspondingly, the fading dew, Prokris, bride of the "Head," became a mortal girl of tragical demise. One more step: the names might become confused with those of actual historical heroes, whereupon the myth would be transformed into a legend.[22]

Müller's theory was the most elaborate attempt to account for the mechanics of personification. Among the "anthropologists" it was, more easily, simply assumed that savages and poets tend to attribute souls to things and to personify.[23] The childlike fantasy of primitive man, his poetic feeling, and his morbid, dream-ridden imagination, played into his attempts to describe and explain the world around him and thus produced a phantasmagoric counterworld. But the savage's effort, at the core, was to discover the cause of things, and then, through spells, prayer, sacrifice, and sacrament, to control them. Mythology, therefore, was only a false etiology; ceremonial a misguided technology. With the gradual, unmethodical, but nevertheless inevitable recognition of error upon error, man progressed through the labyrinth of wonder to the clearer-headed stand of today.*

Another view (and it rather supplemented than contradicted the descriptive-etiological theory) represented primitive man as terrified by the presences of the grave, hence ever anxious to propitiate and turn them away. The roots of myth

---

* "Reflection and enquiry should satisfy us that to our [savage] predecessors we are indebted for much of what we thought most our own, and that their errors were not wilful extravagances or the ravings of insanity, but simply hypotheses, justifiable as such at the time when they were propounded, but which a further experience has proved to be inadequate. It is only by the successive testing of hypotheses and rejection of the false that truth is at last elicited." (Sir James G. Frazer, *The Golden Bough*, one-volume edition [New York and London: The Macmillan Company 1922], p. 264.)

and ritual went down to the black subsoil of the grave-cult and the fear of death.[24]

A fourth point of view was propounded by the French sociologist Emile Durkheim. He argued that the collective superexcitation (*surexcitation*) of clan, tribal, and intertribal gatherings was experienced by every participating member of the group as an impersonal, infectious power (*mana*); that this power would be thought to emanate from the clan or tribal emblem (*totem*); and that this emblem, therefore, would be set apart from all other objects as filled with *mana* (sacred versus profane). This *totem*, this first cult object, would then infect with *mana* all associated objects, and through this contagion there would come into being a system of beliefs and practices relative to sacred things, uniting in a single moral community all believers.[25] The great contribution of Durkheim's theory, and what set it apart from all that had gone before, was that it represented religion not as a morbid exaggeration, false hypothesis, or unenlightened fear, but as a truth emotionally experienced, the truth of the relationship of the individual to the group.

This recognition by Durkheim of a kind of truth at the root of the image-world of myth is supported, expanded, and deepened by the demonstration of the psychoanalysts that dreams are precipitations of unconscious desires, ideals, and fears, and furthermore, that the images of dream resemble— broadly, but nevertheless frequently to the detail—the motifs of folk tale and myth. Having selected for their study the symbol-inventing, myth-motif-producing level of the psyche —source of all those universal themes ("Elementary Ideas") * which men have read into the phenomena of nature, into the shadows of the tomb, the lives of the heroes, and the emblems of society—the psychoanalysts have undoubtedly touched the central moment of the multifarious problem. In the light of their discussion, theories which before seemed mutually contradictory become easily coordinated. Man, nature, death, society—these have served simply as fields into which dream-

* See below, p. 44.

meanings have been projected. Hence the references of the wild motifs are not really (no matter what the rationalizing consciousness may believe) to the sun, the moon, the stars, to the wind and thunder, to the grave, to the hero, or even to the power of the group, but *through* these, back again to a state of the psyche. Mythology is psychology, misread as cosmology, history, and biography.

A still further step can and must be taken, however, before we shall have reached the bounds of the problem. Myth, as the psychoanalysts declare, is *not* a mess of errors; myth is a picture language. But the language has to be studied to be read. In the first place, this language is the native speech of dream. But in the second place, it has been studied, clarified, and enriched by the poets, prophets, and visionaries of untold millenniums. Dante, Aquinas, and Augustine, al-Ghazali and Mohammed, Zarathustra, Shankaracharya, Nagarjuna, and T'ai Tsung, were not bad scientists making misstatements about the weather, or neurotics reading dreams into the stars, but masters of the human spirit teaching a wisdom of death and life. And the thesaurus of the myth-motifs was their vocabulary. They brooded on the state and way of man, and through their broodings came to wisdom; then teaching, with the aid of the picture-language of myth, they worked changes on the patterns of their inherited iconographies.

But not only in the higher cultures; even among the so-called primitives, priests, wizards, and visionaries interpret and reinterpret myth as symbolic of "the Way": "the Pollen Path of Beauty," as it is called, for example, among the Navaho. And this Way, congenial to the wholeness of man, is understood as the little portion of the great Way that binds the cosmos; for, as among the Babylonians, so everywhere, the crux of mythological teaching has always been that "an everlasting reiteration of unchanging principles and events takes place both in space and in time, in large as in small." * [26] The

---

* The Babylonian astrological mythology, as described by Hugo Winckler, is a local specification, amplification, and application of themes that are of the essence of mythology everywhere.

Way of the individual is the microcosmic reiteration of the Way of the All and of each. In this sense the reasonings of the sages are not only psychological but metaphysical. They are not easily grasped. And yet they are the subtle arguments that inform the iconographies of the world.

Myths, therefore, as they now come to us, and as they break up to let their pregnant motifs scatter and settle into the materials of popular tale, are the purveyors of a wisdom that has borne the race of man through the long vicissitudes of his career. "The content of folklore," writes Ananda K. Coomaraswamy, "is metaphysics. Our inability to see this is due primarily to our abysmal ignorance of metaphysics and its technical terms." [27]

Therefore, in sum: The "monstrous, irrational and unnatural" motifs of folk tale and myth are derived from the reservoirs of dream and vision. On the dream level such images represent the total state of the individual dreaming psyche. But clarified of personal distortions and propounded by poets, prophets, and visionaries, they become symbolic of the spiritual norm for Man the Microcosm. They are thus phrases from an image-language, expressive of metaphysical, psychological, and sociological truth. And in the primitive, Oriental, archaic, and medieval societies this vocabulary was pondered and more or less understood. Only in the wake of the Enlightenment has it suddenly lost its meaning and been pronounced insane.

[b] THE TALES

The folk tale, in contrast to the myth, is a form of entertainment. The storyteller fails or succeds in proportion to the amusement he affords. His motifs may be plucked from the tree of myth, but his craft is never precisely of the mythological order. His productions have to be judged, at last, not as science, sociology, psychology, or metaphysics, but as art— and specifically, art produced by individuals at discoverable periods, in discoverable lands. We have to ask: What princi-

ples of craftsmanship inspired the narrators who gave shape to
these stories in the long reaches of the past?

The Indian, Celtic, Arabian, and medieval masters of narrative to whom we owe the most exquisite of our European
tales were the practitioners of a craft that strove to reveal
through mortal things the brilliance of eternal forms.[28] The
quality of their work was not a naturalistic but a spiritual precision, and their power, instructive wonder. To us there may
seem to be little distinction between such a craft and metaphysics; for we have enlarged the connotation of our term,
"metaphysical," to include everything untranslatable into positivistic discourse. But peoples of the premodern type,
whether Gothic, Oriental, archaic, totemistic, or primitive,
typically took for granted the operation of a transcendent energy in the forms of space and time. It was required of every
artist, no matter what his craft, that his product should show
its sign of the spirit as well as serve its mechanical end. The
function of the craft of the tale, therefore, was not simply to
fill the vacant hour but to fill it with symbolic fare. And since
symbolization is the characteristic pleasure of the human
mind, the fascination of the tale increased in proportion to the
richness of its symbolic content.

By an ironic paradox of time, the playful symbolism of the
folk tale—a product of the vacant hour—today seems to us
more true, more powerful to survive, than the might and
weight of myth. For, whereas the symbolic figures of mythology were regarded (by all except the most sophisticated of
the metaphysicians) not as symbolic figures at all but as actual
divinities to be invoked, placated, loved, and feared, the personages of the tale were comparatively unsubstantial. They
were cherished primarily for their fascination. Hence, when
the acids of the modern spirit dissolved the kingdoms of the
gods, the tales in their essence were hardly touched. The elves
were less real than they were before; but the tales, by the
same token, were more alive. So that we may say that, out of
the whole symbol-building achievement of the past, what sur-

vives to us today (hardly altered in efficiency or in function) is the tale of wonder.

The tale survives, furthermore, not simply as a quaint relic of days childlike in belief. Its world of magic is symptomatic of fevers deeply burning in the psyche: permanent presences, desires, fears, ideals, potentialities that have glowed in the nerves, hummed in the blood, baffled the senses since the beginning. The one psyche is operative in both the figments of this vision-world and the deeds of human life. In some manner, then, the latter must stand prefigured in the former. History is the promise of *Märchen* realized through, and against the obstacles of, space and time. Playful and unpretentious as the archetypes of fairy tale may appear to be, they are the heroes and villains who have built the world for us. The debutante combing her hair before the glass, the mother pondering the future of a son, the laborer in the mines, the merchant vessel full of cargo, the ambassador with portfolio, the soldier in the field of war—all are working in order that the ungainsayable specifications of effective fantasy, the permanent patterns of the tale of wonder, shall be clothed in flesh and known as life.

And so we find that in those masterworks of the modern day which are of a visionary rather than of a descriptive order the forms long known from the nursery tale reappear, but now in adult maturity. While the Frazers and the Müllers were scratching their necks to invent some rational explanation for the irrational patterns of fairy lore, Wagner was composing his *Ring of the Nibelung*, Strindberg and Ibsen their symbolical plays, Nietzsche his *Zarathustra*, Melville his *Moby Dick*. Goethe had long completed the *Faust*, Spenser his *Faerie Queene*. Today the novels of James Joyce, Franz Kafka, Thomas Mann, and many another, as well as the poems of every season, tell us that the gastric fires of human fantasy still are potent to digest raw experience and assimilate it to the creative genius of man. In these productions again, as in the story world of the past which they continue and in essence duplicate, the denotation of the symbols is human destiny: destiny recognized, for all its cannibal horrors, as a marvelous, wild, "monstrous, irrational and unnatural" wonder-tale to fill the void. This is the story our spirit asked for; this is the story we receive.

Through the vogues of literary history, the folk tale has survived. Told and retold, losing here a detail, gaining there a new hero, disintegrating gradually in outline, but re-created occasionally by some narrator of the folk, the little masterpiece transports into the living present a long inheritance of story skill coming down from the romancers of the Middle Ages, the strictly disciplined poets of the Celts, the professional story-men of Islam, and the exquisite, fertile, brilliant fabulists of Hindu and Buddhist India. This little tale that we are reading has the touch on it of Somadeva, Shahrazad, Taliesin, and Boccaccio, as well as the accent of the story-wife of Niederzwehren. If ever there was an art on which the whole community of mankind has worked—seasoned with the philosophy of the codger on the wharf and singing with the music of the spheres—it is this of the ageless tale.

The folk tale is the primer of the picture-language of the soul.

Appendix

TALE NUMBERS AND NAMES

1. The Frog-King, or Iron Henry
2. Cat and Mouse in Partnership
3. Our Lady's Child
4. The Story of the Youth Who Went Forth to Learn What Fear Was
5. The Wolf and the Seven Little Kids
6. Faithful John
7. The Good Bargain
8. The Strange Musician
9. The Twelve Brothers
10. The Pack of Ragamuffins
11. Brother and Sister
12. Rapunzel
13. The Three Little Men in the Wood
14. The Three Spinners
15. Hänsel and Gretel
16. The Three Snake-Leaves

17. The White Snake
18. The Straw, the Coal, and the Bean
19. The Fisherman and His Wife
20. The Valiant Little Tailor
21. Cinderella
22. The Riddle
23. The Mouse, the Bird and the Sausage
24. Mother Holle
25. The Seven Ravens
26. Little Red-Cap
27. The Bremen Town-Musicians
28. The Singing Bone
29. The Devil with the Three Golden Hairs
30. The Louse and the Flea
31. The Girl without Hands
32. Clever Hans
33. The Three Languages
34. Clever Elsie
35. The Tailor in Heaven
36. The Wishing-Table, the Gold-Ass, and the Cudgel in the Sack
37. Thumbling
38. The Wedding of Mrs. Fox
39. The Elves
40. The Robber Bridegroom
41. Herr Korbes
42. The Godfather
43. Frau Trude
44. Godfather Death
45. Thumbling's Travels
46. Fitcher's Bird
47. The Juniper Tree
48. Old Sultan
49. The Six Swans
50. Little Briar-Rose
51. Fundevogel
52. King Thrushbeard
53. Little Snow-White
54. The Knapsack, the Hat, and the Horn
55. Rumpelstiltskin
56. Sweetheart Roland
57. The Golden Bird
58. The Dog and the Sparrow
59. Frederick and Catherine
60. The Two Brothers
61. The Little Peasant
62. The Queen Bee
63. The Three Feathers
64. The Golden Goose
65. Allerleirauh
66. The Hare's Bride
67. The Twelve Huntsman
68. The Thief and His Master
69. Jorinda and Joringel
70. The Three Sons of Fortune
71. How Six Men Got On in the World
72. The Wolf and the Man
73. The Wolf and the Fox
74. Gossip Wolf and the Fox
75. The Fox and the Cat
76. The Pink
77. Clever Gretel
78. The Old Man and His Grandson
79. The Water-Nixie
80. The Death of the Little Hen
81. Brother Lustig
82. Gambling Hansel
83. Hans in Luck

205. God's Food
206. The Three Green Twigs
207. Our Lady's Little Glass
208. The Aged Mother
209. The Heavenly Wedding
210. The Hazel-Branch

CLASSIFICATION OF TALES ACCORDING TO TYPE

I. *Animal tales:* Wild animals, 2, 23, 38, 73, 74, 132. Wild animals and domestic, 5, 27, 48, 75. Man and wild animals, 8, 72, 157. Domestic animals, 10, 41 (compare 18). Birds, 58, 86, 102, 171. Fish, 172. Other animals and objects, 105, i; 187.

II. *Ordinary folk tales:* A. *Tales of magic:* * Supernatural adversaries, 4, 5, 12, 15, 26, 42, 44, 46, 51, 56, 60, 66, 79, 81, 82, 85, 91, 99, 101, 106, 111, 113, 120, 121, 133, 181, 186, 191, 193, 197. (Compare 163.) Supernatural or enchanted husband (wife) or other relatives, 1, 9, 11 (compare 141), 13, 25, 49, 50, 63, 69, 88, 92, 93, 106, 108, 123, 127, 135, 144, 160, 161, 169, 193. Supernatural tasks, 24, 29, 100. Supernatural helpers, 6, 14, 17, 19, 21, 55, 57, 62, 65, 71, 89, 97, 126, 130, 134, 136. Magic objects, 16, 36, 54, 60, 64, 103, 107, 110, 116, 122, 165, 188. Supernatural power or knowledge, 16, 33, 76, 90, 118, 124, 129, 142, 149. Other tales of the supernatural, 3, 31, 37, 45, 47, 53, 96. B. *Religious tales:* 28, 35, 81, 87, 92, 125, 145, 147, 167, 178, 194, 195, 206. C. *Novelle (romantic tales):* 22, 40, 52, 67, 94, 112, 114, 115, 152, 179, 198, 199. D. *Tales of the stupid ogre:* 20, 183, 189 (compare 148).

III. *Jokes and anecdotes:* Numskull stories, 70, 174. Stories about married couples, 34, 59, 83, 104, 128, 164, 168. Stories about a woman (girl), 34, 139, 155, 156. Stories about a man (boy), 61 and 192 (the clever man); 7, 20, 59, 70, 98, 104 (lucky accidents); 32, 120, 143 (the stupid man). Tales of lying, 146, 151, 158, 159, 185.

* Albert Wesselski (*Versuch einer Theorie des Märchens*, 1931, pp. 12, 32, etc.) is of the opinion that the term *Märchen* should be reserved for this category, II A.

CLASSIFICATION OF TALES
ACCORDING TO ORIGIN

I. *Primitive belief:* 28, 39, 55, 60, 85, 105: i and ii, 109, 154.

II. *Hero sagas from the period of the Migrations:* 47, 52, 89, 111, 198.

III. *Minstrel work of the tenth century:* 8, 18, 20, 33, 37, 45, 61, 64, 90, 91, 103, 112, 114, 146, 151, *151, 166, 183.

IV. *Chivalrous work of the Middle Ages:* 1, 3, 4, 9, 11, 12, 13, 15, 19, 21, 24, 25, 31, 42, 43, 46, 49, 53, 57, 62, 63, 65, 67, 76, 88, 97, 106, 108, 113, 121, 123, 126, 127, 130, 135, 136, 137, 144, 169, 186, 192, 193, 201-210.

V. *Oriental influences:* 6, 16, 29, 36, 51, 54, 56, 68, 71, 79, 92, 93, 94, 98, 107, 122, 129, 134, 143, 152, 165, 182.

VI. *Animal stories:* 2, 17, 23, 27, 48, 58, 72, 73, 74, 75, 102, 132, 148, 157, 171, 173, 177, 187.

VII. *Work of the townsmen of the fourteenth to sixteenth centuries:* 7, 14, 32, 34, 35, 44, 59, 70, 77, 81, 82, 83, 84, 87, 95, 100, 101, 104, 110, 115, 116, 118, 119, 120, 124, 125, 128, 147, 149, 153, 162, 164, 167, 168, 170, 174, 175, 176, 177, 178, 180, 183, 184, 189, 194, 195, 199.

VIII. *From the seventeenth and eighteenth centuries:* 5, 22, 26, 40, 50, 69, 78, 96, 99, 117, 133, 141, 142, 145, 150, 155, 156, 160, 161, 163, 179, 181, 188, 191, 197.

IX. *Jokes and anecdotes:* 10, 30, 38, 41, 66, 80, 86, 105: iii, 131, 138, 139, 140, 158, 159, 190, 196, 200.

[II]

Bios and Mythos

[1]

Sociological and Psychological Schools of Interpretation

The archetypes of mythology are constant enough for six-teenth- and seventeenth-century Roman Catholics, adequately trained in their own symbology, to have regarded the myths and images, sacraments and temples of the New World as dia-bolical mockeries of the truths of the one True Church. Fray Pedro Simón wrote of his mission in seventeenth-century Co-lombia:

> The demon of that place began giving contrary doctrines, and among other things sought to discredit what the priest had been teaching concerning the Incarnation, declaring that it had not yet come to pass, but that presently the Sun would bring it to pass by taking flesh in the womb of a virgin of the village of Guacheta, causing her to conceive by the rays of the sun while she yet remained a virgin. These tidings were proclaimed throughout the region. And it so happened that the headman of the village named had two virgin daugh-ters, each desirous that the miracle should become accom-plished in her. These then began going out from their father's dwelling and garden enclosure every morning at the first peep of dawn. And mounting one of the numerous hills about the village, in the direction of the sunrise, they disposed themselves in such a way that the first rays of the sun were free to shine upon them. This going on for a number of days, it was granted the demon by Divine Permission (Whose judgments are incomprehensible) that things should come to pass as he had planned, and in such fashion that one of the

daughters became pregnant, as she declared, by the sun. Nine months and she brought into the world a large and valuable *hacuata*, which in their language is an emerald. The woman took this, and wrapping it in cotton, placed it between her breasts, where she kept it a number of days, at the end of which time it was transformed into a living creature: all by order of the demon. The child was named Goranchacho, and he was reared in the household of the headman, his grandfather, until he was some twenty-four years old—

whereupon he proceeded, in great state, to the capital of the nation and became known throughout the provinces as "Child of the Sun." [1]

Fray Pedro's testimony is but one of many. The Mexican symbols and myths of Quetzalcoatl so closely resemble those of Jesus that the Padres in that area supposed that Saint Thomas's mission to India must have reached Tenochtitlán, where, cut off from the pure source of Rome, the Waters of Redemption were muddied by fallen angels. Three centuries later, Adolf Bastian (1826–1905), voyaging in China and Japan, India, Africa, and South America, also recognized the uniformity of what he termed the "Elementary Ideas" (*Elementargedanke*) of mankind,[2] but he took a scientifically maturer view of the implicit problem. Instead of attributing the local variations to the distorting power of a devil, he considered the force of geography and history in the processing of the "Ethnic Ideas" (*Völkergedanke*), that is to say, in the shaping of the local transformations of the universal forms. "First," he writes, "the idea as such must be studied . . . and as a second factor, the influence of climatic-geological conditions must be studied." [3] A third factor, to which he devotes many chapters of his innumerable volumes, is that of the impact and influence upon each other of the various "folk" traditions throughout the course of history. Bastian's insight is basic, and has not yet been supplanted.

Tylor, Frazer, and the other comparative anthropologists of the late nineteenth and early twentieth centuries likewise recognized the obvious constancy in mankind's Elementary

Ideas. Franz Boas, for example, in the first edition of his early work, *The Mind of Primitive Man*,[4] stated without qualification that "in the main the mental characteristics of man are the same all over the world"; and that "certain patterns of associated ideas may be recognized in all types of culture." [5] But these avowals were expunged from his second, "revised" (actually, recomposed) edition;[6] for the vogue had by that time begun of stressing differences, even to the point of denying correspondences, between the dialects of the common human language.

We owe this new tendency in large measure to the muddleheaded Emile Durkheim. Read his confused discussion of Kant's *a priori* forms of sensibility,[7] and his quackery about the distinction between the Zuni and European experiences of space,* and the shallowness of his whole parody of profundity will be apparent! The entire culturalist movement in our contemporary Anglo-American anthropological literature is touched with this Durkheimian myopia. Bronislaw Malinowski's misreading of Sigmund Freud's technical term "Oedipus complex" and his refutation, then, of his own misconception added new dignity to the movement,[8] which in the midnineteen thirties culminated in a kind of professorial *curia*, dedicated to the proposition that mankind is not a species but an indefinitely variable dough, shaped by a self-creating demiurge, "Society." The idea that man may have a psychological as well as physical character was anathematized *ex cathedra* as "mystical." †

---

* Durkheim quotes F. H. Cushing to the effect that space in Zuni has seven quarters, and declares this to be an essentially different space from ours, which has but four. The seven Zuni quarters are, to wit: north, south, east, west, above, below, and middle. Very different indeed! Durkheim's problem, obviously, was semantic and absolutely elementary. "Les divisions de l'espace," he concludes, "changent avec sociétés; c'est la preuve qu'elles ne sont pas fondées exclusivement dans la nature congénitale de l'homme." This he regarded as a refutation of Kant's concept of space as an *a priori* "form of sensibility."

† The denotation of this neologism in the polemical literature of the social sciences, where it is employed as a term of abuse, is obscure. It seems to mean, roughly, "unscientific."

The *curia's* characteristic mistake, specifically, has been that of confusing function with morphology—as though a congress of zoologists, studying the wing of the bat, the flipper of the whale, the foreleg of the rat, and the arm of man, should not know that these organs, though shaped to differing functions, are structurally homologous, and were to suppose that the wing of the bat might be compared, morphologically, with that of a butterfly, the flipper of a whale with the fin of a trout, the leg of a rat with that of a beetle, and the arm of a man with that of a lobster. Skipping the first task of a comparative science—that, namely, of distinguishing precisely the sphere of analogy from that of homology—these students of mankind proceeded to the second task—that of the monograph; and the result has been a complete dismemberment of what, at the opening of our century, promised to become a science.

In contrast, we have the sundry schools of the diffusionists, stressing cultural affinities that obviously unite vast portions of the human race. The philologists of the nineteenth century (Bopp, the Grimm brothers, Max Müller, etc.) studied the wide diffusion of the verbal roots and deities of the Indo-Europeans. Hugo Winckler and his school then indicated Mesopotamia as the area from which the world image and concomitant social structure that we find in all the high cultures of the planet must have been diffused;[9] James H. Breasted, G. Elliot Smith, and W. J. Perry spoke for Egypt;[10] Harold Peake and Herbert John Fleure tentatively championed Syria;[11] while V. Gordon Childe supposed that it was somewhere in the area between the Nile and the Indus that the crucial step was taken from paleolithic food gathering to neolithic food production which underlies the structure of settled civilizations throughout the world.[12] Sylvanus G. Morley, on the other hand, held out for an independent origin of the agricultural civilization of the New World in Middle America,[13] thus maintaining the traditional isolationism of the American Anthropological Society; whereas Leo Frobenius, long before, had recognized evidences of a diffusion

across the Pacific.[14] Adolf E. Jensen supported Frobenius's
view in a study of the trans-Pacific diffusion of the mythological complex of an early gardening culture; [15] G. F. Scott Elliot thought it probable that fugitives from Japan, c. 1000 B.C.,
had been responsible for the Middle American development; [16] Robert von Heine-Geldern showed that late Chou
Dynasty art motifs had been somehow diffused from China to
Indonesia and Middle America; [17] and now, most recently, in
a richly documented joint publication by Betty J. Meggers,
Clifford Evans, and Emilio Estrada, it has been shown that,
possibly as early as 3000 B.C., an early type of Japanese cord-
marked (Jomon) ceramic ware was carried from Kyushu to
the coast of Ecuador.[18] We know, furthermore, that the
sweet potato, called *kumar* in Peru, is in Polynesia *kumara*.[19]
Moreover, as Carl O. Sauer has pointed out, a number of
domesticates besides the sweet potato appear to have crossed
the Pacific in pre-Columbian times: West to East, the bottle
gourd, jack bean, coconut, and plantain, a diploid cotton, the
dog (and the custom of eating dogs), the chicken, and the art
of brewing chicha beer; East to West, sweet potatoes, grain
amaranths, and a tetraploid cotton; kapok and maize also were
known on both shores of the great Pacific water.[20] C. C.
Uhlenbeck has pointed to a fundamental affinity between the
Western Eskimo languages, the Uralo-Altaic, and the so-
called "A" complex of the Indo-European tongues,[21] and
there is, moreover, increasing evidence of some kind of
Semitic-Indo-European continuity.[22] In short, there can be
no question but that vast areas of culture diffusion have been
distinguished, and that these represent not only late diffusions
but also very ancient ones. We cannot fail to be impressed,
furthermore, by the clean-cut definition and self-consistency
of many of these culture spheres, as well as by the tenacity
with which their fundamental patterns of ritual and mythology have been retained in differing landscapes and even in
spite of greatly differing economic conditions.[23]

However, it is of first importance not to lose sight of the
fact that the mythological archetypes (Bastian's Elementary

Ideas) cut across the boundaries of these culture spheres and are not confined to any one or two, but are variously represented in all. For example, the idea of survival after death seems to be about conterminous with the human species; so also that of the sacred area (sanctuary), that of the efficacy of ritual, of ceremonial decorations, sacrifice, and of magic, that of supernal agencies, that of a transcendental yet ubiquitously immanent sacred power (*mana, wakonda, śakti,* etc.), that of a relationship between dream and the mythological realm, that of initiation, that of the initiate (shaman, priest, seer, etc.), and so on, for pages.[24] No amount of learned hairsplitting about the differences between Egyptian, Aztec, Hottentot, and Cherokee monster-killers can obscure the fact that the primary problem here is not historical or ethnological but psychological—even biological; that is to say, antecedent to the phenomenology of the culture styles; and no amount of scholarly jargon or apparatus can make it seem that the mere historian or anthropologist is dealing with the problem at all.

In this sensitive and trickish field (Goethe's wondrous realm of "The Mothers") the poet, the artist, and a certain type of romantic philosopher (Emerson, Nietzsche, Bergson, for example) are more successful; for, since in poetry and art, beyond the learning of rhetorical and manual techniques, the whole craft is that of seizing the idea and facilitating its epiphany, the creative mind, adequately trained, is less apt than the analytic to mistake a mere trope or concept for a living, life-awakening image. Poetry and art, whether "academic" or "modern," are simply dead unless informed by Elementary Ideas: ideas, not as clear abstractions held in the mind, but as cognized, or rather re-cognized, vital factors of the subject's own being. Though it is true that such living ideas become manifest only in the terms and style of some specific historical moment, their force nevertheless lies not in what meets the eye but in what dilates the heart, and this force, precisely, is their essential trait. Hence, since mythology is a compendium of such ideas, the historian or anthropologist heeding only his objective eye is gelded of the organ that would have made it possible for him to distinguish his materials. He may note and classify circumstances, but can no more speak authoritatively of mythology than a man without taste buds of taste.

On the other hand, however, though the poet or the artist, with immediate recognition, experiences the idea and grows to meet it; though it thus affects him as initiatory to his own nature, and in such a way that through it he comes into possession of himself and simultaneously into increased understanding of the Elementary Idea—he is finally an amateur in the fields of history and ethnology. There is certainly no comparison between the profundity of Wagner's masterful realization of the import of Germanic mythology in his *Ring of the Nibelungs* and Max Müller's sentimental theory about solar allegories; nevertheless, for detailed information concerning the materials involved, one would properly turn to the unilluminated philologist, not to the genius of Bayreuth.

Is it then impossible to have a science of myth?

Since Wagner's and Max Müller's day, C. G. Jung and Sigmund Freud have opened the way to the new prospect. With their recognition that myth and dream, ceremonial and neurosis, are homologous—their psychological readings of the phenomena of magic, sorcery, and theology, demonstrating the identity of the mythological realm and age with the unconscious, and the relationship, consequently, of myth to dream and of ceremonial to the symptomatology of a neurosis—a total transformation of our control of the problem of the Elementary Idea has taken place. Freud, mainly stressing the parallelism to neurosis, and Jung, recognizing the educative (in the primary sense of the term *e-ducere*) power of the life-binding images, have laid the foundations of a possible science of the universals of myth. Bastian's order of study was correct: (1) the Elementary Idea; (2) the influence of local climatic-geological factors in the processing of the Ethnic Ideas; and, (3) the impact upon each other of the varying local traditions in the course of history. Psychoanalysis now makes it possible to go beyond Bastian's mere listing and description of the Elementary Ideas to a study of their biological roots. To criticize the method as unscientific is ridiculous, since objective scholarship, in this particular field, has shown itself helpless—and absolutely so; helpless by definition, since the materials are not optically measureable, but must, on the contrary, be experienced, if not as in the craftmanship of the poet and the artist, then somehow in life.

There is no need to rehearse the demonstration by psychoanalysis of the parallelism of dream and myth, and the consequent theory of the possibility of mythology developing spontaneously, along traditional lines, wherever mankind may be nesting. "Anyone who really knows what a dream is will agree," writes Géza Róheim, "that there cannot be several 'culturally determined' ways of dreaming just as there are no two ways of sleeping. . . . The dream work is the same for everybody although there are differences in the degree and technique of secondary elaboration." [25] The relationship of dream and vision to mythological symbolism, from Dante to the dreamers (*oko-jumu*) of the Andamanese,[26] is too well known, now, to require demonstration. There is a close relationship between the protective, ego-defending religious symbolism of any people and the dreams of its most talented dreamers. The medicine men, as Róheim so aptly phrases it, are "the lightning conductors of common anxiety. They fight the demons so that others can hunt the prey and in general fight reality." [27] They fight the demons and, while doing so, achieve a measure of psychological wisdom that is denied their extraverted fellows. They are, in fact, the forerunners of those really great dreamers whose names are the names of the pedagogues of the race: Ptahhotep, Akhnaton, Moses, Socrates, Plato, Lao-tzu, Confucius, Vyasa, Homer, the Buddha, Jesus, Quetzalcoatl, and Mohammed. The intentional fathoming of the interior darkness of the psyche in the long tradition of the disciplines of yoga has perhaps given India a larger share than other lands of the wisdom bestowed by the "Eternal Ones of the Dream"; nevertheless, some portion of that wisdom is shared by all the world. Hence Ananda K. Coomaraswamy could maintain that the metaphysical principles symbolized in India in the dreamlike imagery of myth are implicit in mythology everywhere. "All mythology," he wrote in a paper comparing Platonic and Indian thought, "involves a corresponding philosophy; and if there is only one mythology, as there is only one 'perennial philosophy,' then that 'the myth is not my own, I had it from my mother' (Euripides) points to a spiritual unity of the human race already predetermined long before the discovery of metals. It may be really true that, as [Alfred] Jeremias said, the various cultures of mankind are no more than the dialects of one and the same spiritual language." [28]

"Myth," he states again, "is the penultimate truth, of which all experience is the temporal reflection. The mythical narrative is of timeless and placeless validity, true nowever and everywhere"; [29] precisely, one might add, as the dream is the penultimate truth about the dreamer, of which all his experience is the temporal reflection.

A serious science of mythology must take its subject matter with due seriousness, survey the field as a whole, and have at least some conception of the prodigious range of functions that mythology has served in the course of human history. It is dreamlike and, like dream, a spontaneous product of the psyche; like dream, revelatory of the psyche and hence of the whole nature and destiny of man; like dream—like life—enigmatic to the uninitiated ego; and, like dream, protective of that ego. In the simplest human societies mythology is the text of the rites of passage; in the writings of the Hindu, Chinese, and Greek philosophers (as of all who have ever read them) mythology is the picture language of metaphysics. The first function is not violated by the second but extended; both harmoniously bind man, the growing animal, to his world, simultaneously in its visible and in its transcendent aspects. Mythology is the womb of mankind's initiation to life and death.

[2]

The Biological Function of Myth

How mythology functions, why it is generated and required by the human species, why it is everywhere essentially the same, and why the rational destruction of it conduces to puerility, become known the moment one abandons the historical method of tracing secondary origins and adopts the biological view (characteristic of the medical art of psychoanalysis), which considers the primary organism itself, this universal carrier and fashioner of history, the human body. As Róheim states in his brilliant monograph *The Origin and Function of Culture:*

> The outstanding difference between man and his animal brethren consists in the infantile morphological characters of human beings, in the prolongation of infancy. This prolonged infancy explains the traumatic character of sexual experiences which do not produce the like effect in our simian brethren or cousins, and the existence of the Œdipus Complex itself which is partly a conflict between archaic and recent love objects. Finally, the defence mechanisms themselves owe their existence to the fact that our Soma (Ego) is even more retarded than the Germa (Id) and hence the immature Ego evolves defence mechanisms as a protection against libidinal quantities which it is not prepared to deal with.[30]

"Man," as Adolf Portmann of Basel vividly phrases it, "is the incomplete creature whose style of life is the historical process determined by a tradition."[31] He is congenitally dependent on society and society, commensurably, is both oriented to and derived from the distinctive psychosomatic structure of man. This structure, furthermore, is rooted not in any local landscape, with its economic-political potentials, but in the germa of a widely distributed biological species. Whether on the ice of Baffin Land or in the jungles of Brazil, building temples in Siam or cafés in Paris, "civilization," as Dr. Róheim shows, "originates in delayed infancy and its function is security. It is a huge network of more or less successful attempts to protect mankind against the danger of object-loss, the colossal efforts made by a baby who is afraid of being left alone in the dark." [32] In such a context, the symbolical potentialities of the various environments are at least as important as the economic; symbolism, the protection of the psyche, no less necessary than the nourishment of the soma. Society, as a fostering organ, is thus a kind of exterior "second womb," wherein the postnatal stages of man's long gestation—much longer than that of any other placental—are supported and defended.

One thinks of the marsupial pouch, likewise auxiliary to a foetal development that overreaches the intrauterine possibilities of the species. The young of the kangaroo, for example, born after a gestation period of but three weeks, measure an inch in length and are entirely naked and blind; their hind limbs are undeveloped, but the forelimbs are robust with claws. William King Gregory, of the American Museum of Natural History, describes the climbing of these little creatures, by means of their sturdy forelimbs, up the mother's belly, immediately upon birth, and into her pouch, where they reach for the teats, one of which each eventually seizes. The tip of the teat then expands within the mouth, so that the young cannot be released. "Thus the marsupials," Gregory summarizes, "specialized in the early and brief internal development of the embryo, which depends for food chiefly upon its own yolk-sack and which completes its development after birth while attached to the teat. The higher or placental mammals gave the young a longer and better uterine development and a more flexible system of nursing, with greater maternal responsibility." [33]

The marsupials (kangaroo, bandicoot, wombat, opossum, etc.) represent an intermediate stage between monotremes (the duck-billed platypus, spiny anteater of Australia, etc.), whose progeny, like those of reptiles, are born from eggs, and placentals (mice, antelopes, leopards, gorillas, etc.), whose young appear only after a comparatively long gestation pe-

riod within the mother (made possible by the placenta) and at
birth are almost ready for life. Man, biologically, is a placental. The period of gestation, however, has become again
inadequate—indeed, even less adequate than that of the marsupials; for instead of the mere few months spent by the
young kangaroo in the auxiliary womb of its mother's pouch,
the infant *Homo sapiens* requires years before it can forage
for its food, and as many as twenty before it looks and be-
haves like an adult.

George Bernard Shaw played on this anomaly in his biological fantasy *Back to Methuselah*, where he viewed man, in
Nietzsche's manner, as a bridge to the superman. Looking forward to the year 31,920 A.D., he showed us the birth from a
huge egg of a pretty girl, who, in the twentieth century,
would have been thought to be about seventeen.[34] She had
been growing within the egg for two years; the first nine
months, like the nine of the present gestation period of the
human embryo, recapitulated the biological evolution of man;
the remaining fifteen then matured the organism, briefly but
securely, to the condition of the young adult. Four years
more, spent among youthful playmates in the sort of childhood that we remain in today until seventy, would terminate
when her mind changed and the young woman, tiring suddenly of play, became wise and fit for the wielding of such
power as today, in the hands of children, is threatening to
wreck the world.

Human adulthood is not achieved until the twenties: Shaw
put it in the seventies: not a few look ahead to Purgatory.
Meanwhile, society is what takes the place of the Shavian egg.

Róheim has indicated the problem of man-growing-up, no
matter where—defense against libidinal quantities with which
the immature ego is not prepared to deal;[35] and he has analyzed the curious "symbiotic mode of mastering reality,"[36]
which is the very fashioner, the master builder, of all human
societies. "It is the nature of our species," he writes, "to
master reality on a libidinal basis and we create a society, an
environment in which this and only this is possible."[37] "The

psyche as we know it, is formed by the introjection of primary objects (super-ego) and the first contact with environment (ego). Society itself is knitted together by projection of these primary introjected objects or concepts followed by a series of subsequent introjections and projections." [38] This tight-knitting of defensive fantasy and external reality is what builds the second womb, the marsupial pouch that we call society. Hence, though man's environment greatly varies in the corners of the planet, there is a marvelous monotony about his ritual forms. Local styles of the century, nation, race, or social class obviously differ; yet what James Joyce calls the "grave and constant in human sufferings," [39] remains truly constant and grave. It arrests the mind, everywhere, in the rituals of birth, adolescence, marriage, death, installation, and initiation, uniting it with the mysteries of eternal recurrence and of man's psychosomatic maturation. The individual grows up, not only as a member of a certain social group, but as a human being.

[3]
The Image of a Second Birth

Rites, then, together with the mythologies that support them, constitute the second womb, the matrix of the postnatal gestation of the placental *Homo sapiens*. This fact, moreover, has been known to the pedagogues of the race, certainly since the period of the Upanishads, and probably since that of the Aurignacian caves. In the Mundaka Upanishad we read, for example: "There are two knowledges to be known—as indeed the knowers of Brahman are wont to say: a higher and also a lower. Of these, the lower is the Rig Veda, the Yajur Veda, the Sama Veda, the Atharva Veda, Pronunciation, Ritual, Grammar, Definition, Metrics, and Astrology. The higher is that whereby the Imperishable is apprehended." [40] "Those abiding in the midst of ignorance, self-wise, thinking themselves learned, hard smitten, go around deluded, like blind men led by one who is himself blind. Thinking sacrifice

and merit the chiefest thing, naught better do they know.
. . . But they who practise austerity and faith in the forest,
the peaceful knowers who live on alms, depart passionless
through the door of the sun, to where is that immortal Person, even the imperishable Spirit." [41]

In India the objective is to be *born* from the womb of
myth, not to remain in it, and the one who has attained to this
"second birth" is truly the "twice born," freed from the pedagogical devices of society, the lures and threats of myth, the
local *mores*, the usual hopes of benefits and rewards. He is
truly "free" (*mukti*), "released while living" (*jivan mukti*);
he is that reposeful "superman" who is man perfected—
though in our kindergarten of libidinous misapprehensions he
moves like a being from another sphere.

The same idea of the "second birth" is certainly basic to
Christianity also, where it is symbolized in baptism. "Except a
man be born of water and of the spirit, he cannot enter into
the kingdom of God. That which is born of the flesh is flesh;
and that which is born of the Spirit is spirit." [42] One could
ask for no more vivid rendition of the doctrine of the two
wombs: the womb of the mammal and the womb of perfected
man.

Within the Christian Church, however, there has been a
historically successful tendency to anathematize the obvious
implications of this idea, and the result has been a general obscuration of the fact that regeneration means going beyond,
not remaining within, the confines of mythology. Whereas in
the Orient—India, Tibet, China, Japan, Indo-China, and
Indonesia—everyone is expected, at least in his final incarnation, to leave the womb of myth, to pass through the sundoor and stand beyond the gods, in the West—or at least
throughout the greater part of the Judaeo-Christian–Mohammedan development—God remains the Father, and none
can step beyond Him. This accounts, perhaps, for the great
distinction between the manly piety of the Orient and the infantile of the recent Occident. In the lands of the truly "twice
born" man is finally superior to the gods, whereas in the West

even the saint is required to remain within the body of the Church, and the "second birth" is read rather as being born *into* the Church than born out of it. The historical result was a shattering of this particular marsupial pouch in the fifteenth century.

There is no need to multiply examples of the rebirth motif in the philosophies and religious rites of the civilized world. The Neoplatonic and Taoist philosophies, the Greek Mysteries, the myths and rites of Phoenicia, Mesopotamia, and Egypt, as well as those of the Celts and Germans, Aztecs and Mayas, abound in applications of the idea. Nor is it less prominent in the myths and rites of the primitive peoples of the world. "Death and rebirth," declares Róheim, "are the typical contents of all initiation rites." [43]

Among the Keraki of New Guinea bull-roarers play a prominent role in the ceremonies of initiation. The boys are made to sit with their eyes covered by the older men and then the bull-roarers begin to sound. The boys think they are hearing the voice of the presiding crocodile-deity of the ritual; the sound comes nearer, as though the monster were approaching to swallow them, and when it is directly over their heads, the old men's hands are removed and the boys see the bull-roarers.[44] Thus they become aware, abruptly, of the source of the sound that throughout their childhood had been thought to be the voice of a living monster.

Such sudden awakenings are characteristic of the tradition of initiation everywhere. What for the child were disciplinary terrors become the symbolic implements of the adult who knows. Nevertheless, the result is not that the symbols are understood as frauds; on the contrary, the bull-roarers of the Keraki receive food offerings.[45] They are divinities: the guardians of the Way of life. "At the creation of the world," said a medicine man of the Pawnee of Kansas and Nebraska, "it was arranged that there should be lesser powers. Tirawa-atius, the mighty power, could not come near to man, could not be seen or felt by him, therefore lesser powers were permitted. They were to mediate between man and Tirawa." [46]

The myths and paraphernalia of the rites of passage represent such powers, and so are informed with the force of the source, support, and end of existence.

The fact that some of the burials of the Mousterian cave men include implements and joints of meat suggests that the idea of regeneration beyond the veil of life must have been entertained some fifty thousand years B.C. Later paleolithic burials with the corpse in the crouch-position of the foetus in the womb give point to the same theme by stressing the idea of a second birth. And, finally, the picture of a dancing, masked medicine man in the Aurignacian cave of the Trois Frères, Ariège, France, suggests that there must have been, fifteen thousand years ago, initiates aware of the force and meaning of the symbols. It would perhaps be going too far to suggest that in any primitive society pedagogues, or mystagogues, can have existed whose reading of the rebirth idea drove as far as that of the Hindus; nevertheless, it cannot be denied that in primitive mythologies and rites we find the image of the sun-door, the clashing rocks, death and resurrection, the Incarnation, the sacred marriage and father atonement, employed not haphazardly but in the same relationships as in the myths of the higher cultures.[47]

The actual unity of folklore represents on the popular level [declared Ananda K. Coomaraswamy] precisely what the orthodoxy of an élite represents in a relatively learned environment. The relation between the popular and the learned metaphysics is, moreover, analogous to and partly identical with that of the lesser to the greater mysteries. To a very large extent both employ one and the same symbols, which are taken more literally in the one case and in the other understood parabolically: for example, the "giants" and "heroes" of popular legend are the titans and gods of the more learned mythology, the seven-league boots of the hero correspond to the strides of an Agni or a Buddha, and "Tom Thumb" is no other than the Son whom Eckhart describes as "small, but so puissant." *So long as the material of folklore is transmitted,*

so long is the ground available on which the superstructure
of full initiatory understanding can be built.[48]

Whether, in any given culture, the individual is enabled to
be really born again or required to remain spiritually foetal
until released from purgatory, myth is everywhere the womb
of man's specifically human birth: the long-tried, the tested
matrix within which the unfinished being is brought to maturity; simultaneously protecting the growing ego against
libidinal quantities which it is not prepared to deal with and
furnishing it with the necessary foods and saps for its normal,
harmonious unfoldment. Mythology fosters a balanced intui-
tive and instinctive, as well as rational, ontogenesis, and
throughout the domain of the species the morphology of this
peculiar spiritual organ of *Homo sapiens* is no less constant
than that of the well-known, readily recognizable human
physique itself.

[4]

The Anxiety of the Misborn

Misbirth is possible from the mythological womb as well as
from the physiological: there can be adhesions, malforma-
tions, arrestations, etc. We call them neuroses and psychoses.
Hence we find today, after some five hundred years of the
systematic dismemberment and rejection of the mythological
organ of our species, all the sad young men, for whom life is a
problem. Mythology leads the libido into ego-syntonic chan-
nels, whereas neurosis (to cite, once again, Géza Róheim)
"separates the individual from his fellows and connects him
with his own infantile images." [49] Psychoanalysis and certain
movements in contemporary art and letters represent an effort
to restore the biologically necessary spiritual organ. Blake, for
example, Goethe and Emerson, saw the need for it. Their
effort was to restore the poet to his traditional function of
seer and mystagogue of the regenerative vision. James Joyce
has supplied the whole blueprint. The morphology of the or-

gan will remain the same as ever, but the materials of which it is composed and the functions served will have to be those of the new world: the materials of the machine age and the functions of the world society that is today in its throes of birth— as myth.

[III]

Primitive Man as Metaphysician

> "The name of the song is called 'Haddocks' Eyes.' "
> "Oh, that's the name of the song, is it?" Alice said, trying
> to feel interested. "No, you don't understand," the
> Knight said, looking a little vexed. "That's what the
> name is called."
>
> —LEWIS CARROLL, *Through the Looking Glass*

[1]

Tender- and Tough-Minded Thinking

"The metaphysical notions of man may be reduced to a few
types which are of universal distribution"; so wrote Franz
Boas in the first edition (1911) of *The Mind of Primitive
Man.*[1] However, in the second edition of the same authoritative work, published a quarter of a century later (1938), this
observation, as already remarked,* does not appear; for there
had developed in American anthropology, meanwhile, a tendency to emphasize the differentiating, not the shared, traits
of primitive societies; so that any mention of common features would simply have branded an author as out of touch
with the fashions of his guild. By the early fifties, on the other
hand, the tide again had turned, and in a formidable inventory
of anthropological lore, prepared under the chairmanship of
A. L. Kroeber and published (1953) as *Anthropology Today,*[2] there appeared a substantial article by Clyde Kluck-
hohn, "Universal Categories of Culture," as well as a number

---

* Supra, p. 45.

of references by the other recognized authorities to the need for comparative evaluations. No one at that time, however, brought forward again the idea developed by Paul Radin some thirty years before, when, in *Primitive Man as Philosopher* (1927), he offered a formula by which the two points of view successively represented by Boas might have been reconciled and brought together in a single general theory. His eminently sensible observation that among primitive as well as highly civilized peoples the two types of man are to be found that William James long ago characterized as the tough-minded and tender-minded [3]—and that the myths and symbols of all societies are interpreted in differing senses by these two—had apparently been forgotten by the representatives of a science which, in the words of Boas himself, "does not deal with the exceptional man." [4]

"From the man of action's viewpoint," wrote Dr. Radin, describing the attitude of the tough-minded type, "a fact has no symbolic or static value. He predicates no unity beyond that of the certainty of continuous change and transformation. For him a double distortion is involved in investing the transitory and ceaselessly changing object with a symbolic, idealistic, or static significance." The thinker, on the other hand, the tender-minded type, "is impelled by his whole nature, by the innate orientation of his mind, to try to discover the reason why there is an effect, what is the nature of the relation between the ego and the world, and what part exactly the perceiving self plays therein. Like all philosophers, he is interested in the subject as such, the object as such, and the relations between them. . . . An original, moving, shapeless or undifferentiated world must be brought to rest and given stable form. . . . Philosophers have always given the same answer to this problem and predicated a unity behind these changing aspects and forms. Primitive philosophers are at one with their European and Asiatic brothers here." [5]

Now it appears to me that any science that takes into consideration only or even primarily the vulgar, tough-minded interpretation of symbols will inevitably be committed to a study largely of local differentiations, while, on the other hand, one addressed to the views of thinkers will find that the ultimate references of their cogitations are few and of universal distribution. Anthropologists, by and large (or, at least, those of the current American variety) are notoriously tough-minded. (There is a Haitian proverb, I am told: "When the anthropologist arrives, the gods depart!") They have tended to give reductive interpretations to the symbols of primitive thought and to find their references only in the particularities of the local scene. The following pages offer an alternative, an amplification and supplement, to that view.

[2]

The Image and Its Meaning

The first problem to be confronted by anyone wishing to deal with the metaphysical notions of mankind is that of distinguishing between symbols and their references—between what we may term the *vehicles* and their *tenor*. For instance, the three or four instances of "metaphysical notions" enumerated by Franz Boas in his chapter on "The Universality of Cultural Traits" are not metaphysical notions at all: they are simply images, symbols, or vehicles, which by a tough-minded individual might be interpreted physically, as references not to any metaphysical realization whatsoever but to remote facts, realms, or lands much like our own—whereas the term "metaphysical" refers to no place, no time, no thing, no fact, not even wonders of such stuff as dreams are made of. "Belief in a land of the souls of the deceased," for example,[6] "located in the west, and reached by crossing a river": this is not in itself a metaphysical notion, though it may be given a metaphysical reading. Nor can we call metaphysical "the idea of a multiplicity of worlds,—one or more spanned over us, others stretching under us, the central one the home of man; the upper or lower, the home of the gods and happy souls; the other, the home of the unhappy." [7]

Such images are not the final terms of our subject, if it is of metaphysics that we are treating. They have often served, indeed, as vehicles of metaphysical expression, and part of our problem, certainly, is to collect, compare, and classify them; but we miss our proper point if we rest with them as they stand. For an image may signify various things in various contexts and to various minds. Furthermore, where an image has disappeared, it need not follow that the tenor of its reference has disappeared: this may be lurking under another image entirely. Nor in cross-cultural comparisons can we safely assume that because the symbolic figures differ from culture to culture the tenors of their references must differ also.

Let us consider, therefore, a brief series of mythological images culled from a number of cultures, which may be discovered to be the vehicles of a single metaphysical tenor.

[3]

Imagery of the Manifold and Its "Cause"

Natalie Curtis, in *The Indians' Book*, published years ago (1907) a remarkable origin myth recounted to her by an aged Pima chief, Hovering Hawk:

> In the beginning there was only darkness everywhere—darkness and water. And the darkness gathered thick in places, crowding together and then separating, until at last out of one of the places where the darkness had crowded there came forth a man. This man wandered through the darkness until he began to think; then he knew himself and that he was a man; he knew that he was there for some purpose.
>
> He put his hand over his heart and drew forth a large stick. He used the stick to help him through the darkness, and when he was weary he rested upon it. Then he made for himself little ants; he brought them from his body and put them on the stick. Everything that he made he drew from his own body even as he had drawn the stick from his heart. The stick was of grease-wood, and of the gum of the wood the ants made a round ball upon the stick.

Then the man took the ball from the stick and put it down in the darkness under his foot, and as he stood upon the ball he rolled it under his foot and sang:

> I make the world, and lo!
> The world is finished.
> Thus I make the world, and lo!
> The world is finished.

So he sang, calling himself the maker of the world. He sang slowly, and all the while the ball grew larger as he rolled it, till at the end of his song, behold, it was the world. Then he sang more quickly:

> Let it go, let it go,
> Let it go, start it forth!

So the world was made, and now the man brought forth from himself a rock and divided it into little pieces. Of these he made stars, and put them in the sky to light the darkness. But the stars were not bright enough.

So he made Tau-mik, the milky-way. Yet Tau-mik was not bright enough. Then he made the moon. All these he made of rocks drawn forth from himself. But even the moon was not bright enough. So he began to wonder what next he could do. He could bring nothing from himself that could lighten the darkness.

Then he thought. And from himself he made two large bowls, and he filled the one with water and covered it with the other. He sat and watched the bowls, and while he watched he wished that what he wanted to make in very truth would come to be. And it was even as he wished. For the water in the bowl turned into the sun and shone out in rays through the cracks where the bowls joined.

When the sun was made, the man lifted off the top bowl and took out the sun and threw it to the east. But the sun did not touch the ground; it stayed in the sky where he threw it and never moved. Then in the same way he threw the sun to the north and to the west and to the south. But each time it only stayed in the sky, motionless, for it never touched the ground. Then he threw it once more to the east, and this time it touched the ground and bounced and

started upward. Since then the sun has never ceased to
move. It goes around the world in a day, but every morning it must bounce anew in the east.[8]

It is impossible to read this story without thinking of the
far-flung Old World theme of the primordial giant out of
whose body the universe proceeds, and who, until the end of
time, remains within the forms of the universe as the "self of
all."

"In the beginning, this universe was only the self, in a human form," we read in the Sanskrit Brihadaranyaka Upanishad.

He looked around and saw nothing but himself. Then,
at the beginning, he cried out, "I am he!" Whence came
the name, I. That is why, even today, when a person is
addressed, he first declares, "It is I," and then announces
the other name that he goes by.

He was afraid. That is why people are afraid to be alone.
He thought, "But what am I afraid of? There is nothing
but myself." Whereupon his fear was gone. . . .

He was unhappy. That is why people are not happy
when they are alone. He wanted a mate. He became as big
as a woman and man embracing. He divided this body,
which was himself, in two parts. From that there came
husband and wife. . . . Therefore this body [before one
marries a wife] is like one of the halves of a split pea. . . .
He united with her; and from that were born men.

She considered: "How can he unite with me after producing me from himself? Well then, let me hide myself."
She became a cow; but he became a bull and united with
her: from that were born cattle. She became a mare, he a
stallion; she a she-ass, he a he-ass and united with her; from
that were born the one-hoofed animals. . . . She became a
goat, he a buck; she a ewe, he a ram and united with her:
from that were born goats and sheep. Thus did he project
everything that exists in pairs, down to the ants.

Then he knew: "Indeed, I am myself the creation, for
I have projected this entire world." Whence he was called
Creation. . . .[9]

Sometimes, as here, the projection of the world is pictured in Brahminical mythology as voluntary; sometimes, as in the Kalika Purana,[10] where the gods spring spontaneously from the yogic contemplation of the demiurge, Brahma, the creation is a succession of surprises even to the creator. In the Icelandic Eddas, it will be recalled, the cosmic hermaphrodite, Ymir, gives off Rime-Giants from his living hands and feet, but is attacked during a later age by the young gods, Wotan, Wili, and We, to be cut up and transformed into the entire theater of the cosmos.[11] Comparably, in the celebrated Babylonian "Epic of Creation," the young god Marduk kills, cuts up, and fashions the universe from the body of the primal chaos monster Tiamat. Ovid, in the first chapter of his *Metamorphoses*, states that a god, in the beginning, brought order out of chaos.[12] And we learn from the ancient Egyptian Memphite theogony that Egypt, the universe, and all the gods came forth from Ptah, "The Great One," "Him-with-the-lovely-face." [13]

In the Indian metaphysical system of the Vedanta, which purports to be a translation of the metaphorical imagery of Brahminical myths into abstract philosophical terms, the primordial entity out of which the universe proceeds is described as a fusion of Pure Consciousness (*brahman*, *vidyā*) and Ignorance (*māyā*, *avidyā*), where Ignorance (*māyā*) is compared to the female of the mythological pair, furnishing at once the womb and the substance of creation. By virtue of her obscuring power she occludes the Absolute Brahman, and by virtue of her projecting power she refracts the radiance of that Absolute in the forms of the world mirage, somewhat as a prism breaks the white light of the sun into the seven colors of the rainbow—for, as Goethe has phrased the same concept in his *Faust*: "*Am farbigen Abglanz haben wir das Leben.*" *
In the fifteenth-century Vedantasara, this marriage of Ignorance and Consciousness, Illusion and Truth, Maya and Brahman, is described as at once the efficient and the material cause of all things. "Consciousness associated with Ignorance

---

* *Faust*, Part II, 1.1, last line. "We have our life in the colorful reflection."

(and the latter possessed of the two powers) is both the efficient cause and the material cause of the universe . . . ; just
as the spider, when considered from the standpoint of its own
self, is the efficient cause of the web, and, when looked upon
from the standpoint of its own body, is also the material cause
of the web." [14]

Translated into Kantian terms, Ignorance as here interpreted corresponds to the *a priori* forms of sensibility (time
and space), which are the inmost and outmost boundaries and
the preconditions of all empirical experience: these *a priori*
forms occlude the metaphysical realm of absolute reality and
project the universe of phenomenality. But what the "true
being" of the ultimate reality, dissociated from our modes of
experience, might be, we shall never know; for, as the "great
Chinaman of Königsberg" phrases it: *"Was es für eine Be-
wandniss mit den Gegenständen an sich und abgesondert von
aller dieser Receptivität unserer Sinnlichkeit haben möge,
bleibt uns gänzlich unbekannt."* *

Thus Hovering Hawk, the Brihadaranyaka Upanishad, the
Kalika Purana, the Eddas, the Babylonian "Epic of Creation,"
Ovid, the Memphite theogony, Vedantic philosophy, Kant,
and Goethe, through varieties of metaphor, have stated and
stated again a single thought—and what would appear to be
an easy thought to state, namely: the One, by some sleight of
hand or trick of the eye, has become the Manifold. Yet, instead of stating this thought directly, they have employed
allegorical vehicles, now of pictorial, now of abstract character, and, curiously, though each of the vehicles succeeds in
conveying at least a hint of the tenor of the message, none
actually elucidates it—none really explains, or even directly
represents, the mystery of the coming of the Manifold out of
the One. And in this respect Kant's formulation is no more
satisfactory than Hovering Hawk's.

But the problem, again regarded, is seen to be not suscepti-

* Immanuel Kant, *Kritik der reinen Vernunft*, I.8.i. "What might be said
of the things in themselves, separated from all relationship to our senses,
remains for us absolutely unknown."

ble of outright elucidation; for it is a problem of the relationship of a known term (the universe) to an unknowable (its so-called source): that is to say, it is, strictly speaking, a metaphysical, not an empirical problem. Whether such a problem be presented for contemplation in the picture language of the myth or in the abstract of philosophy, it can only be presented, never elucidated. And since it is thus finally ineffable, no single metaphor, no combination of metaphors, can exhaust its implications. The slightest change of standpoint, and the entire conception undergoes kaleidoscopic transformation, as do likewise the correlative vehicles of imagery and communication. The primordial One, for instance, may be represented as masculine (as in the case of Brahma), feminine (as in the World Mother), hermaphrodite (as in the cases of "I" and Ymir), anthropomorphic (as in most of the above-presented examples), theriomorphic (as in the Persian myth of the dismembered World Ox), botanomorphic (as in the Eddic image of the World Ash, Yggdrasil), simply ovoid (as in the stories of the World Egg), geometrical (as in the Tantric yantras), vocal (as in the cases of the Vedic sacred syllable OM and the Kabbalistic Tetragrammaton), or absolutely transcendent (as in the cases of the Buddhistic Void and the Kantian Ding-an-sich). But even the notion of the Oneness of the primordial is finally only a metaphor—referring past itself to an inconceivable term beyond all such pairs of opposites as the One and the Manifold, masculinity and feminity, existence and nonexistence.

[4]

The "Cause" Understood as Absolutely Unknown

Kant supplies an extraordinarily simple formula for the proper reading of a metaphysical symbol.[15] What he offers is a four-term analogy (*a* is to *b* as *c* is to *x*), which points not to an incomplete resemblance of two things but to a complete resemblance of two relationships between quite dissimilar things ("*nicht etwa, eine unvollkommene Ähnlichkeit zweier*

Dinge, sondern eine vollkommene Ähnlichkeit zweier Verhält-nisse zwischen ganz unähnlichen Dingen"): not "*a* somewhat resembles *b*," but "the relationship of *a* to *b* perfectly resembles that of *c* to *x*," where *x* represents a quantity that is not only unknown but absolutely unknowable—which is to say, metaphysical.

Kant demonstrates this formula in two examples:

1. As the promotion of the happiness of the children (*a*) is related to the parents' love (*b*), so is the welfare of the human race (*c*) to that unknown in God (*x*) which we call God's love.

2. The causality of the highest cause is precisely, in respect to the world, what human reason is in respect to the work of human art.

He then discusses the implication of the second of these examples, as follows: "Herewith the nature of the highest cause itself remains unknown to me; I only compare its known effect (namely, the constitution of the universe) and the rationality of this effect with the known effects of human reason, and therefore I call that highest cause a Reason, without thereby attributing to it as its proper quality, either the thing that I understand by this term in the case of man, or any other thing with which I am familiar."

Mythological, theological, metaphysical analogies, in other words, do not point indirectly to an only partially understood knowable term, but directly to a *relationship between two terms*, the one empirical, the other metaphysical; the latter being, absolutely and forever and from every conceivable human standpoint, unknowable.

If this be so then we shall have misread the series presented in section 2 if we suppose that we have fully caught its tenor in the simple statement, "the One, by some sleight of hand, has become the Multiple." Such a statement furnishes, indeed, a terse summary of the vehicular aspect of the analogous metaphors but leaves unclarified their metaphysical tenor; that is to say, it summarizes only the first two terms of an implied four-term analogy, which would read, fully rendered, as follows: "As many (a) proceed from one (b), so does the universe (c) from God (x)." But the term x, it must be insisted, remains absolutely unknown and unknowable. Oneness can no more be a quality of this x than can Love or Reason. Hence, as Kant has declared, it is only by analogy that we speak of Love or Reason, Unity, or even Being, as of God.

X remaining unknown, then, the precise nature of its relationship to c must likewise remain unknown. Magic, simple fission, sexual procreation, violent dismemberment, refraction, effusion, and delusion are among the relationships suggested—suggested, not as proper to the mystery of creation itself, but as vehicles to carry the analogy. And there are no end of possible vehicular relationships; no end of possible a terms and related b terms; for instance: as Earth Maker (b^1) is related to the things drawn from his body (a^1); as All-father (b^2) is related to the creatures that he has begotten (a^2); as meditating Brahma (b^3) is related to the visions of his meditation (a^3); as occluded light (b^4) to its refractions (a^4); as the spider (b^5) to its web (a^5); etc., etc., etc., ad infinitum (b^n: a^n); so is "God" (x) related to creation (c).

[5]

Theology as a Misreading of Mythology

Unless the myths can be understood—or felt—to be true in some such way as this, they lose their force, their magic, their charm for the tender-minded and become mere archaeological curiosities, fit only for some sort of reductive classification. And this, indeed, would appear to be the death that the heroes of the myths themselves most fear. Continually, they are pointing past and through their phenomenal to their universal, transcendental, aspect. "I and the Father are One," declares the Christ, for example (John 10:30). And Krishna, in the Bhagavad Gita, shows that all the forms of the world are rooted in his metaphysical essence, just as that essence itself, reciprocally, is rooted in all things:

Neither the hosts of gods, nor the great saints, know my
origin, for in every way I am the source of all the gods and
great saints. He who knows Me, birthless and beginning-
less, the great Lord of worlds—he, among mortals, is un-
deluded, he is freed from all sins. . . . I am the Self existing in the heart of all beings; I am the beginning, the
middle, and also the end of all beings. Of the gods, I
am Vishnu; of luminaries, the radiant sun; . . . of bodies
of water, I am the ocean; . . . of measures, I am time; of
beasts, I am the lord of beasts; of birds, I am the lord of
birds; . . . of fishes, I am the shark; of streams, I am the
Ganges; . . . I am the gambling of the fraudulent; I am
the power of the powerful; I am victory, I am effort, I am
the harmony of the harmonious; . . . of punishers, I am the
scepter; of those who seek to conquer, I am the statesman-
ship; of things secret, I am silence, and the knowledge of the
knowers am I. . . .[16]

Comparably, Killer-of-Enemies, the hero of the Jicarilla
Apache tribe of New Mexico, declares, when he is about to
depart from the people:

The earth is my body. The sky is my body. The seasons
are my body. The water is my body too. . . . The world
is just as big as my body. The world is as large as my
word. And the world is as large as my prayers. The seasons
are only as great as my body, my words, and my prayer.
It is the same with the waters; my body, my words, my
prayers are greater than the waters. Whoever believes me,
whoever listens to what I say, will have long life. One who
doesn't listen, who thinks in some evil way will have a
short life. Don't think I am just in the east, south, west, or
north. The earth is my body. I am there. I am all over.
Don't think I stay only under the earth or up in the sky,
or only in the seasons, or on the other side of the waters.
These are all my body. It is the truth that the underworld,
the sky, the waters, are all my body. I am all over. I have
already given you that with which you have to make an
offering to me. You have two kinds of pipe and you have
the mountain tobacco.[17]

Or once again, in the words of Aeschylus:

Zeus is air, Zeus is earth, Zeus is heaven;
Zeus is all things, and whatsoever is higher than all things.[18]

"We should understand well," said an old Sioux medicine man, Black Elk, the Keeper of the Sacred Pipe of his tribe, "that all things are the works of the Great Spirit. We should know that He is within all things: the trees, the grasses, the rivers, the mountains, and all the four-legged animals, and the winged peoples; and even more important, we should understand that He is also above all these things and peoples. When we do understand all this deeply in our hearts, then we will fear, and love, and know the great Spirit, and then we will be and act and live as He intends." [19]

Wherever myths still are living symbols, the mythologies are teeming dream worlds of such images. But wherever systematizing theologians have appeared and gained the day (the tough-minded in the gardens of the tender) the figures have become petrified into propositions. Mythology is misread then as direct history or science, symbol becomes fact, metaphor dogma, and the quarrels of the sects arise, each mistaking its own symbolic signs for the ultimate reality—the local vehicle for its timeless, ineffable tenor.

"But he who is called Krishna," said the nineteenth-century Indian teacher, Ramakrishna, "is also called Shiva and bears the names Shakti, Jesus, and Allah as well—the one Rama with a thousand names. . . . The substance is one under different names and everyone is seeking the same substance; nothing but climate, temperament, and names vary." [20]

[6]

Esoteric and Exoteric Anthropology

And so now we have to ask whether mythology can have originated in the camps of the tough-minded and only later have become sublimated and sophisticated into metaphysical poetry by the broodings of the tender-minded; or whether its course of development must not have been in precisely the opposite direction, from the poetical imagery of the tender-minded to the clumsy misreadings of the ungifted many. Franz Boas appears to have been a champion of the former view. In his article already referred to, "The Ethnological Significance of Esoteric Doctrines," he wrote:

> It may be said that the exoteric doctrine is the more general ethnic phenomenon, the investigation of which is a necessary foundation for the study of the problems of esoteric teaching. It is, therefore, evident that we must not, in our study of Indian life, seek for the highest form of thought only, which is held by the priest, the chief, the leader. Interesting and attractive as this field of research may be, it is supplementary only to the study of the thoughts, emotional life, and ethical standards of the common people, whose interests center in other fields of thought and of whom the select class forms only a special type.[21]

Professor R. R. Marett, on the other hand, in his article "Mana," in the *Encyclopaedia Britannica* (fourteenth edition), appears to take the opposite view. "By the very virtue of his profession," he writes, "the medicine man or the divine king must hold himself apart from those who by status or by choice are *noa*, laymen. The latter may live in brutish contentment; but to the end they lack enlightenment, participating in the highest mysteries at best from without. Every member of a primitive society is in some degree versed in experience of the occult, though for the most part some better qualified person is present to help him through it."

Whether primary or secondary in temporal terms—that is to say, in terms of "Which came first?"—the tender-minded, esoteric view is clearly the one that has played the chief role in the significant shaping of traditions, since it is everywhere the priests and shamans who have maintained and developed the general inheritance of myths and symbols. Radin, I observe, like Boas, regarded the role of the intellectual as secondary in primitive societies.[22] He gave due recognition to the force of philosophical thought in the shaping of their cultural heritage, however; and since we cannot go back, even hypothetically, to the moment when a metaphysical insight first dawned in a human mind, to learn whether myths, rituals, and symbols had already given shape to the society in which the first genius lived who thought like a philosopher, perhaps Dr. Radin's balanced recognition of the dialogue of the two types in the continuance and development of primitive traditions is about as far as we can go. "How are we ever to trace properly the development of thought and, more specifically, that of our fundamental philosophical notions," he asks, "if we begin with false premises? If it can be shown that the thinkers among primitive peoples envisage life in philosophical terms, that human experience and the world around them have become subjects for reflection, that these ponderings and searchings have become embodied in literature and ritual, then obviously our customary treatment of cultural history, not to mention that of philosophical speculation, must be completely revised." [23]

For myself, I believe that we owe both the imagery and the poetical insights of myth to the genius of the tender-minded; to the tough-minded only their reduction to religion. As far as I know, in the myths themselves the origins of their symbols and cults have always been attributed to individual visionaries —dreamers, shamans, spiritual heroes, prophets, and divine incarnations. Hovering Hawk, for example, when asked how his people made their songs, replied: "We dreamed them. When a man would go away by himself—off into solitude— then he would dream a song." [24]

In any case, the time has certainly come—as Paul Radin told us long ago—for the collectors and classifiers to regard the pretensions of their materials to a deep significance. From every corner of the globe they have gathered images, tales, and myths; yet the science of interpreting the materials can hardly be said to have broached even the first outposts of the psychology of man's approach to and experience of the metaphysical; for up to now the interest of the scholars has been almost exclusively ethnological and historical. They have analyzed from many points of view what may be termed the stylistic variations of the vehicles. Yet, what such stylistic variations signify it will certainly be impossible to say until the tenors of clusters of analogous metaphors have been established and understood. For the bedrock of the science of folklore and myth is not in the wisps and strays of metaphor, but in the ideas to which the metaphors refer.

［𝕃𝕃𝕃𝕃𝕃𝕃𝕃𝕃𝕃𝕃𝕃𝕃𝕃𝕃𝕃𝕃𝕃𝕃𝕃𝕃𝕃𝕃𝕃𝕃𝕃𝕃𝕃𝕃𝕃𝕃𝕃𝕃𝕃𝕃𝕃𝕃𝕃］

[IV]

Mythogenesis

[1]

An American Indian Legend

If an authority on architecture, looking at the buildings of New York, were to observe that most of the older ones were of brick, then, viewing the ruins of ancient Mesopotamia, remarked that the buildings were all of brick, and finally, visiting Ceylon, made the point that many of the early temples were of brick, should we say that this man had an eye for architecture? It is true that bricks appear in many parts of the world; true, also, that a study might be made of the differences between the bricks of Ceylon, those of ancient Sumer, those, say of the Roman aqueducts still standing in southern France, and those of the city of New York. However, these observations about brick are not all that we should like to hear about the architecture of the cities of the world.

Now let me suggest a problem in the architecture of myth.

Early one morning, long ago, two Sioux Indians with their bows and arrows were out hunting on the North American plains; and as they were standing on a hill, peering about for game, they saw in the distance something coming toward them in a strange and wonderful manner. When the mysterious thing drew nearer, they perceived that it was a very beautiful woman, dressed in white buckskin, bearing a bundle on her back, and one of the men immediately became lustful. He told his friend of his desire, but the other rebuked him, warning that this surely was no ordinary woman. She had come close now and, setting her bundle down, called to the first to approach her. When he did so, he and she were covered suddenly by a cloud and when this lifted there was the woman alone, with the man nothing but bones at her feet, being eaten by terrible snakes. "Behold what you see!" she said to the other. "Now go tell your people to prepare a large ceremonial lodge for my coming. I wish to announce to them something of great importance."

The young man returned quickly to his camp; and the chief, whose name was Standing Hollow Horn, had several tepees taken down, sewn together, and made into a ceremonial lodge. Such a lodge has twenty-eight poles, of which the central pole, the main support, is compared to the Great Spirit, Wakan Tanka, the supporter of the universe. The others represent aspects of creation; for the lodge itself is a likeness of the universe.

"If you add four sevens," said the old warrior priest, Black Elk, from whom this legend was derived, "you get twenty-eight. The moon lives twenty-eight days and this is our month. Each of these days of the month represents something sacred to us: two of the days represent the Great Spirit; two are for Mother Earth; four are for the four winds; one is for the Spotted Eagle; one for the sun; and one for the moon; one is for the Morning Star; and four are for the four ages; seven for our seven great rites; one is for the buffalo; one for the fire; one for the water; one for the rock; and finally, one is for the two-legged people. If you add all these days up you will see that they come to twenty-eight. You should know also that the buffalo has twenty-eight ribs, and that in our war bonnets we usually wear twenty-eight feathers. You see, there is a significance for everything, and these are the things that are good for men to know and to remember." [1]

This wonderful old Oglala Sioux priest explained to the young scholar, Joseph Epes Brown, who had come to the Pine Ridge Reservation (South Dakota) expressly to gain knowledge first hand of the mystic dimension of American Indian mythology, the image of the man consumed by snakes.

"Any man who is attached to the senses and things of this world," he said, "is one who lives in ignorance and is being consumed by the snakes that represent his own passions." [2]

One is reminded by this Indian image of the Greek legend of the young hunter Actaeon, who, in quest of game, following a forest stream to its source, discovered there the goddess Artemis bathing, perfectly naked, in a pool: and when she saw that he looked lustfully upon her, she transformed him into a stag that was then pursued by his own hounds, torn to pieces, and consumed.[3] And not only are the two legends comparable, but the old Sioux priest's interpretation of his own accords with the sense of the Greek. Moreover, his interpretation of the symbolism of the ceremonial lodge suggests a number of themes familiar to us as well: so that we are moved to wonder what the explanation of these accords might be.

When the people of Black Elk's legend had made their large ceremonial lodge that was symbolically a counterpart of the universe, they all gathered within it, extremely excited, wondering who the mysterious woman could be and what she wished to say to them. Suddenly, she appeared in the door, which was facing east, and proceeded sunwise around the central pillar: south, west, north, and again east. "For is not the south the source of life?" the old teller of the tale explained. "And does not man advance from there toward the setting sun of his life? Does he not then arrive, if he lives, at the source of light and understanding, which is the east? And does he not return to where he began, to his second childhood, there to give back his life to all life, and his flesh to the earth whence it came? The more you think about this," he suggested, "the more meaning you will see in it." [4]

This sturdy old son of the American earth, now nearly blind, had been born in the early eighteen-sixties, fought as a young man at the battle of the Little Bighorn and the battle of Wounded Knee, had known the great chiefs, Sitting Bull, Crazy Horse, Red Cloud, and American Horse, and at the time of this retelling of his legend, the winter of 1947–1948, was Keeper of the Sacred Pipe. He had received the treasured talisman, together with its legend, from the earlier Keeper, Elk Head, who had prophesied at that time that as long as the pipe was used and its legend known, the Oglala Sioux would live, but as soon as the legend was forgotten, they would lose their center and perish.[5]

The pipe and its legend, then, were of indeterminate age, anonymous, practically timeless. Yet actually, more closely regarded, they could not have been much older than a couple of hundred years; for the Oglala Sioux did not migrate to the plains and become buffalo hunters there until the end of the seventeenth century—1680 or so. They had formerly been a forest folk of the Upper Mississippi, a region of lakes and marshes, where they traveled in birchbark canoes.[6] And yet, as already remarked, although we may never have heard before of the Sacred Pipe of the Oglala Sioux, or have numbered the buffalo's ribs, all the elements of this myth are curiously familiar. We recognize the bricks, so to say, though the way in which they have been put together is surprising.

The ceremonial lodge is exactly comparable to a temple, oriented to the quarters, with its central pole symbolic of the world axis. "We have established here the center of the earth," the nearly blind old medicine man explained to his attentive listener, "and this center, which in reality is everywhere, is the dwelling place of Wakan Tanka." [7] But this figure of the "center" that is "everywhere" is a counterpart, exactly, of that of the hermetic twelfth-century "Book of the Twenty-four Philosophers," from which Nicholas Cusanus and a number of other distinguished European thinkers—Alan de Lille, Rabelais, Giordano Bruno, Pascal, and Voltaire, for example—derived their definition of God as "an intelligible sphere, whose center is everywhere and circumference nowhere." [8] It is amazing indeed to catch the echo of such a metaphysical statement as this from the lips of an absolutely illiterate old Sioux, living out his fading day as the guardian of an aboriginal Amerindian fetish and its myth.

What are we to think of all these coincidences? Whence come these timeless, placeless themes?

Shall we join our voice to those who write of a great Perennial Philosophy, which, from time out of mind, has been the one, eternally true wisdom of the human race, revealed somehow from on high? How came this, then, with all its symbols, to the Sioux? Or shall we seek our answer, rather, in some psychological theory, like many of the most distinguished nineteenth-century ethnologists—Bastian, for instance, Tylor, and Frazer—attributing such cross-cultural accords to "the effect," as Frazer put it, "of similar causes acting alike on the similar constitution of the human mind in different countries and under different skies"? [9] Do such images, that is to say, take form naturally in the psyche? Can they be assumed and even expected to appear spontaneously, in dreams, in visions, in mythological figurations, any place on earth, wherever man has made his home?

Or must it be said, on the contrary, that, since mythological orders—like architectural orders—serve specific, historically conditioned cultural functions, where any two can be shown to be homologous they must be assumed to be historically related? Can the Greeks and the Sioux, that is to say, be supposed to have received any part or parts of their mythological heritages from a common source?

Or, finally, shall we simply set aside this whole question of shared motifs (whether religiously, psychologically, or historically explained) as unworthy of a scientist's speculation, since —as a number of important field-anthropologists now hold— myths and rituals are functions of local social orders, hence meaningless out of context and, consequently, not to be abstracted and compared across cultural lines? Comparisons of that sort, enjoyed by dilettantes and amateurs, are, according to this view, neither significant nor of interest to a properly tutored scientific intelligence.

Let us look further, with an uncommitted eye, and try to judge for ourselves.

We note in Black Elk's commentary to his legend the formula four times seven, giving twenty-eight supports of the universe, the numbers four and seven being standard symbols of totality in the iconographies of both the Orient and the Occident; and this game of sacred numbers itself is a shared trait worth remarking. One of the twenty-eight supports is in the center of the great tepee, as the axis, the pivot of the universe. The number surrounding it then is twenty-seven: three times nine: three times three times three. One thinks of the psychologist C. G. Jung's numerous discussions of the symbolism of the four and three. One thinks of the nine choirs of angels (three times three) that surround and celebrate the central throne of the Trinity. Three is the number of time: past, present, and future; four is the number of space: east, south, west, and north. Space (four) and time (three) constitute the field—the universe—in which all phenomenal forms become manifest and disappear. (Another way would be to think of the vertical—above, here, and below—plus the four directions: which again yields three plus four.) The number four recurs in the "sacred turn," the clockwise circumambulation of the center, which is here associated not only with the four directions but also with the life stages of the individual, so that the symbolism is applied as well to the microcosm as to the macrocosm: the two being tied by the related number twenty-eight to the cycle of the moon, which dies and is resurrected and is accordingly a sign of the cycle of renewal.

Furthermore, as we are told, the buffalo has twenty-eight ribs and is therefore himself a counterpart of the moon—and the universe. Do not the buffaloes return every year, miraculously renewed like the moon? We think of the Moon Bull of the archaic Near East, the animal-vehicle of Osiris, Tammuz, and, in India, of Shiva. The horns of the moon suggest those of the moon-god Sin, after whom Mount Sinai was named, so that it should represent the cosmic mountain at the center of the world, from the summit of which Moses descended. And his face then shone with horns of light, like the moon, so that when he stood before the people he had to wear a veil (Exodus 34:29–35)—like the veils of archaic kings who, for centuries before his time, had been revered as incarnations of the self-renewing power of the moon. At the foot of Mount Sinai, the

High Priest Aaron was found conducting a festival of the Moon Bull in the image of a golden calf, which Moses angrily committed to the fire, ground to bits, mixed with water, and caused the people to drink, in a kind of communion meal (Exodus 32:1-20). And—remarkably—it was only after this sacrifice that, returning to the mountaintop (where the earth-goddess and heaven-god are joined in eternal connubium), he received the full assignment of the Law and promise of the Promised Land, not for himself—for he was now, himself, to become the sacrifice—but for the Holy Race.

In the mythology of Christ crucified, three days in the tomb and resurrected, there is implicit the same symbolism of the moon that is three days dark. The Sacrificial Lamb, the Sacrificial Bull, and the Cosmic Buffalo: their symbology was perfectly interpreted by the old Sioux medicine man, Black Elk, when he explained that the buffalo was symbolic of the universe in its temporal, lunar aspect, dying yet ever renewed, but also (in its twenty-eighth rib) of the Great Spirit, which is eternal, the center that is everywhere and around which all revolves.

Chief Standing Hollow Horn—as Black Elk recounted in his tale—was seated at the west of the lodge, the seat of honor, when the beautiful woman entered: because there he faced the door, the east, whence comes the light, namely wisdom, which a leader must possess. And the woman, arriving before him, lifted the bundle from her back and held it out to him with both hands.

"Behold this bundle," she said, "and always love it! It is *lela wakan* [very sacred], and you must treat it as such. No impure man should ever be allowed to see it; for within this bundle there is a very holy pipe. With this pipe you will, during the years to come, send your voices to Wakan Tanka, your Father and Grandfather."

She drew forth the pipe and with it a round stone, which she placed on the ground. Holding the pipe with its stem to the heavens, she said: "With this sacred pipe you will walk upon the Earth; for the Earth is your Grandmother and

Mother, and she is sacred. Every step that is taken upon her should be as a prayer. The bowl of this pipe is of red stone; it is the Earth. Carved in the stone and facing the center is a buffalo calf, who represents all the quadrupeds who live upon your Mother. The stem of the pipe is of wood, and this represents all that grows upon the Earth. And these twelve feathers that hang here, where the stem fits into the bowl, are feathers of the Spotted Eagle. They represent that eagle and all the winged things of the air. When you smoke this pipe all these things join you, everything in the universe: all send their voices to Wakan Tanka, the Great Spirit, your Grandfather and Father. When you pray with this pipe you pray for and with all things." [10]

The proper use of the pipe, as expounded by its guardian priest, required that it should be ceremonially identified with both the universe and oneself. From the fire in the center of the lodge, the fire symbolic of Wakan Tanka, an attendant with a split stick lifted a coal, which he placed before the Keeper of the Pipe. The latter, holding in his left hand the pipe, took with his right a pinch of a sacred herb, and elevating this to heaven four times, prayed:

"O Grandfather, Wakan Tanka, I send you, on this sacred day of yours, this fragrance that will reach to the heavens above. Within this herb is the Earth, this great island; within it is my Grandmother, my Mother, and all four-legged, winged, and two-legged creatures who walk in a holy [*wakan*] manner. The fragrance of this herb will cover the entire universe. O Wakan Tanka, be merciful to all."

The bowl of the pipe was then held over the burning aromatic herb in such a way that the fragrant smoke, entering, passed through the stem and out the end, toward heaven. Thus Wakan Tanka was the first to smoke, and the pipe, by that act, was purified.[11] It was then filled with tobacco that had been offered in the six directions: to the west, north, east, and south, to heaven, and to earth. "In this manner," said the medicine man, "the whole universe is placed in the pipe." [12] And, finally, the man who fills the pipe should identify it with himself. There is a prayer in which this identity is described. It runs as follows:

These people had a pipe,
Which they made to be their body.

O my Friend, I have a pipe that I have made to be my body;
If you also make it to be your body,
You shall have a body free from all causes of death.

Behold the joint of the neck, they said,
That I have made to be the joint of my own neck.

Behold the mouth of the pipe,
That I have made to be my mouth.

Behold the right side of the pipe,
That I have made to be the right side of my body.

Behold the spine of the pipe,
That I have made to be my own spine.

Behold the left side of the pipe,
That I have made to be the left side of my body.

Behold the hollow of the pipe,
That I have made to be the hollow of my body. . . .

Use the pipe as an offering in your supplications,
And your prayers shall be readily granted.[13]

This game, this holy game of purifying the pipe, expanding the pipe to include the universe, identifying oneself with the pipe, and igniting it in symbolic offering, is a ritual act of the kind represented, also, in Vedic Brahmanic ceremonials, where the altar and every implement of the sacrifice is identified allegorically with both the universe and the sacrificing individual. "He who is in the fire," we read in the Maitri Upanishad, for example, "he who is here in the heart, and he who is yonder in the sun: he is one." [14] Likewise, in the great Chandogya: "Now the light that shines higher than this heaven, on the backs of all, on the backs of everything, in the highest worlds, than which there are no higher—verily, that is the same as this light which is here within a person. . . ."[15]

"One should reverence the mind as *brahman.* —Thus with reference to oneself. And now, with reference to the gods: One should reverence space as *brahman.* —That is the twofold instruction with reference to oneself and with reference to the gods.

"That *brahman* has four quarters. One quarter is speech. One quarter is breath. One quarter is the eye. One quarter is the ear. —Thus with reference to oneself. And now, with reference to the gods: One quarter is Fire. One quarter is Wind. One quarter is the Sun. One quarter is the quarters of the sky. —That is the twofold instruction with reference to oneself and with reference to the gods." [16]

Now, as we have heard, the feathers of the sacred pipe are those of the spotted eagle, which is the highest-flying bird in North America and therefore equivalent to the sun. Its feathers are the solar rays—and their number is twelve, the number, exactly, that we too associate with the cycle of the sun in the months of the solar year and twelve signs (three times four) of the zodiac. There is a verse in a sacred song of the Sioux: "The Spotted Eagle is coming to carry me away." [17] Do we not think here of the Greek myth of Ganymede transported by Zeus, who came in the form of an eagle to carry him away? "Birds," declares Dr. Jung in one of his dissertations on the process of individuation, "are thoughts and flights of the mind. . . . The eagle denotes the heights . . . it is a well-known alchemistic symbol. Even the *lapis*, the *rebis* [the Philosopher's Stone], made out of two parts, and thus often hermaphroditic, as a coalescence of Sol and Luna, is frequently represented with wings, in this way standing for premonition—intuition. All these symbols in the last analysis depict that state of affairs that we call the Self, in its role of transcending consciousness." [18]

Such a reading nicely accords with the part played by our North American spotted eagle in the rites of the Indian tribes. It explains, also, the wearing of eagle feathers. They are counterparts of the golden rays of a European crown. They are the rays of the spiritual sun, which the warrior typifies in his life. Furthermore—as we have been told—their number in the war bonnet is twenty-eight, the number of the lunar cycle of temporal death and renewal, so that here Sol and Luna have again been joined.

There can be no doubt whatsoever that this legend of the Sioux is fashioned of at least some of the same materials and thoughts as the great mythologies of the Old World—Europe, Africa, and Asia. The parallels both in sense and in imagery are too numerous and too subtle to be the consequence of mere accident. And we have not yet finished!

For when the holy woman, standing before Chief Standing Hollow Horn, had taught him how to use the pipe, she touched its bowl to the round stone that she had placed upon the ground. "With this pipe you will be bound," she said, "to all your relatives: your Grandfather and Father, your Grandmother and Mother."

The Great Spirit, the medicine man explained, is our Grandfather and Father; the Earth, our Grandmother and Mother. As Father and Mother, they are the producers of all things; as Grandfather and Grandmother, however, beyond our understanding.[19] These suggest the two modes of considering God that Rudolf Otto, in *The Idea of the Holy*, has termed the "ineffable" and the "rational": [20] the same, as Joseph Epes Brown points out in his commentary on Black Elk's rite, that are referred to in India as *nirguṇa* and *saguṇa brahman*, the "Absolute without Qualities" and the "Absolute with Qualities," respectively *That* beyond names, forms, and relationships, and *That* personified as "God."

"This round rock," the very beautiful woman continued, "which is made of the same red stone as the bowl of the pipe, your Father Wakan Tanka has also given to you. It is the Earth, your Grandmother and Mother, and it is where you will live and increase. This Earth which he has given to you is red, and the two-legged people who live upon the Earth are red; and the Great Spirit has also given to you a red day, and a red road."

"The 'red road,'" Joseph Brown explains, "is that which

runs north and south and is the good or straight way, for to
the Sioux the north is purity and the south is the source of
life. . . . On the other hand, there is the 'blue' or 'black
road' of the Sioux, which runs east and west and which is the
path of error and destruction. He who travels on this path,
Black Elk has said, is 'one who is distracted, who is ruled by
his senses, and who lives for himself rather than for his people.' " [21] The latter was the road followed by the man at the
opening of the story, who was eaten by snakes. And so we
notice now that even the ethical polarity that we recognize
between the bird and serpent as allegoric of the winged flight
of the spirit and the earth-bound commitment of the passions,
has been suggested here, as well.

"These seven circles that you see upon the red stone," the
woman said, "represent the seven rites in which the pipe will
be used. . . . Be good to these gifts and to your people; for
they are *wakan* [holy]. With this pipe the two-legged people
will increase and there will come to them all that is good." She
described the rites and then turned to leave. "I am leaving
now, but I shall look back upon your people in every age; for,
remember," she said, "in me there are four ages: and at the end
I shall return."

Passing around the lodge, in the sunwise way, she left, but
after walking a short distance, looked back toward the people
and sat down. When she got up again, they were amazed to see
that she had turned into a young red and brown buffalo calf.
The calf walked a little distance, lay down and rolled, looked
back at the people, and when she got up was a white buffalo.
This buffalo walked a little distance, rolled upon the ground,
and when it rose was black. The black buffalo walked away,
and when it was far from the people it turned, bowed to each
of the four directions, and disappeared over a hill. [22]

The *wakan* woman had thus been the feminine aspect of
the cosmic buffalo itself. She herself was the earthly red
buffalo-calf represented on the pipe bowl, but also its mother,
the white buffalo, and its grandmother, the black. She had
gone to be restored to her eternal portion, having rendered to

man those sacred thoughts and visible things by which he was to be joined to his own eternity, which is here and now, within him and all things, in this living world.

Let us try, therefore, to follow her to her source.

[2]
The Neolithic Background

Let us peer, first, down the well of the past—the very deep well of history and prehistory; for actually, a good deal is known concerning the history of our North American tribes and their mythologies. We know, for example, as already remarked, that the Oglala Sioux had not always been hunters of the buffalo, dwelling on the great plains. In the sixteenth and early seventeenth centuries they had lived among the lakes and marshes of the upper Mississippi, in the woods of Minnesota and Wisconsin, traveling mainly in bark canoes. They had been a people of the forest, not the plains, and knew practically nothing of the buffalo.[23] The White Buffalo Woman cannot possibly have been a factor in their mythology at that time.

However, many of the other elements of this myth might have been known to them from of old: the symbolism, for instance, of the sacred sunwise turn, the cosmic ceremonial lodge, and the cycle of four ages. The ritual of the sacred pipe itself would seem to point, furthermore, not to an origin among hunters but to a planting-culture background, and indeed, the Sioux, before moving to their sixteenth-century station at the source of the "Father of Waters"—where they paddled delicate birchbark canoes on woodland rivers and lakes—had dwelt in that more southerly part of the long Mississippi valley, between the mouths of the Ohio and Missouri, which scholarship now identifies with the maize-growing "Middle Mississippi" culture complex, many elements of which are known to have come from Middle American sources. For, from as early as about 500 B.C., influences had been entering and ascending the great Mississippi waterway from Mexico,[24] where, as the Spaniards found when they arrived in the sixteenth century (about the time the Siouan tribes were moving from the Middle Mississippi, northward), there was flourishing a mighty civilization, with many religious practices strangely similar to their own,* based on agriculture, governing its festival year by an astronomically correct calendar, and supporting cities comparable in size, grandeur, and sophistication to the greatest in the Old World. The use of tobacco in the holy pipe—which is not a wild but a cultivated plant—should have let us know that its ritual could not have been originally of hunters. Besides, the Sioux and their neighbors on the plains were not simply hunters. They planted maize, squash, and lima beans, and these, like tobacco, had come to them from the south.

In all, some sixty-odd varieties of domesticated plants are known to have been cultivated in pre-Columbian Middle and South America, including maize, squash, the lima bean, pineapple, peanut, and avocado, kidney bean, pumpkin, white and sweet potato, watermelon, and tomato. Chocolate, rubber, and quinine, too, were first produced from these soils; [25] likewise tobacco.†

An impressive amount of productive research has lately been conducted in those parts of Mexico and South America

---

* Compare supra, p. 43.

† Tobacco was introduced to Europe, first as a healing herb (*herba panacea, sana sancta Indorum*), by a Spaniard, Francisco Fernandes, whom the Emperor Philip II had commissioned to Mexico to investigate the products of the Empire; but it was a Frenchman, Jean Nicot, who gained the fame (his name now immortalized as "nicotine"), when, as French ambassador to Portugal, he sent seeds of the plant to Catherine de' Medici, his queen. Meanwhile, an Englishman, Ralph Lane, the first governor of Virginia, had presented a native Indian pipe to his honored friend and guest, Sir Walter Ralcigh, and it was from England, then, that the art of smoking "divine tobacco" (as Edmund Spenser called the weed) was "diffused" (to use the technical anthropological term), first to the Continent and then, in the seventeenth century, to the world. The most ancient pipes of which remains exist have been found in the early Indian mounds of Ohio, Indiana, Illinois, and Iowa. (See the article, "Tobacco," by D. A. Gracey, *Encyclopaedia Britannica*, 14th Edition, Vol. 22, pp. 260–63.)

where the basic food plants of the New World are now believed to have been translated from their wild to domesticated
states. The prehistoric period reviewed extends from c. 7000
to c. 1500 B.C., with the millennium from c. 4000 to 3000
emerging as the critical one within which the first trust-
worthy signs of plant domestication can now be said to have
been "fairly certainly" detected.[26] The best-rewarded excavations were those in the Valley of Tehuacán and southwest
Tamaulipas, Mexico, where a series of strictly controlled studies of the deeply stratified layers of debris in the floors of a
number of once-inhabited caves yielded results that may be
summarized as follows:

A. In layers of the Tehuacán Valley caves:
   (1) In the deepest, so-called *El Riego phase, c. 7200–
   5200* B.C., signs are recognized of a number of wild plants
   later domesticated: a wild squash, chili peppers, avocado,
   and a wild cotton.
   (2) During the following *Coxcatlán phase, c. 5200–
   3400* B.C., indications become evident of several more
   food plants: gourds, amaranths, tepary beans, white and
   yellow zapotes, another squash, and primitive maize—a
   few of which plants *may* have been domesticated, though
   certainly not the maize, which here appears for the first
   time in the archaeological record.
   (3) Apparently it was during the next, the *Abejas
   phase, c. 3400–2300* B.C., that maize came under cultivation,
   and from that period on, dependable signs increase of
   the practice of some sort of horticulture, supplemen-
   tary to the timeless primitive arts of foraging, hunting,
   and fishing—the people, be it noted, dwelling still in
   caves.
B. Concurrently, in Tamaulipas:
   (1) In the *Infiernillo phase, c. 7000–5000* B.C., evidences
   again are registered of certain wild plants later domesticated: agave, opuntia, runner beans, chili peppers, a
   gourd, and a pumpkin.
   (2) The *Ocampo phase, c. 5000–3000* B.C., shows
   pumpkins of a larger seed and both yellow and red

large beans—any or all of which may have been domesticated.

(3) During the so-called *La Perra phase, c. 3000–
2200 B.C.*, domesticated maize appears, derived, apparently, from the Tehuacán development.

C. There is a possibility, also, that domesticated maize may
have reached South America at about this time, and that
in Peru, as early as c. 3800–3000 B.C., lima beans and
bottle gourds may have begun to be cultivated.

In any case, it is from these last dates onward, 3800–2200
B.C., that signs of a primitive type of garden cultivation, practiced by cave-dwelling hunting and fishing folk, first appear
in the Americas, increasing until, by c. 1500 B.C., the beginnings of something resembling a genuine neolithic stage of village farming can be said to have been attained.

But the critical period thus indicated corresponds exactly to
that of the first securely documented trans-Pacific landings of
visitors from Asia—and these, furthermore, may not have
been the *first* trans-Pacific voyagers, either!

In *The Masks of God*,[27] I reviewed the evidences for a trans-
Pacific contribution to the so-called "Formative Period" of
the New World civilizations as the case stood in 1959, when
the earliest verified date for plant domesticates in the New
World was c. 1016 B.C. ± 300 years, and the materials in hand
—found on the northern coast of Peru at a site called Huaca
Prieta—consisted of twined net and woven fabrics of what
appeared to be an Asiatic cotton, together with two small bottle gourds bearing highly stylized carved figures suggesting
trans-Pacific themes (a double bird-head and the mask of a
sort of cat- or jaguar-man)—the bottle gourd being a plant
not known to be native to America. In addition, there had
been unearthed in association with these remains a few bits of
bark cloth (i.e., tapa), which is an Oceanic culture-trait.

Today, however, as remarked above,* there is more to
tell. For in December 1960 a fragment of Japanese "cord-
marked" (Jomon) pottery of a date c. 3000 B.C. was unearthed

* Supra, p. 47.

on the coast of Ecuador, and subsequent digs along that coast soon yielded many fragments more, these being the earliest evidences of ceramic ware yet found anywhere in the New World. Moreover, a number of ceramic female figurines were included in the finds, and these are the earliest figurines known for the Americas. Significantly, a pilot chart of the North Pacific Ocean, published by the Hydrographic Office of the Navy, U.S.A.,[28] shows the course of one of the strongest west-to-east ocean currents running northward from the neighborhood of the Japanese island of Kyushu, bending eastward in a great arc, over Hawaii and then down, exactly to the Guayas coast of Ecuador. Japanese pottery of the Early to Middle Jomon period has now been dated by the Carbon-14 method, c. 3140 B.C. ± 400 years, and that of this so-called Valdivia phase of the Ecuadorian coast, c. 3190 B.C. ± 150.

"Words," state the finders, "do not adequately express the degree of similarity between early Valdivia and contemporary Jomon pottery. . . . In most categories of decorative technique, examples can be found so similar in appearance that they might almost have come from the same vessel." [29] And in a series of handsomely photographed plates of numerous matching samples they have demonstrated their point so well that the viewer, to keep the two orders apart, must draw a line between.[30]

The designs in Figure 1 are from an American Indian mound of the Mississippi period, c. 1000–1500 A.D., excavated in Spiro, Oklahoma. Those of Figure 2 are from Iraq, c. 4000 B.C. Figure 3 is a map of the world distribution of the swastika, and Figure 4, of the idea of the colors of the four directions. Already in the first years of the present century, that is to say, it was evident to Frobenius—who is responsible for these maps—that (in his words), "a bridge existed, and not a chasm, between America and Asia." [31] Subsequently, Dr. Adolf Jensen, Director of the Forschungsinstitut für Kulturmorphologie, Frankfurt am Main, demonstrated in his studies of the myths and rites of tropical planting cultures [32] that, even on the primitive mesolithic level, there is a cultural continuum

Figure 1. Painted Pottery Designs; Samarra ware, Iraq, c. 4000 B.C.

Figure 2. Designs from Shell Gorgets; Spiro Mound, Oklahoma, c. 1000 A.D.

extending from Africa eastward, through India, Southeast Asia, and Oceania, to America, and that one of the characteristic features of this equatorial *Kulturkreis* is the myth of a killed and cut up ancestral being from whose buried remains food plants grow.[33] In every province of the early planting cultures of the world this archetypal origin myth has been adapted to the local vegetation. In primitive Indonesia it is referred to the banana, coconut, and yam; in Polynesia, to the same; in Japan, to rice; in Mexico, to maize, and in Brazil, to manioc; in ancient Egypt, the plant was wheat. Can the Sioux have been touched by this widely known equatorial tradition?

It would be amazing had they not.

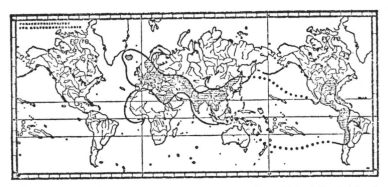

Figure 3. World Distribution of the Swastika. (After Frobenius.)

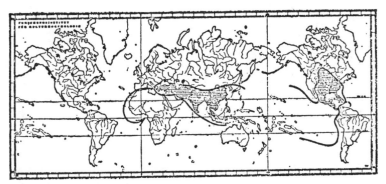

Figure 4. World Distribution of Color Symbolism of the Four Directions. (After Frobenius.)

Longfellow, in *The Song of Hiawatha*, Part V, "Hiawatha's Fasting," has rendered into verse an instance of the planting myth in question, drawn from Henry Schoolcraft's *Algic Researches*.[34] Its source was an Ojibwa legend of the origin of maize from a slain, cut up, and buried divinity—the Ojibwa being an Algonquin tribe inhabiting the same general region at the headwaters of the Mississippi that the Sioux had known in the sixteenth century. Moreover, at the time of the earlier residence of the Sioux further south, in the Middle Mississippi, there had been a mighty concentration there of truly agricultural towns of many thousand souls, raising crops of maize, squash, and beans, with immense rectangular temple mounds arranged around central plazas, spiritual as well as secular governors, and recondite iconographies. This culture had struck its roots, as we have said,* as early as the fifth century B.C. It culminated in the fifteenth A.D., with extensions eastward to the Atlantic and westward into both Arkansas and eastern Oklahoma, as well as north through Illinois.[35] The culture level was about equivalent to that of France in the period of Caesar's Gallic Wars, the period of Vercingetorix. And the temple mounds—as well as a number of other features—let us know that influences from Mexico had been of considerable force.

In sum, then, the possibility, or even probability, of extremely early trans-Pacific contacts of a more than passing influence on equatorial America, the evidence of Japanese ceramic wares of a date c. 3000 B.C. found on the coast of Ecuador, and the evidence, somewhat southward, on the shoreline of Peru, from c. 1016 B.C., of tapa, an Asiatic cotton, and bottle gourds carved with mythic figures of a style suggesting Shang China (Shang is now dated c. 1523–1027 B.C.), suggest very strongly that Frobenius can have been right. And such early, primitive contacts are not the only ones of which we have signs; for there is notable evidence, also, of a sequence of later contributions from China and Southeast Asia, affecting the nuclear centers of Middle and South America. These commence at least as early as the eighth century B.C., when China was already halfway through its great period of the Chou dynasty (Early Chou, c. 1027–772 B.C.; Middle Chou, 722–480 B.C.; Late Chou, 480–221 B.C.), and continue to the twelfth century A.D., when the marvelous Khmer civilization of Ankor (c. 600–c. 1300 A.D.) seems to have influenced the Mayan architecture and sculpture of Chiapas, Tabasco, Campeche, and the Petén, as well as the Toltec arts of the fabled feathered-serpent king, Quetzalcoatl.[36]

It is entirely possible, therefore, that all those elements that

* Supra, p. 89.

have impressed us as familiar in the mythology of the Sioux are actually constituents of the same great mythological complex of the agriculturally based high civilizations from which our own mythological heritage derives, and that, consequently, they do not represent either an accident of cultural convergence or any generally valid archetypology of the human psyche, but an archetypology only of the higher, agriculturally based civilizations—which, as we know from the archaeology of the nuclear Near East, had its beginnings in the proto- and early neolithic towns and villages of that area, c. 9000 B.C., and came to its first full flowering in the early cities of Mesopotamian Sumer, c. 3500-2500 B.C.*

[3]

The Paleolithic Background

The enveloping atmosphere of old Black Elk's legend, however, is very different from that of the myths of planting cultures, whether of the Old World or of the New. It is definitely of a hunting race, and resembles in spirit and tone the Blackfoot legend of the origin of the Buffalo Dance that I have retold in *Primitive Mythology* from George Bird Grinnell's *Blackfoot Lodge Tales*.[37] The main point of all such legends is that between the animals hunted and the human communities dependent for survival on their offering of themselves, there has been a covenant established, confirmed, and reconfirmed in certain rites performed in relation to certain fetishes: both the rites and the sacred tokens having been delivered, years ago, by the animals themselves to insure that when they had been slain their lives should be returned to the mother-source for rebirth; and reciprocally, when such rites were performed and the mystery of the order of nature thus recognized, the food supply of the human community would be assured.

Among the hunting tribes of the buffalo plains the legends of this type are innumerable, and they are in many features

* See below, pp. 150–55.

very different from the corresponding myths of tropical planting folk. The rites, of which they tell the origins, are not, for the most part, referred to a remote age of mythological ancestors, but are supposed to have been derived from historical encounters of actual human beings with the Animal Mothers or Master Animals of vision—as we have just seen, for instance, in Black Elk's Sioux legend of the Sacred Pipe. So that even in such a legend as that of the Ojibwa Origin of Maize, where a typical planting myth from the tropical zone has been taken over by a hunting folk together with the plant itself, the divine being cut up and buried is represented, not as a divinity of the Mythological Age, but as a vision appearing to a gifted youth at the time of his puberty fast; hence Longfellow's title for his version of the episode: "Hiawatha's Fasting."

Now the Sioux and the Blackfeet were enemies and of very different racial stocks. The Blackfeet were Algonquins from the forested north, snowshoe and toboggan folk, whereas the Sioux, as we have seen, were from the south. Yet in their legends of the buffalo plains—to which both (like all their neighbors) were relative newcomers—they were, so to say, of the same mythological stock. Whence then could this shared mythological stock have been derived—which, moreover, was shared (with modifications) by all the other, racially various, contending peoples of the plains—Paiutes, Kiowas, Pawnees, Comanches, and the rest—none of whom had known anything of the buffalo before migrating to the plains?

There is now considerable evidence that in the symbolic lore of the North American buffalo plains there survived to the end of the nineteenth century, and even into the twentieth, a powerful late formation of truly paleolithic culture forms. There is a variety of North American stone spearhead, called the Clovis Point, for which a radiocarbon date has been established c. 35,000 B.C. plus.[38] A number of examples have been found associated with the mammoth. There have been reports of an excavation, fifteen miles northeast of Barstow, in the Mojave Desert, California, where nearly two hundred

chalcedony chips and blades have been brought to light from
a depth assigned by radiocarbon tests to c. 40,000 B.C.[39] The
first discovered example of another very early stone spearhead,
the Folsom Point, was found amidst the bones of an extinct
species of bison: its date, not later than 8000 B.C. But these
are dates of the range, approximately, of the great paleolithic
grottoes of southern France and northern Spain—Altamira,
Lascaux, etc.—which have now been assigned to a period of
some twenty thousand years, from c. 30,000 to c. 10,000 B.C.

It is really an amazing, thrilling experience for anyone familiar with the legends of our North American Indians to enter any one of those French or Spanish caves. One is immediately transported to the same visionary field, where the
mystery-dimension of man's residence in the universe opens
through an iconography of animal messengers. The great
caves were not domestic sites but sanctuaries of the men's
rites: rituals of the hunt, of generations living by the hunt,
and of initiation to the mythological substratum of their rigorous lives. The caves are dangerous and absolutely dark.
And the pictures on the rocky walls are never at the entrances
but begin where the light of day is lost and unfold, then, deep
within. The painted animals, living there forever in that
darkness beyond the tick of time, are the germinal, deathless
herds of the cosmic night, from which zone those on earth—
which appear and disappear in continuous renewal—proceed,
and back to which they return. And where human forms appear among them, they are generally male, costumed as
shamans, wearing such animal-like masquerade as American
Indian shamans wear to this day.

One sees, also, on these cavern walls many silhouetted
handprints—hands of the hunters of those times; and from a
number of them certain finger joints are missing. Our plains
Indians, too, chopped off their finger joints—as offerings to
the sun or to Wakan Tanka, with prayers for power and success.

In several of the caves, deep and special chambers have been
found, where rites of exceptional power must have been cele-

brated. In the grotto of Trois-Frères, in the Pyrenees, for example, there is a long, tubelike passage—a flume, hardly two feet in mean diameter—through which one has to crawl and wriggle on one's belly for a distance of some fifty yards, to come to a large chamber with animal forms engraved everywhere on the walls, and among them, directly opposite and facing the mouth of the very difficult passage, is the celebrated dancing Sorcerer of Trois-Frères (Figure 5), with the antlers of a stag, a beard flowing to his chest, the body and front paws of a lion, tail of a horse, and legs of a man.

At Lascaux, in a kind of crypt or lower chamber, there is what appears to be a shaman lying in a shamanistic trance, wearing the mask and costume of a bird (Figure 6). His shaman staff is beside him, bearing on its top the figure of a bird. And standing before him is a great bison bull, struck from behind, mortally, by a lance. Mysteriously, a rhinoceros strolls by.

Then again in the Pyrenees, in the cave Tuc d'Audoubert, which is neighbor to Trois-Frères, there is a little chamber entered only by a very small hole, through which a man can scarcely squeeze. Within are two clay figures in high relief— unique in paleolithic art—representing a bison bull and cow, the bull following the cow, while on the ground, round about, are what appear to be the footprints of a boy dancing on his heels, possibly in imitation of the hoof prints of the buffalo.[40] Moreover, there were also in this chamber a number of phallic forms, roughly modeled in clay.

With these caves and, in particular, with this last sanctuary in mind, I believe we can now presume to say that we have followed our goddess Buffalo to the sanctum sanctorum of her source and now know from what far land and time, beyond their ken, the very beautiful woman came whom the two Sioux Indians saw on the North American plain. For there can be no question concerning the land of origin of the hunting tribes of North America. The vast area of the paleolithic Great Hunt, which stretched in a single sweep from the Pyrenees to Lake Baikal, in Siberia, actually went on to the Missis-

Figure 5. The Sorcerer of Trois Frères; Ariège, France, c. 15,000–11,000 B.C.

Figure 6. The Shaman of Lascaux; Dordogne, France, c. 20,000–15,000 B.C.

sippi. And the peoples who first came to America from northern Asia, and continued to come in many waves, brought with them the rites and hunting methods of that world.

These rites and methods, that is to say, were not separately invented in Europe, Asia, and America, but were carried from one area to the other. And the *mythogenetic zone*, the primary region of origin of the myths, was certainly the Old World, not the New. North America was, therefore, not a primary zone, but a *zone of diffusion*, to which the myths and rites were transported.

However, in the course of a transfer of this kind myths do not rest inert. There are two transforming processes of secondary creativity that come into play inevitably when a mythology is transferred from one landscape to another. The first I would term (following Ananda K. Coomaraswamy) [41] *land-taking*. In the case, for example, of the ubiquitous planting myth, above mentioned, the mythological being who was sacrificed, buried, and now lives in the food plants, is variously associated, in Brazil with manioc, in Japan with rice, and in Mexico with maize. It is everywhere the same myth, the same mystery play, but in each province the local landscape has become its theater and local animals and plants are its actors. Land-taking, then, is the act of taking spiritual possession of a newly entered land with all its elements, by assimilation to a myth already carried in the immigrant's heart as the spiritual support of a continuing culture. We are not to suppose that in every province of the tropical continuum the one same myth was separately developed.

The second transforming process to be noted is one that has been closely studied, lately, in many ethnological works, namely, *acculturation*. Here motifs from an alien culture complex are taken into a native tradition by a process of syncretistic assimilation; and the rapidity with which such a process can yield results is amazing. In the case of the recent Cargo Cults of Melanesia, for example, which arose throughout that area immediately following the Second World War

(when the natives, who had enjoyed for a time the magical
bounty of goods supernaturally derived from American mili-
tary cargoes, thought to bring back those fabulous days by
enacting millenarian rites of expectation), like a flash fire the
new rituals penetrated far beyond the colonial culture zone,
deep into the bush, the wild country of peoples who had
never seen a white man.[42] New ideas travel fast. And so it
was, of old, also, in America, when the mythologies of Mexico penetrated the Mississippi: the motifs of the higher mythology were syncretistically assimilated by the northern
hunters and applied to their own concerns.

Both the Sioux and the Pawnee, for example, assimilated to
the image of the Master Buffalo of the paleolithic hunting era
(Figure 5) the Mexican astronomical myth of the four world
ages (the same four that were known to Hesiod as the ages of
gold, silver, bronze, and iron, and to India as the cycle of four
yugas, during the course of which the cow of virtue lost with
each passing *yuga* one leg—standing first on four, then on
three legs, then two, and now, in our miserable last age of the
cycle, on one). Both the Pawnee and the Sioux declare that
their Cosmic Buffalo, the Father and Grandfather of the universe, stands at the cosmic gate through which the game animals pour into this temporal world and back through which
they go when they are slain, to be reborn. And in the course
of the cycle of the four world ages, with the passage of each
year, that Master Buffalo sheds one hair, and with the passage
of each of the World Ages, one leg.[43]

The resemblance of this striking image to that of India is
amazing; and the more so when it is compared not only with
the cow losing its legs but also with a tale from the Brah-
mavaivarta Purana that Heinrich Zimmer recounts at the
opening of his volume *Myths and Symbols in Indian Art
and Civilization.*[44] There the Lord of the Universe, the god
Shiva, whose animal is the white bull Nandi, appears in the
form of an old yogi named Hairy, who has on his chest a circular patch of hair from which one hair falls at the end of

each cosmic cycle. At the end of a Brahma year of such cosmic cycles all the hairs are gone and the universe dissolves into the night sea, the Ocean of Milk, to be renewed.

Who will say by what miracle—whether of history or of psychology—these two homologous images came into being, the one in India and the other in North America? It is, of course, possible that either one of the two paths of diffusion just described may have been followed. However, it is also possible that the two images were independently developed by some process of *convergence,* as an "effect," to use Frazer's words again, "of similar causes acting alike on the similar constitution of the human mind in different countries and under different skies" : for in India, too, there was a meeting and joining of animal and plant cultures when the Aryans with their herds arrived in the Dravidian agricultural zone. Analogous processes may have been set in play—as in two separate alchemical retorts.

So that we must now confess that our tracking down of the goddess Buffalo may have brought us to a problem not of history only, but of psychology as well. We have perhaps broken beyond the walls of time and space, and should ask by what psychological as well as historical laws these primitive myths and their counterparts in the higher cultures might have been formed.

[4]

The Psychological Base

There is no such thing, however, as an uncommitted psychology of man *qua* "Man," abstracted from a specific historical field. For, as I have already pointed out in Chapter II, "Bios and Mythos," the human infant is born (biologically speaking) a year too soon, completing in the social sphere a development that other species accomplish within the womb; in fact, developing in the social sphere precisely those powers most typically human: upright posture, rational thought, and speech. Man—as "Man"—develops in a manner that is simultaneously biological and social, and this development continues through adolescence—indeed, through life.

Moreover, whereas the instinct system of the animal is relatively inflexible, fixed, stereotyped, according to species, that of man is not so, but open to imprint and impression. The "innate releasing mechanisms" of the human central nervous system, through which man's instincts are triggered to action, respond to sign stimuli that are not fixed for all time and general to the species but vary from culture to culture, even from century to century and individual to individual, according to imprints indelibly registered during the long course of a sociologically conditioned childhood.[45] And, if I have read aright the works of the specialists in this field of psychological research, there has not yet been identified a single triggering image, a single sign stimulus, that can be firmly verified as innate to the human psyche.

How, then, shall we rest secure in any theory of psychological archetypes based upon our own culturally conditioned mode of responses, or upon a study of the myths and symbols of our own tradition, or even upon a comparative study of that large complex of primitive planting and higher agricultural traditions, which, as I have just indicated, are both historically and prehistorically related to our own?

We have to accept the fact that the walls have lately been knocked from around all mythologies—every single one of them—by the findings and works of modern scientific discovery. The four ages, the four points of the compass, the four elements! What can those mean to anyone today, in the light of what we are learning? Today we have one hundred and three elements, and the number is still growing. The old soul and the new universe—the old microcosm and the new macrocosm—do not match; and the disproportion is about equivalent to that of 4 to 103. No wonder, then, if a lot of us are nervous! The little tower of Babel, which to some in its day seemed to be threatening God in his heaven, we see now surpassed many times in every major city of the world, and rockets fly where once the angels sang. One cannot *tutoyer*

God any more: the mystery is infinite, both without and within. That is the *tremendum* that our modern mind—this flower of creation—has revealed for us to absorb, and it cannot be willed or walled away by any system of archaic feeling. It will not be screened from us, nor will we be protected, by any organization of archaic images. There has not yet been identified a single image (the point cannot be too often repeated) that can be definitely guaranteed as innate to man.

And so, it would seem, we are compelled to face the problem of the imagery of myth largely from a historical point of view, after all. There is a remarkable passage in a letter of Charles Darwin (addressed to a certain W. Graham who had inquired concerning his religious beliefs), where it is suggested that even the image of God may be only an imprint impressed upon the mind of man through centuries of teaching.

Darwin wrote, first in justification, but then in criticism, of his own somewhat shaky faith:

> Another source of conviction in the existence of God follows from the extreme difficulty or rather impossibility of conceiving this immense and wonderful universe, including man with his capacity of looking far backwards and far into futurity, as the result of blind chance or necessity. When thus reflecting I feel compelled to look to a First Cause having an intelligent mind in some degree analogous to that of man; and I deserve to be called a Theist. . . .
>
> *But then arises the doubt*—can the mind of man, which has, as I fully believe, been developed from a mind as low as that possessed by the lowest animal, be trusted when it draws such grand conclusions? May not these be the result of the connection between cause and effect which strikes us as a necessary one, but probably depends merely on inherited experience? Nor must we overlook the probability of the constant inculcation in a belief in God on the minds of children producing so strong and perhaps an inherited effect on their brains not yet fully developed, that it would be as difficult for them to throw off their

belief in God, as for a monkey to throw off its instinctive
fear and hatred of a snake.[46]

That would seem to fit the case precisely—at least as far as
anything but faith can tell us: and faith itself would then, of
course, be only a reflex of the imprint to which it referred.

To attempt to account, then, psychologically for those
common images (the bricks) that keep turning up alike in all
mythologies, let us review, briefly, some of the inevitable imprints to which the human infant and adolescent, no matter
where he may have developed, must always have been subject. These should account for at least a significant part of
those sign stimuli by which our human energies are triggered
to action and organized for life, as are the instincts of the animals by the various sign systems of their species: those energy-
releasing signals by which the organism is struck and moved,
as it were, from within.

The first of such imprintings are, of course, those to which
the infant is subjected in its earliest years. These have been ex-
tensively discussed in the literature of psychoanalysis, and
may be summarized somewhat as follows: (1) those of the
birth trauma and its emotional effects; (2) those of the
mother and father images in their benevolent and malevolent
transformations; (3) those associated with the infant's own
excrement and the measures of discipline imposed upon it in
relation to this area of experience; (4) those of the child's sexual researches and findings (whether in the male or in the female mode); and then, (5) those related to his discovery of
his place and rating among his peers. There can be little doubt
that no matter where in the world an infant may ever have
been born, as long as the nuclear unit of human life has been a
father, mother, and child, the maturing consciousness has had
to come to a knowledge of its world through the medium of
this heavily loaded, biologically based triangle of love and ag-
gression, desire and fear, dependency, command, and urge for
release; nor can there ever have been a school for life where
the individual did not have to come to terms, one way or an-

other, at a very early age, with his position in the "peck series" of his intimates.

But now, in every primitive society on earth—whether of the hunting or of the planting order—these inevitable imprints and conceptions of infancy are filled with new associations, rearranged and powerfully reimprinted, under the most highly emotional circumstances, in the puberty rites, the rites of initiation, to which every young male (and often every female too) is subjected. That long flume in the paleolithic grotto of Trois-Frères, with the vivid image of the staring sorcerer in the chamber to which it led, may have been employed in such a rite. A fundamental motif in such ceremonials is that of death to infancy and rebirth to adulthood, and this grotto shows every sign of having been used to suggest and effect such a crisis. Moreover, in these rites, the child's body is generally painfully altered—through circumcision, subincision, tattooing, scarification, ritual defloration, clitoridectomy, or what not; so that there is no childhood to which the child can now return. And through these forceful rearrangements of the references of the father image, mother image, birth idea, etc., the reflex system of the whole psyche is decisively transformed. The infantile system of responses is erased and the energies carried forward, away from childhood, away from the attitude of dependency that the long infancy characteristic of our species tends to enforce—on to adulthood, engagement in the local tasks of man- and womanhood, to an attitude of adult responsibility and a sense of integration with the local group.

A neurotic, then, might be defined as one in whom this initiation has failed of its effect, so that in him those socially organized sign stimuli that carry others on to their adult tasks continue to refer only backward—to the imprint system of the infant. The mother image then is experienced only as a reference to the human mother of one's childhood, not to the life-producing, disciplining, and supporting aspect of the world (which is our Mother and Grandmother), and the father is not Wakan Tanka, but that "undemonstrative relative," as James Joyce terms him, "who settles our hash bill for us." [47] All attempts, therefore, to interpret myths through a study of the imagery of neurotics necessarily run the risk of failing to consider precisely that aspect of mythology which is distinctive, namely, its power to carry people *away* from childhood—from dependency—on to responsibility.

Furthermore, the peculiar interests of adulthood differ radically from one society to another, and since it is a primary function of myth and ritual in all traditional societies not only to shape youngsters into adults but then, also, to hold the adults to their given roles, mythology and ritual, in so far as they serve this local, moral, ethical aim, cannot be called functions of any generally valid human psychology but only of local history and sociology.

Professor A. R. Radcliffe-Brown of Cambridge University has well discussed this aspect of our subject in his work on the pigmies of the Andaman Islands, where he writes as follows:

> (1) A society depends for its existence on the presence in the minds of its members of a certain system of sentiments by which the conduct of the individual is regulated in conformity with the needs of the society. (2) Every feature of the social system itself and every event or object that in any way affects the well-being or the cohesion of the society becomes an object of this system of sentiments. (3) In human society the sentiments in question are not innate but are developed in the individual by the action of the society upon him. (4) The ceremonial customs of a society are a means by which the sentiments in question are given collective expression on appropriate occasions. (5) The ceremonial (i.e. collective) expression of any sentiment serves both to maintain it at the requisite degree of intensity in the mind of the individual and to transmit it from one generation to another. Without such expression the sentiments involved could not exist.[48]

A mythological system, in short, according to this view, is not a natural, spontaneous production of the individual psyche, but a socially controlled reorganization of the imprints of childhood, so contrived that the sign stimuli that move the individual will conduce to the well-being of the local culture, and of that local culture alone. What is effective, as well as distinctive, in every mythology, therefore, is its locally ordered architecture, not the bricks (the infantile imprints and their affects) of which this structure is composed: and this architecture, this organization, differs significantly, according to place, time, and culture stage.

However, there is one more great aspect and function of mythology to be noted—and here we find ourselves moving away again from local, back to general terms; for man has not only to be led by myth from the infantile attitude of dependency to an adult assumption of responsibility in terms of the system of sentiments of his tribe, but also, in adulthood, to be prepared to face the mystery of death: to absorb the *mysterium tremendum* of being: for man, like no other animal, not only knows that he is killing when he kills but also knows that he too will die; and the length of his old age, furthermore, is—like his infancy—a lifetime in itself, as long as the entire life span of many a beast. Furthermore, even in the period of childhood, and certainly throughout one's adult years, the wonder of death—the awesome, dreadful transformations that immediately follow death—strike the mind with an impact not to be dismissed. The reconciliation of consciousness with the monstrous thing that is life—which lives on death, terminates in death, and begins with the curiously dreamlike event of a birth—is a function served by all primitive and most high-culture mythologies that is of no less weight and consequence than the function of imprinting a sociology. Indeed, the local sociology itself rides upon the mystery of life, which, like the mythological sea beneath the earth, is always there. And so, even when serving their social function, mythologies are dealing not only with sentiments *not* innate to man, "developed in the individual by the action of the society upon him," but also with what James Joyce termed, in *A Por-*

trait of the Artist as a Young Man, the "grave and constant in human sufferings." *

"You have noticed," said the old Sioux medicine man, Black Elk, to the poet John G. Neihardt, "that the truth comes into this world with two faces. One is sad with suffering, and the other laughs; but it is the same face, laughing or weeping." [49]

The Greeks subsumed a like insight in the image of their two contrasting masks, of tragedy and of comedy.

"In the heyoka ceremony," Black Elk said, "everything is backwards, and it is planned that the people shall be made to feel jolly and happy first, so that it may be easier for the power to come to them. . . . When people are already in despair, maybe the laughing face is better for them; and when they feel too good and are too sure of being safe, maybe the weeping face is better for them to see. And so I think that is what the heyoka ceremony [the Comic Mask] is for." [50]

Mythology and the rites through which its imagery is rendered open the mind, that is to say, not only to the local social order but also to the mystery dimension of being—of nature —which is within as well as without, and thereby finally at one with itself. Moreover, the sentiments of this nature within are indeed innate: of love, for example, hate, fear, and disdain, wonder, terror, and joy. They are not *"developed* in the individual," as the anthropologist states, "by the action of the society upon him," but *evoked* by these means and *directed* to sociological ends. Nature is prime: it is there at birth; Society is next: it is only a shaper of Nature, and a function, moreover, of what it shapes; whereas Nature is as deep and, finally, inscrutable as Being itself. Or, as Thomas Mann once phrased this·truth:

Man is not only a social, but also a metaphysical being. In other words, he is not merely a social individual, but also a personality. Consequently, it is wrong to confuse

* Supra, p. 39.

what is above the individual in us with society, to translate it completely into sociology. Doing that, one leaves the metaphysical aspect of the person, what is truly above the individual, out of account; for it is in the personality, not the mass, that the actual superordinated principal is to be found.[51]

[5]

The Personal Factor

And so we find that even in the most emphatically group-oriented traditions the preservation of the mythological lore is entrusted not to the merely practical men, alert to the needs of the day, but to individuals believed to be uncommonly endowed, whose visionary consciousness transcends the claims of the light world. "It is hard," said the old Sioux Black Elk to his friend, the poet John G. Neihardt, "to follow one great vision in this world of darkness and of many changing shadows. Among these shadows men get lost."[52] And indeed, even among the very primitive pigmies of the Andaman Islands—to the study of whose extremely simple stone-age culture the anthropologist Dr. Radcliffe-Brown devoted the very volume from which his above-quoted pronouncement concerning social sentiments was taken—it was not the social leaders but the "dreamers" (*oko-jumu*), the medicine men, who were honored as the authorities on all legendary lore. Moreover, this legendary lore was the base on which the social order itself was founded: all the rites, private and public, all the aims and all the means of life.[53] And these medicine men, who spoke from dreams, had gained their group-supporting wisdom through experiences of their own, *outside* the social compound, through personal contact, one way or another, with the spirits; as classified by Radcliffe-Brown: (a) through dying and coming back to life again; (b) through meeting spirits in the jungle; or (c) through extraordinary dreams.[54] Likewise Black Elk, the Oglala Keeper of the Sacred Pipe, had had a vision of his own—already at the age of nine: and it was to this that he owed those spiritual powers that had qualified him for the priestly office he held.

As a boy he had fallen strangely ill and was lying with his father and mother sitting by him in the tepee, when through the opening above he saw two men coming down from the clouds, head first like arrows, each with a spear from the point of which lightning flashed. He had already seen these two, four years before, when he was five, and they had sung to him then a sacred song:

> "Behold, a sacred voice is called you;
> All over the sky a sacred voice is calling. . . ."

After which they had wheeled toward where the sun goes down, and suddenly were geese. This time, however, they came to the ground, stood a little way off, and said to him: "Hurry! Come! Your Grandfathers are calling you!" He felt himself rise to follow them, and it was a truly wonderful great vision that then unfolded.

The vision has been rendered beautifully by Neihardt in the volume *Black Elk Speaks*, where it opens out, page after page, stage beyond stage, for twenty-five full pages. Confided by the aging seer as a trust, in the spring of 1931, to be given to the new world by which his own had been wiped away in the span of his single lifetime, it sings, still, in those pages, with the melody of a distant day that was our own, also, in our fathers: the long brave day of the paleolithic Great Hunt.

The sick child in the tepee spiritually rose, following the two spearsmen, and was carried by a little cloud to a landscape all of cloud, where everything was still. And the two men together said to him: "Behold him, the being with the four legs." He looked, and saw a bay horse standing.

The animal spoke to him. "Behold me! My life history you

shall see." Then it wheeled to the West. "Behold them! Their history you shall know." And there were twelve black horses yonder, all abreast, with necklaces of bison hoofs, their manes lightning, and thunder in their nostrils. The bay wheeled to the North: "Behold!" and there were twelve white horses, their manes flowing like a blizzard wind, and all about them white geese soaring. Eastward he wheeled: twelve sorrel horses, with eyes that glimmered like the daybreak star, and manes of morning light. Then South: and yonder stood twelve buckskins, all with horns on their heads, and manes that lived and grew like trees and grasses. "Your Grandfathers," said the bay "are having a council. These shall take you; so have courage."

All forty-eight horses then stood in formation behind the bay, who again turned and neighed to the quarters, whereupon the sky of each was terrible with a storm of plunging horses in all colors that shook the world, neighing back. "See," said the bay, "how your horses all come dancing!" And there were horses everywhere, a skyful, dancing, that changed then to all kinds of animals and vanished to the quarters.

The pair of spearsmen walked with their charge to a cloud that changed to a tepee, and a rainbow was its open door, through which could be seen the six Grandfathers sitting in a row: like hills, like stars—so old. They were the Powers of the West, North, East, South, Sky, and Earth; and each—to an accompaniment of many marvelous signs—presented tokens to the boy: a bow (the power to destroy) and a cup of water (the power to make live); an herb (the power to make grow); a pipe (the power that is peace); and a bright red stick that was alive, which put forth branches whereon birds sang. "Behold," said the Grandfather of the South, "the living center of a nation I shall give you, and with it many you shall save." The Spirit of the Sky stretched out his arms and turned into a spotted eagle, hovering, while the Spirit of the Earth—who looked, somehow, familiar—began, very slowly chang-

ing, growing backward into youth, and the boy perceived
that it was himself, with all the years that would be his. "My
boy," he said, when he was old again, "have courage, for my
power shall be yours and you shall need it, for your nation
on the earth will have great troubles. Come." He rose
and tottered through the rainbow door, where the boy followed.

Again he was riding the bay with the forty-eight behind
him, four abreast, all now with riders; and they rode along the
Black Road, eastward.* A series of magical adventures followed: drought overcome by the bow and cup; pestilence
cured by the mere passage of this troop; the flowering stick
was planted at the center of the nation's hoop, the sacred pipe
came flying, and a great Voice sounded: "Behold the circle of
the nation's hoop, for it is holy, being endless, and thus all
powers shall be one power in the people without end. Now
they shall break camp and go forth upon the Red Road, and
your Grandfather shall walk with them."

A beautiful procession formed: the black horse riders with
the cup in front, the white with the herb, the sorrel with the
pipe, the buckskins with the flowering stick, then all the children, youths, and maidens: next, the tribe's four chieftains
with young attendants; the four advisers, with the middle-
aged; then the old men and old women, hobbling with canes
and looking at the earth; all followed by the boy on his bay,
with the bow, and with a trail of ghosts behind him, of the
ancestors, like a fog, as far as eye could see. "Behold," said the
Voice, "a good nation walking in a sacred manner in a good
land."

But there were four ascents ahead—the generations now to
come, which Black Elk was to know: first, the land all green;
second, green but getting steeper, leaves falling from the tree,
and the Voice warning, "Remember what your Six Grandfathers gave you, for henceforth your people walk in difficul-
ties: the black road lies ahead"; then third, the people scat-

---

* The Black Road, west-east; the Red, north-south; cf. supra, pp. 87–88.

tering: "for each one seemed to have his own little vision that he followed and his own rules," and all over the universe were winds at war. At the summit of this difficult ascent the nation's hoop was broken, and the next ascent would be horrible: the people were already starving. . . .

And now comes that part of the vision which Black Elk, in later life, took to be the symbol of the spiritual charge placed upon him by the Powers for the benefit of his people. "But now that I can see it all from a lonely hilltop," he said, as an old man, to his friend, "I know it was the story of a mighty vision given to a man too weak to use it; of a holy tree that should have flourished in a people's heart with flowers and singing birds, and now is withered; and of a people's dream that died in bloody snow.

"But if the vision was true and mighty, as I know, it is true and mighty yet; for such things are of the spirit, and it is in the darkness of their eyes that men get lost." [55]

What he saw at this point was a man standing on the north side of the starving camp, his whole body painted red, who held a spear as he walked to the center of the people, where he lay down and rolled and when he got up was a fat bison. Where he stood a sacred herb sprang up, where the tree had been in the center of the nation's hoop. This grew and bore four blossoms: a blue (the West), a white (the North), a scarlet (the East), and a yellow (the South).

"I know now what this meant," old Black Elk told his friend, the poet: "that the bison were the gift of a good spirit and were our strength, but we should lose them, and from the same good spirit must find another strength." [56]

A great number of other marvels followed, of which the culmination was the arrival of the boy, still riding his bay horse, on the highest mountain of the world, Harney Peak in the Black Hills. "But anywhere," said Black Elk, "is the center of the world." [57] And there: "I was seeing in a sacred manner," he said, "the shapes of all things in the spirit, and the shape of all shapes as they must live together like one being. And I saw that the sacred hoop of my people was one of many hoops that made one circle, wide as daylight and as star-light, and in the center grew one mighty flowering tree to shelter all the children of one mother and one father."

Presently the two spearsmen who had first appeared to the boy returned and became four flocks of geese, one above each quarter of the earth, circling. The cloud tepee again appeared: underneath were all the animals and men, rejoicing. The Six Grandfathers within welcomed him: "He has triumphed!" they cried, like thunder, and again each gave the gift he had given before. The tepee rocked and faded: the face of the day of earth was appearing. The sun leaped up and sang as it rose: "With visible face, I am appearing. In a sacred manner I appear. . . ." And when the singing stopped, alone and feeling lost, the boy, on the plain, saw before him his people's village, his own tepee, and inside his mother and father bending over a sick child that was himself. As he entered, someone said, "The boy is coming to. . . ."

Then he was sitting up.[58]

The elements (the bricks) of this marvelous dream—the tree at the world center, the crossing there of the two roads, the world hoop ⊕ , the world mountain, the guides, the world guardians, and their tokens, magical powers, etc.— are such as are known to mythologies of many orders. The landscape and the animals involved, on the other hand, the colors and virtues of the four directions, the attitude toward nature and the supernatural, the high roles of the buffalo and the horse, the peace pipe, spotted eagle, etc., are of the architecture of the mythic world of the North American plains heritage. The intuition that gave rise to this vision in the mental sphere of a nine-year-old boy was personal, however: personal in the sense that no one else had ever had it, though collective indeed, not only in the sense that its imagery was archetypal, but also in that its prophecy was of the destiny, not merely of this boy, but of his folk. It was the foresight of an impending crisis, subliminally intuited, together with a statement of the way it was to be met.

When he was seventeen years old, Black Elk translated a

portion of this dream into a rite, a ceremonial for his people that was actually enacted. "A man who has a vision," he explained, "is not able to use the power of it until after he has performed the vision on earth for the people to see." [59] Thus do mythologies and their rites arise. A ritual is the form through which one participates in a myth, partakes of it, gives oneself to it: and the myth is a group dream projected from the personal-collective vision of a seer: a gifted individual.

And this condition prevails even in such emphatically anti-individualistic mythological traditions as those of the Old Testament and Koran, where what are put forward as the source inspirations are not group experiences at all, but the voices heard and visions seen by individuals alone: Abraham, hearing and heeding the voice of the Lord (Genesis 12); Jacob, dreaming his great dream of the heaven-ladder (Genesis 28); Moses and the burning bush, Moses on Mount Sinai (Exodus 3 and 19 ff.), Mohammed in his meditation cave (Koran, Sura 96). The usual Christian understanding of the "Good News" of Jesus, on the other hand, is that he who brought it—the Lamb of God—was an incarnation of the holy power itself, who had come into the world at the close of an old and opening of a new day: rather in the way of the very beautiful holy woman who came, as it were, from nowhere, in a strange and wonderful manner, with the gift of the Sacred Pipe—just when the Oglala Sioux were exchanging one manner of life (that of the forest) for another (that of the plains).

The vision of Black Elk was a foreview in the year 1873 of the next exchange before his people—from the hunt to agriculture (the buffalo to the sacred herb). The fair promise of his cult, however, was broken at the root, by *force majeure*, in the Year of Our Lord 1890, at Wounded Knee.

"Nothing I have ever seen with my eyes," he said to his friend, at the age of sixty-eight, "was so clear and bright as what my vision showed me; and no words that I have ever heard with my ears were like the words I heard. I did not have to remember these things; they have remembered themselves all these years. It was as I grew older that the meanings came clearer and clearer out of the pictures and the words; and even now I know that more was shown to me than I can tell." [60]

[V]

The Symbol without Meaning

PART I

[1]
The Impact of Modern Science

It was Bertrand Russell, as I recall, who once told a New York audience that all Americans believe the world was created in 1492 and redeemed in 1776. The cultural conditioning of an American, then, may account for the history and theory of mythological symbols that I am about to offer in this chapter. However, since one of the main themes of my subject is to be that of the provincial character of *all* that we are prone to regard as universal, we may let the presentation itself stand as an illustration of its own thesis.

I cannot forget that for many centuries the vast majority of the great as well as minor thinkers of Europe believed that the world was created about 4004 B.C. and redeemed in the first century A.D.; that Cain, the eldest son of the first human couple, was the first agriculturalist, the first murderer, and the first builder of cities; that the Creator of the Universe once held in particular regard a certain tribe of Near Eastern nomads, for whom he parted the waters of the Red Sea and to whom he communicated, in person, his program for the human race; and that, because of the failure of this people to recognize himself when he then became incarnate among them as the son of one of their daughters, the Creator of the Universe transferred his attention to the northern shores of the Mediterranean: to Italy, Spain, and France, to Switzerland, Germany, and England, to Holland and Scandinavia, and for a while, also, to the Austro-Hungarian Empire.

I am quite ready to admit, therefore, that it does seem to me that when the prows of Columbus's three brave little ships (the *Santa Maria* was a vessel of only one hundred tons, the *Pinta* a caravel of fifty, and the *Nina* a mere forty tons)— when the prows of these three nutshells cut through the world-encircling Uroboros, Ocean, the mythological age of European thought was dealt a lethal blow and the modern age of global thinking, adventurous experiment, and empirical demonstration inaugurated.

Hardly two centuries earlier, Saint Thomas Aquinas had sought to show, by reasonable argument, that the garden of paradise from which Adam and Eve had been expelled was an actual region of this physical earth, still somewhere to be found. "The situation of paradise," he had written, "is shut off from the habitable world by mountains, or seas, or some torrid region, which cannot be crossed; and so people who have written about topography make no mention of it." [1] The Venerable Bede, five and a half centuries before, had sensibly suggested that paradise could not be a corporeal place but must be entirely spiritual; [2] Augustine, however, had already rejected such a notion, maintaining that paradise was, and is, both spiritual *and* corporeal; [3] and it was to Augustine's view that Aquinas brought support. "For whatever Scripture tells us about paradise," he wrote, "is set down as a matter of history; and wherever Scripture makes use of this method, we must hold to the historical truth of the narrative as a foundation of whatever spiritual explanation we may offer." [4]

Dante, it will be recalled, placed paradise on the summit of the mountain of purgatory, which his century situated in the middle of an imagined ocean covering the whole of the southern hemisphere; and Columbus shared this mythological image. The earth, wrote Columbus, is shaped "like a pear, of which one part is round, but the other, where the stalk comes, elongated;" or "like a very round ball, on one part of which there is a protuberance, like a woman's nipple." [5] The protuberance was to be found, Columbus believed, in the south; and on his third voyage, when his vessels sailed more rapidly northward than southward, he believed this showed that they had begun to go downhill. And he was the more convinced of his error, since, some weeks earlier, at the southern reach of his voyage, when he had sailed between the island of Trinidad and the mainland of South America, the volume of fresh water pouring into the ocean from the mighty Orinoco, "the roar, as of thunder" that occurred where the river met the sea, and the height of the waves, which nearly wrecked his ships, had assured him that so great a volume of fresh water could have had its origin only in one of the four rivers of paradise, and that he had at last, therefore, attained to the stalk end of the pear.[6] Sailing north, he was leaving paradise behind.

Columbus died without knowing that he had actually delivered the first of a series of blows that were presently to annihilate every image, not only of an earthly, but even of a celestial paradise. In 1497, Vasco da Gama rounded South Africa, and in 1520, Magellan, South America: the torrid region and the seas were crossed, and no paradise found. In 1543, Copernicus published his exposition of the heliocentric universe, and some sixty years later, Galileo commenced his celestial researches with a telescope. And, as we know, these researches led immediately to the condemnation of the new cosmology by the Holy Inquisition.

Whereas you, Galileo, [wrote the holy fathers] son of the late Vincenzio Galilei, of Florence, aged seventy years, were denounced in 1615, to this Holy Office, for holding as true a false doctrine taught by many, namely, that the sun is immovable in the center of the world, and that the earth moves, and also with a diurnal motion; also, for having pupils whom you instructed in the same opinions; also for maintaining a correspondence on the same with some German mathematicians; also, for publishing certain letters on the sun-spots, in which you developed the same doctrine as true; also, for answering the objections which

were continually produced from the Holy Scriptures, by
glozing the said Scriptures according to your own meaning;
and whereas thereupon was produced the copy of a writing,
in form of a letter professedly written by you to a person
formerly your pupil, in which, following the hypothesis of
Copernicus, you include several propositions contrary to the
true sense and authority of the Holy Scriptures; therefore
(this Holy Tribunal being desirous of providing against the
disorder and mischief which were thence proceeding and
increasing to the detriment of the Holy Faith) by the desire
of his Holiness and of the Most Eminent Lords, Cardinals of
this supreme and universal Inquisition, the two propositions
of the stability of the sun, and the motion of the earth, were
qualified by the Theological Qualifiers as follows:

1. The proposition that the sun is in the center of the
world and immovable from its place is absurd, philosophically false, and formally heretical; because it is expressly
contrary to Holy Scriptures.

2. The proposition that the earth is not the center of
the world, nor immovable, but that it moves, and also with
a diurnal action, is also absurd, philosophically false, and,
theologically considered, at least erroneous in faith.

Therefore. . . , invoking the most holy name of our
Lord Jesus Christ, and of His Most Glorious Virgin
Mother Mary, We pronounce this Our final sentence. . . :
We pronounce, judge, and declare, that you, the said
Galileo . . . have rendered yourself vehemently suspected
by this Holy Office of heresy, that is of having believed and
held the doctrine (which is false and contrary to the Holy
and Divine Scriptures) that the sun is the center of the world,
and that it does not move from east to west, and that the
earth does move, and is not the center of the world; also,
that an opinion can be held and supported as probable,
after it has been declared and finally decreed contrary to
the Holy Scripture, and, consequently, that you have in-
curred all the censures and penalties enjoined and promul-
gated in the sacred canons and other general and particular
constituents against delinquents of this description. From
which it is Our pleasure that you be absolved, provided
that with a sincere heart and unfeigned faith, in Our pres-

ence, you abjure, curse, and detest, the said errors and
heresies, and every other error and heresy contrary to the
Catholic and Apostolic Church of Rome. . . .[7]

Three brief centuries later, and even the sun (which, in the
words of Copernicus's English translator, Thomas Digges,
"like a king in the middest of al raigneth and geeveth lawes of
motion to ye rest") has been dethroned. The great telescopes
of America have shown the Milky Way system, of which our
sun is but one member, to be a lens-shaped collection of some
100 billion stars, with our sun, a minor star, out toward the
rim—its distance from the center of the galaxy being about
26,000 light-years (that is to say, a distance that light, going
at the rate of approximately 6000 billion miles a year, would
require 26,000 years to traverse). Moreover, it has been found
that our entire galaxy is spinning around its center at such a
speed as would bring our sun through one full circuit in approximately 200 million years. Nor is our galaxy the only
galaxy in existence. Photographic surveys of the skies, made
from the Mount Wilson observatory in California, have
shown that galaxies tend to cluster in groups of over a thousand, in supergalaxies. Many supergalaxies have been identified. And this discovery has suggested to some the notion that
our own galaxy may be an outrider in one such supergalaxy,
just as the sun that once was "like a king in the middest of al"
was presently found to be an outrider of the Milky Way.

I shall not go on with this story, but simply ask—by way of
introducing at this point one of the main questions of this subject: How, in the way of reason, is any mind confronted with
this new image of the universe to understand, interpret, eval-
uate, or make any use whatsoever of the mythological cosmology of Holy Writ—or of any other of the many archaic
traditions still asserting their superstitions claims in the modern world? Luther brayed at Copernicus, naming him "an ass
who wants to pervert the whole art of astronomy and deny
what is said in the book of Joshua, only to make a show of
ingenuity and attract attention"; while his Holiness, the
Pope, and the most eminent cardinals of the universal Inquisi-

tion, as we have just seen, decreed that the actual form and state of the universe is false and contrary to the Holy Scriptures. Can it not now be said, then, on the word of these competent doctors, that since what then was thought to be false is proven true, what then was deemed to be true is proven false, absurd, and philosophically erroneous, because it is expressly contrary to the facts?

What is the modern mind to make of the pious belief, confirmed as dogma two decades ago and reconfirmed in the Credo of Pope Paul VI, June 30, 1968, of the Assumption of the Blessed Virgin Mary? * Is one to imagine a human body rising from this earth, to pass beyond the bounds of our solar system, beyond the bounds, then, of the Milky Way, beyond the bounds, next, of our supergalaxy, and beyond the bounds even of what may lie beyond that? If so, then—please!—at what velocity is this body moving? For it must still be in flight! Having been launched less than two millenniums ago, even if traveling at the speed of light (which for a physical body is impossible), both the body of our Lord Jesus Christ (which began its own ascent some fifteen years earlier) and that of His Most Glorious Virgin Mother Mary, would now be only some two thousand light-years away—not yet beyond the horizon of the Milky Way. The image is ridiculous. We have to ask, therefore, whether any meaning, spiritual or otherwise, can possibly inhere in such a figure today. Originally conceived when it could have been thought, literally, that Joshua stopped the sun and that God in his heaven dwelt but a short way beyond the orbit of Saturn, a figure of this kind imposes on the modern mind a feat of interpretation far more sophisticated than anything demanded of the faithful in the Middle Ages. And it is obvious, furthermore, that this problem touches not only Catholic Christianity but every one of the great traditions; for it cannot be denied that even

* *The New York Times,* July 1, 1968, p. 23: "Text of the Message and Credo of Pope Paul Marking End of the Year of Faith," Column 3, lines 58–64: "The Blessed Virgin, the immaculate, was at the end of her earthly life raised body and soul to heavenly glory and likened to her risen Son in anticipation of the future lot of all the just."

though some may now be symbolically reinterpreted by those who wish to retain them (pouring very new wine into very old bottles), in the days when they were brought into being as images of the highest truth, they were always literally as well as symbolically understood; or, to use the terms of Saint Augustine, corporeally as well as spiritually. Moreover, they always guaranteed to their believers a spiritual superiority over the other peoples of the earth—and we may well ask whether in our world today there still is room for such dangerous nonsense.

Let us ask, therefore: What can the value or meaning be of a mythological notion which, in the light of modern science, must be said to be erroneous, philosophically false, absurd, or even formally insane? The first answer suggested will no doubt be the one that, in the course of the past century, has been offered many times by our leading thinkers. The value, namely, is to be studied rather as a function of psychology and sociology than as a refuted system of positivistic science, rather in terms of certain effects worked by the symbols on the character of the individual and the structure of society than in terms of their obvious incongruity as an image of the cosmos. Their value, in other words, is not that of science but that of art: and just as art may be studied psychologically, as symbolic or symptomatic of the strains and structures of the psyche, so may the archetypes of myth, fairy tale, archaic philosophy, cosmology, and metaphysics.

This is the point of view that Professor Rudolf Carnap has presented in the chapter "The Rejection of Metaphysics," in his University of London lectures, *Philosophy and Logical Syntax*, which were published in 1935. There he states that metaphysical propositions "are neither true nor false, but expressive." They are like music, or like lyric poems, or like laughter. And yet, he states, they *pretend* to be representative. They *pretend* to have theoretical value—and therewith, not only is the reader or hearer deceived but the metaphysician also. "The metaphysician believes," wrote Dr. Carnap, "that in his metaphysical treatise he has asserted something, and he is

led by this into argument and polemics against the propositions of some other metaphysician. A poet, however, does not
assert that the verses of another are wrong or erroneous; he
usually contents himself with calling them bad." [8]

C. G. Jung, in many passages, has drawn a distinction between the terms "sign" and "symbol," as he employs them.
The first, the sign, is a reference to some concept or object,
definitely known; the second, the symbol, is the best possible
figure by which allusion may be made to something relatively
unknown. The symbol does not aim at being a reproduction,
nor can its meaning be more adequately or lucidly rendered in
other terms. Indeed, when a symbol is allegorically translated
and the unknown factor in its reference rejected, it is dead. [9]

I believe we may say that, in general, the symbols of science
and of symbolic logic are, in this sense, signs; and the figures
of art, in this sense, symbols.

In Indian philosophy two terms occur that are the counterparts of sign and symbol as here interpreted. The first,
pratyakṣa (from *prati*, meaning "near to, over against," plus
akṣa, "the eye" : "over against, or apparent, to the eye") refers to the sensible, obvious, evident, immediate field, perceptible to the senses. This field is described as that of waking
consciousness. Here subject and object are separate from each
other, and the phenomena observed are of "gross matter,"
while the logic of the relationship of things and concepts to
each other can be expressed largely in Euclidean or Aris-
totelian terms: A is not not-A; two objects cannot occupy the
same place at the same time. In modern physics, of course,
those obvious rules have begun to blur at the edges, so that
scientific and logical formulae now exhibit some of the qualities of art. But the *referienda* of these modern formulae are
invisible to the eye, and are composed, furthermore, not of
"gross matter," but of what the Indians call "subtle matter."
Hence they would seem to pertain, actually, to the field of the
second term.

This second term—which would be a counterpart of Jung's
"symbolic"—is *parokṣa* (again from *akṣa*, meaning "eye,"

but now with the prefix *paras:* "beyond, far away, higher than"; so that the meaning is "beyond the reach of the eye"). For the references of a *parokṣa* vocabulary are not immediately perceptible to waking consciousness. They are, rather, like Platonic ideas, purely intelligible, spiritual, or esoteric. They are said to be *adhidaivata,* "divine," or "angelic." But they are perceived by the saints and sages in vision, and so are said to pertain to the field of "dreaming."

The phantasmagorias of dream and vision are of "subtle matter." Extremely fluent and mercurial, they are not illuminated, like gross objects, from without, but are self-luminous. Moreover, their logic is not that of Aristotle. In dream, we all know, the subject and object are not separate from each other —though they seem so to the dreamer—but identical; and two or more objects, furthermore, not only can but always do occupy the same place at the same time. The images, that is to say, are polysynthetic and polysemantic—and, I might add, in both aspects inexhaustible when analyzed from the standpoint of waking consciousness. The law of this sphere is well epitomized in Lévy-Bruhl's term *participation mystique,* which is frequently cited by Jung. In the Orient, the realms of the gods and demons, the heavens, purgatories, and hells, are assigned to this sphere and are of subtle matter. They are the macrocosmic counterpart of the microcosmic images of dream. But since we do not encounter on this level the sort of clear distinction between A and not-A that is proper to the field of waking consciousness, micro- and macrocosm on this level are not as different as they seem, and all the gods, therefore, all the powers of heaven and hell, are within us.

The references of religious art in the Orient—in contrast to the West—are, almost always, not to the phenomenology of waking consciousness but to that of dream; hence the findings of modern science do not as greatly trouble Hinduism and Buddhism as they trouble Christianity and Judaism, where all the symbols have been taught and read as signs. Nevertheless, even in the Orient there is thought to be a real and necessary correspondence between the phenomenology of dream consciousness and that of waking. Micro- and macrocosm, which in dream may be experienced as identical, when we are awake are to be recognized as *anurūpam*, "in the image of each other." [10] In fact, I am sure that it can be said, without exception, that wherever a system of mythological symbols is alive and fully operative, it unites in a single, cohesive order, all phenomena both of the corporeal—"directly obvious" (*pratyakṣa*)—sphere of waking consciousness, and of the spiritual—metaphysical, occult, purely intelligible (*parokṣa*) —sphere of dream. Hence an imprecise fusion of sign and symbol, fact and fancy, is characteristic of the entire range and history of the archaic cultures; and we may well say, consequently, that one of the chief philosophical effects of the crisis represented by my crucial date 1492 was that of the fracturing of this vague mythological order: the drawing of a distinct dividing plane between the world of dream consciousness and that of waking, together with a radical shift of the commitment of the waking intellect from the logic of the former to that of the latter. This we term the scientific revolution—which is still in progress; and it is amounting, indeed, to the creation of a new world—or, to use a mythological image, to a separation of heaven and earth.

Mythological cosmologies, it now must be recognized, do not correspond to the world of gross facts but are functions of dream and vision; and therefore, the meanings (if any) inherent in or implied by the propositions of theology and metaphysics are not to be sought at the other end of either the microcope or the telescope. They are not verifiable through any science of physical research but belong, rather, to the science of the psyche—and here, as we know, considerable progress has already been made toward a reconstruction of our understanding of their terms.

Indeed, for some, this ancient lore, now interpreted psychologically instead of cosmologically, has actually seemed to restore the old religions to their former place both in the center and around the bounding horizon of the sphere of the human spirit, as representing not merely a passing phase in the history of the evolution of consciousness but a permanent spiritual legacy, symbolic of the very structure of the psyche. The Assumption of the Virgin and the Ascension of her Divine Son (who was, and is forever, both true God and true Man) may now be sensitively glozed in a manner that would have brought us all to the stake a mere three centuries ago; and on the groundswell of this fortunate heresy (*O felix culpa!*) the ship of the "City of God" is lifted off the rocks and carried powerfully on its way.

But now, let us ask, very calmly, objectively, and honestly: Is it true that these discredited cosmological dogmas, which are now returning to us as psychological symbols—is it true that all these archaic propositions, which have been disqualified, from top to bottom, as representations of the macrocosm —can now be safely restored to favor as a universal revelation of the microcosm? Are these forms—these sacred *mandalas*, icons, and yantras, these gods who sit about the world, hand down their moral edicts, or come down to man as incarnations and fly back to heaven again—are these actually the symbolic guardians of some kind of natural or supernatural Law, qualifying the meaning and destiny of man; bounding, binding, and yet guiding him to his proper end? Do they have meaning, that is to say, as microcosmic universals—and hence, perhaps, finally, in some mysterious manner, as macrocosmic universals, after all? Or must we judge them, rather, as functions merely of a certain phase or form of human culture— not of universal psychological validity but sociologically determined? In the latter event, like the carapace of a crayfish or cocoon of a butterfly that has been cracked, sloughed off, and left behind, they too have been cracked (for they were certainly cracked in 1492) and should now be left behind.

[2]

The Mythic Forms of Archaic Civilization

One of the most interesting and important of the many critical developments that have taken place in the field of archaeological research in recent decades has been that of the steady progress of excavations in the Near East, which have now begun to bring into clear focus the chief centers of origin and the main paths of diffusion of the earliest neolithic culture forms. To present very briefly the main result of this work pertinent to our present theme, let me commence by saying that the arts of grain agriculture and stock breeding, which are the basic forms of economy on which all of the high cultures of the world are based, now appear to have been developed in the Near East, commencing about 9000 B.C., and to have spread eastward and westward from this center in a broad band, displacing the earlier, much more precariously supported hunting and food-collecting cultures, until both the Pacific coast of Asia and the Atlantic coasts of Europe and Africa were reached about 3500 B.C. Meanwhile, in the nuclear zone from which this diffusion had originated, a further development was accomplished, and both the mythological and the technological effects of this continuing development were subsequently diffused along the ways already blazed— until, again, the coasts were attained.

That is to say: the transformation of society from a food-collecting, hunting, and root-gathering structure to an agrarian, stock-breeding, food-producing one, took place, specifically and uniquely, in a certain definite region of the globe, at a certain definite time. And the development from this center of all the basic arts and myths of the agriculturally based archaic civilizations can be described in four great stages, briefly as follows:

[a] THE PROTO-NEOLITHIC: FROM C. 9000 B.C.

Stage one, which we may term the *Proto-Neolithic*, is represented by an assemblage of artifacts discovered in the middle twenties by Dr. Dorothy Garrod at the so-called Mount Carmel caves in Palestine.[11] Similar artifacts have since been found as far south as to Helwan, in Egypt, as far north as to Beirut and Yabrud, and as far east as to the Kurdish hills of

Iraq. The industry is known to archaeology as the Natufian and has been variously assigned by differing scholars to dates as far apart as c. 9000 and c. 4500 B.C.[12] What the evidence suggests is a congeries of hunting tribes, not yet dwelling in fixed villages, yet supplementing their food supply with some variety of grainlike grass; for sickle-blades of stone have been found among the remains, and these suggest a harvest. Many bones of the pig, goat, sheep, ox, and an equid of some sort let us know, furthermore, that even if the Natufians were not yet domesticating, they were nevertheless slaughtering the same beasts that would later constitute the basic barnyard stock of all the higher cultures. Their style of life, then, was transitional, and let us mark the date. Mankind had inhabited this planet already for nearly two million years, yet here, not twelve thousand years ago, is the first hint even of the beginnings of a turn to agriculture.

[b] THE BASAL NEOLITHIC:
C. 7500–4500 B.C.

Stage two in the development of village farming in the Near East, which I have termed in *The Masks of God* the *Basal Neolithic* and there dated c. 5500–4500 B.C., has been so greatly expanded by the archaeology of the last ten years that its dates must now be assigned to c. 7500–4500 B.C., and within this span as many as three distinct substages have been identified.

Substage 1. Aceramic Neolithic: from c. 7500 B.C. The earliest of these substages, the *Pre-Pottery or Aceramic Neolithic*, was first disclosed and registered by Dr. Kathleen Kenyon in the lowest strata of the ancient mound of Jericho, in Palestine; and Dr. James Mellaart, in southern Turkey, on the Anatolian plain, has since discovered an impressive series of sites of equivalent age. According to Miss Kenyon, the earliest settlers at the great spring of Jericho were Natufians who built there a sanctuary of some kind that was subsequently burned down, leaving a charcoal deposit that has been dated by the Carbon-14 method at 7800 B.C. ± 210 years. The fragile shelters of these proto-neolithic hunters gave place presently to houses built of plano-convex bricks (bricks with a flat base and curved top), the round or curvilinear forms of the little buildings imitating the earlier primitive huts. In time this settlement—known as *Pre-Pottery Neolithic A Jericho*—was protected by a town wall of stone, some twelve feet high and six feet six inches wide, with an associated stone watch tower rising to a height of at least thirty feet, suggesting that somewhere on the horizon there were enemies.

"It looks," Miss Kenyon writes, "as though there were two lines of development. One Lower Natufian group settled down at Jericho, and it is surely to be presumed that other groups established settlements in comparable positions. . . . But the cousins of the settled groups, living mainly in the hills, in areas less favorable for agriculture, continued in a Mesolithic way of life, still living as hunters and food-gatherers. The caves and shelters in which they lived have produced the implements which have been classified as Middle and Upper Natufian." [13] And this, then, accounts for the great spread of differing dates for the Natufians suggested by earlier scholars.

Somewhere about 7000 B.C. this earliest settlement at Jericho was deserted and its site appropriated by a people of another culture, building houses of a different type, to which the name *Pre-Pottery Neolithic B Jericho* has been assigned. And these may have been the enemies foreseen. Their buildings were of another, more highly evolved type. "The newcomers arrived," Miss Kenyon states, "with this architecture fully developed." [14] The houses were not circular but rectangular, built of bricks of another shape, and with several rooms, having hard lime-plaster floors, reddish or cream colored and finished with a high burnish. The same kind of floors and rectangular dwellings have now been found in the Anatolian sites of Hacilar and Çatal Hüyük, where they are of an earlier date than at Jericho; and not only the architecture, but the evidences of religion, too, provide, as the excavator

James Mellaart has pointed out, "an unmistakable link" between the Pre-Pottery levels at Hacilar (which he dates between c. 7000 and c. 6000 B.C.) and the Pre-Pottery B phase of Jericho (which he places c. 6500–5500 B.C.).[15]

The principal shared religious feature of Jericho and the Anatolian sites was an unmistakable skull cult. In the Pre-Pottery levels at Hacilar, "human skulls, propped up with stones on the floors of many houses and at the corners of the hearths, indicate," according to Dr. Mellaart, "that the inhabitants practiced an ancestor cult, preserving heads to protect the homes."[16] And in Pre-Pottery B Jericho, not only were skulls set up the same way, but a number were found that had been lightly covered with plaster shaped to the likeness of human features, the eyes being of inset shells.[17]

So much, then, for the first substage of the Basal Neolithic.

Substage 2. Ceramic Neolithic: from c. 6500 B.C.   The second substage appeared at Çatal Hüyük, abruptly, at an astonishingly early date, and has been termed the *Pottery or Ceramic Neolithic.* "At Çatal Hüyük," states Dr. Mellaart, "we can actually study the transition from an aceramic Neolithic with baskets and wooden vessels to a ceramic Neolithic with the first pottery."[18] The deeper levels of this large and luxurious town site have not yet been investigated systematically, but a probe to Level XIII has revealed the presence of pottery already at that depth, roughly 6500 B.C. And with the pottery, there has come to view an astonishing display of religious imagery in the wall paintings, mother-goddess statuettes, bucrania, etc., of some forty or more richly decorated shrines, which have advanced by some two thousand years our knowledge of the backgrounds of the great mother-goddess myths and cults of the ancient world.

Figure 7[19] is a figurine that was found at Level II (c. 5800 B.C.), in a grain bin, showing the goddess supported by leopards and giving birth to a child, whereas in Figure 8,[20] from a shrine at Level VI (c. 5950 B.C.), she is shown giving birth to a bull. It is recalled that Osiris, Tammuz, Dionysus,

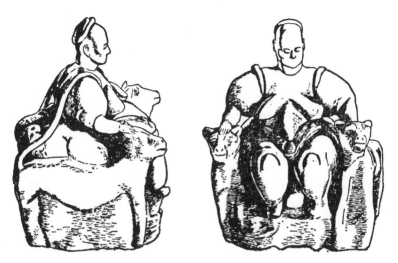

Figure 7. Goddess Supported by Leopards, Giving Birth to a Child; Çatal Hüyük (Anatolia), Turkey, c. 5800 B.C.

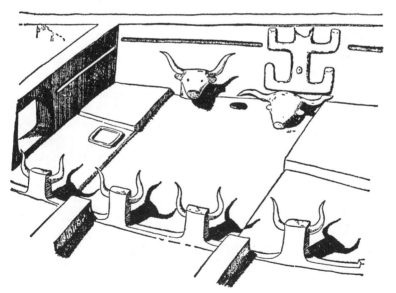

Figure 8. Goddess Giving Birth to a Bull; west wall of Shrine VI.B.8. Çatal Hüyük (Anatolia), Turkey, c. 5950 B.C.

and many other great divinities symbolic of a resurrection beyond death, were in later centuries identified with the moon bull, who was both the child and the consort of the cosmic goddess. The Pharaoh, identified in death with Osiris, was called, for example, "the bull of his own mother." [21] Taken back to the universal mother in death, he became, as it were, the seed of his own rebirth: like the moon that dies each month into the sun, to become in three days reborn. "The male," declares Mellaart, discussing his finds at Çatal Hüyük, "appears either as husband or as son." [22] And indeed, again from Level VI there is an interesting dual figure, showing the goddess back-to-back with herself: in one character embraced by an adult male and in the other holding a child. [23]

Figure 9 [24] presents a reconstructed view of three walls—west, north, and east—of the so-called Second Vulture Shrine of Level VII, c. 6200 B.C., and of the greatest interest here, in the light of what we have learned of the Pre-Pottery skull cult, are the four human skulls ceremonially disposed: one beneath the mighty bucranium of the west wall, two on the northeast corner platform beneath a stylized female breast, and one more, beneath an arrangement of three rams' heads, a bucranium, and a row of six stylized female breasts. The entire north wall is decorated with paintings of vultures attacking headless human bodies, while on the southernmost panel of the long east wall there is what Dr. Mellaart describes as "a large ram's head with actual horns and painted with a bold meander pattern . . . beneath a bold clay horn from which a single breast protrudes. Out of the open breast springs the lower jaw of a gigantic boar." [25] Nor is this the only shrine at this site where the lower jaws of boars are contained within models of the female breast. [26] Fox and weasel skulls have been used in this way as well. And there is a shrine on Level VI where the heads of two Griffin vultures are sealed within a pair of breasts, with the beaks protruding from the open red-painted nipples. [27] The idea suggested would seem to be of a mother who eats back the lives she has nourished—the mother to whom the dead are returned for rebirth. "Contrasting sym-

Figure 9. Reconstruction of "The Second Vulture Shrine," with human skulls as found. *Top:* west and north walls. *Bottom:* north and east walls. Çatal Hüyük (Anatolia), Turkey, c. 6200 B.C.

bols of life and death," states Dr. Mellaart, "are a constant feature of Çatal Hüyük." [28]

Substage 3. Early Chalcolithic: from c. 5500 B.C. The third and final substage, then, of the Basal Neolithic, as it has been brought to light from the mounds of the Anatolian Plain, is termed (for this area) the *Early Chalcolithic,* since there have been found among the remains a few artifacts of metal. The beginnings of metallurgy, specifically the smelting and working of copper and lead into beads, tubes, and other trinkets, are already evident at Çatal Hüyük as early as Level IX, c. 6300 B.C.[29] (which is the earliest date for the knowledge of metals yet registered anywhere on earth). However, it is not until nearly a millennium later, c. 5500 B.C., that metal tools become numerous enough (though still relatively unimportant) to warrant the recognition of a "copper-stone" (chalcolithic) phase of this basal neolithic development. Dr. Mellaart has been able to mark in detail a gradual progression from Ceramic Neolithic to Early Chalcolithic particularly well at Hacilar, where, as he declares, "the first copper implements appear, and with them painted pottery in force." "The truly superb pottery of this period developed," he continues, "out of the late Neolithic, some still in monochrome but most of it gaily painted in red or cream. Geometric patterns, many derived from textiles or woven mats, prevailed in the early phases of the period; later [c. 5200–5000 B.C.] the patterns took on bold curves, the so-called fantastic style." [30]

And a somewhat surprising observation touching the art styles of the neolithic female figurines can also be made at this point. For, whereas those of the earlier Ceramic Neolithic had been naturalistic and lifelike, giving us, as Mellaart declares, "for the first time in Near Eastern prehistory, a reliable picture of what late Neolithic woman looked like," [31] those of this early chalcolithic period (c. 5500–4500 B.C.) are "conventionalized fertility symbols." And as time goes on, the figurines become more and more stylized and unlifelike.

[c] THE HIGH NEOLITHIC: C. 4500–3500 B.C. (MIDDLE AND LATE CHALCOLITHIC)

And so we are brought to the next great stage in the evolution of civilization, which I have termed in *The Masks of God* the *High Neolithic: 4500–3500 B.C.*: that of the beautiful, geometrically conceived, painted ceramic wares of Halaf, Samarra, and Obeid, which has also been called the *Middle and Late Chalcolithic*.

Miss Kenyon explains:

The difficulty in deciding where to place the transition from the Neolithic to the Chalcolithic is reflected in the existing confusion in nomenclature. Sometimes the one and sometimes the other name is given to allied groups. The transition is in fact a gradual one. The dawn of the new era is not marked by the sudden appearance of copper implements on a site, but by the gradual breakdown of isolation and the resultant spreading of ideas and cultures over a considerable area. In Palestine, in fact, as far as our evidence goes, metal seems to have played a relatively small part among the materials employed until quite a late date, about the end of the third millennium. But in spite of this, the change in outlook is reflected in the gradual growth of widespread cultures, and the eventual amalgamation of isolated groups into a cultural whole.

In the northern part of the Fertile Crescent, this stage is marked by the appearance of a widespread culture, called Halafian, after Tell Halaf in northern Iraq where it was first found. Site after site, from Mesopotamia across to the Mediterranean coast, has shown that after the stage of the Neolithic villages with all their diverse ways of life, a remarkably similar economy appears, with, as a characteristic feature, a type of pottery with geometric decoration in red on a light background. This is usually dated to the late fifth millennium.[32]

The arts of carpentry and house building, weaving, ceramic crafts, and even metallurgy have been added to the sum of human skills. An imposing mythology—to be echoed through all subsequent high traditions to the present—has been articulated in a well-developed constellation of iconographic arts, which in the rendition of certain themes were already losing immediacy and devolving into abstractions. Settled village life based on a barnyard economy is now, throughout the nuclear Near East, a firmly established pattern, the grains being chiefly wheat and barley, and the animals, the pig, goat, sheep, and ox (the dog having already joined the human family as early, perhaps, as about 15,000

B.C., as an aid and companion of hunters of the late Paleolithic). And society, apparently, has already become differentiated, with specialist craftsmen producing articles of lux-
ury, a special priestly order of some kind, and possibly also
governing authorities: as Miss Kenyon has observed, already
at the level of Pre-Pottery A Jericho, "the evidence that there
was an efficient communal organization is to be seen in the
great defensive system," [33] the great wall and tower of stone.

Then suddenly—quite suddenly—in the highly styled,
painted ceramic wares of the high neolithic (middle and
late chalcolithic) towns, c. 4500 B.C., a totally new concept
of art becomes apparent in the very beautiful, strictly balanced, circular organizations of abstract aesthetic forms applied to the decoration of vessels of all kinds.

In the earlier, paleolithic art of the great caves of southern
France and northern Spain, which are now being dated c.
30,000–c. 9000 B.C.,[34] we do *not* find evidence of a concept
of *geometrical* organization. Professor André Leroi-Gourhan
has recently demonstrated that the positioning of the figures
engraved and painted on the walls of the caves was not at all
haphazard but strictly ordered by a mythology in which the
form of the cave itself participated. "The cavern," he states,
"is truly, as it were, an organized world." [35] And he com-
pares the organization to that of a cathedral. What images are
normally at the entrance? What, halfway down the nave?
What in the apse, the Lady Chapel? What and where is the
high altar? etc. The organization, that is to say, is mythological and three-dimensional—architectural, as it were; and the
figures are, for the most part, beautifully alive. We do not
find anywhere in this cave art aesthetically conceived signs
and abstractions, symmetrically arranged in a closed, geometrically organized, *two*-dimensional aesthetic field—no mandalas or anything of the kind (Figures 2 and 10). In fact,
the painted or incised surfaces of the cave walls are so little
regarded as fields of aesthetic interest in themselves that the
animals frequently overlap each other in great tangles.[36] Nor

do we find anything like an aesthetic organization of the field in the works surviving to us from the later, terminal stages of the Paleolithic, where many of the petroglyphs have lost the earlier impressionistic beauty and precision and some have even deteriorated into mere geometric scrawls or abstractions. On certain flat, painted pebbles that have been found in what apparently were religious sanctuaries, geometrical symbols appear: the cross, the circle with a dot in the center, a line with a dot on either side, stripes, meanders, and something resembling the letter E.[37] Yet we do not find, even in this late stage of the hunting period, anything that could be termed a geometrical organization—anything suggesting the concept of a definitely circumscribed field in which a number of disparate elements are united and fused into one aesthetic whole by a rhythm of beauty. Whereas suddenly, in the period of the high neolithic towns, there breaks into view, from a number of centers, an elegant display of the most gracefully and tastefully organized mandalas—in the painted ceramic wares of the so-called Halaf and Samarra styles.[38]

And so now—returning to the argument of the first part of this chapter—we have to ask ourselves whether it can be properly claimed that these geometrical forms, which have become the commonplaces of our modern psychological discussion of archetypal symbols, actually do represent basal structures of the human psyche, or may not, rather, be functioned only of a certain type or phase of social development incidental to the history of a limited portion of the race.

The question is one of considerable moment; for on it depends our whole interpretation of the so-called "spiritual," "divine," "esoteric," or "mystical," *parokṣa* references of our psychological vocabulary. Yet, as far as I know, it has not been systematically studied. What I should like to propose, therefore, is a preliminary hypothesis: an idea that occurred to me some years ago, during the course of a comparative study of the myths and art of certain living hunting races with those of the archaic Near East.

Figure 10. Polychrome Pottery Designs; Halaf ware, Iraq, c. 4000 B.C.

THE NEOLITHIC-PALEOLITHIC
CONTRAST

To begin with, then, let me call attention to the fact that among hunting peoples the young male adult, or even the normal youngster of ten or twelve, is a more or less competent master of the entire technological inheritance of his culture. The late Dr. Géza Róheim remarked on this, with reference to the hunting peoples of Australia. In one of his last publications he wrote:

I shall never forget the Pijentara children, who, at the age of eight or ten, went roaming about the desert and were practically self-supporting. A boy, with his keen eyes and spear, can catch what he needs in small fry and keep going from morning until evening. Even an adult male cannot do very much more. The outstanding characteristic of primitive economies is the absence of a true differentiation of labor. An incipient or rudimentary division of labor may exist along sexual or age lines, and there may be some incipient and part-time specialization in matters of ritual and magic. But true specialization is lacking. This means that every individual is technically a master of the whole

culture or, where certain modest qualifications are necessary, of almost the whole culture. In other words, each
individual is really self-reliant and grown up.

We however do not grow up as simply as that. If the
testimony of anthropology indicates anything, it shows
that primitive man is free, untrammeled, and truly self-
reliant in comparison with Medieval or Modern Man.[39]

It was this remark of Dr. Róheim's that seemed to me to
offer the clue to the interpretation of the sudden appearance
of the mandala, and of other geometrical organizations of en-
closed fields, after the passing of the hunting age and with the
development of the agricultural. For, whereas in the camps of
the hunters the community was constituted of a group of
practically equivalent individuals, each in adequate control of
the whole inheritance, in the larger, more greatly differentiated communities that developed when agriculture and stock
breeding had made for a settled, more richly articulated social
structure, adulthood consisted in acquiring, first, a certain
special art or skill, and then, the ability to support or sustain
the resultant tension—a psychological and sociological tension
—between oneself (as merely a fraction of a larger whole)
and others of totally different training, powers, and ideals,
who constituted the other necessary organs of the body social.

The problem of existing as a mere fraction instead of as a
whole imposes certain stresses on the psyche which no primitive hunter ever had to endure, and consequently the symbols
giving structure and support to the development of the primitive hunter's psychological balance were radically different
from those that arose in the settled villages, in the Basal and
High Neolithic, and which have been inherited from that age
and continued into the present by all the high civilizations of
the world. Furthermore, by far the greatest number of the so-
called primitive peoples today are not actually primitive in
their culture, but regressed—regressed neolithic, regressed
bronze, or even regressed iron age culture provinces. For example, even the pigmoid negritos of the Andaman Islands,

who are certainly among the most primitive peoples now living on earth, cannot be studied simply as primitives; for there is a good deal of evidence, not only in their kitchen middens, which have been piling up for thousands of years, but also in their myths and folkways, of important cultural influences which arrived from the southeast Asian mainland, beginning perhaps three or four thousand years ago, and which brought to them not only pottery and the pig but also a new method of cooking and even the art of smoking pipes. They have, besides, an extremely beautiful type of bow, which is not, by any means, a primitive weapon, but one that appears only as late as the Mesolithic—that is to say, in the culture period just preceding that of the dawn of the arts of food cultivation.[40]

Now it should certainly not be necessary to point out that one cannot safely draw conclusions concerning the typology and archetypology of the human psyche in general from any body of evidence, no matter how abundant, that has been gathered almost exclusively from one province—even though a very great one: the province, namely, of the range and influence of the food-producing, settled villages, towns, and cities of the comparatively brief neolithic and post-neolithic era of the human race. When it is recalled—as already remarked—that the earliest evidences of man in this world date from the neighborhood of two million years ago, and that the period during which he has been an agriculturalist embraces no more than some ten thousand (a segment, that is to say, of less than one half of one per cent of the known arc), and when it is considered, further, that this physical body of ours, of which our psyche is a function, evolved under the conditions not of agriculture but of the hunt—then perhaps it may be asked whether this whole history and mythology of the earth-rooted, walled town or village, with its temple tower in the center, lifting the goddess earth to her divine connubium with the all-father of the overarching fertilizing sky, is not, perhaps, only a highly specialized formula, not normal to the psyche of the species, but rather, an effect of the tensions, fears, and expectations generated in a society based on an agricultural economy. And we may ask, also, then, whether today, when that economy is giving way to one based on industry, and the cosmological image commensurate with an agricultural horizon has been shattered for us forever—whether today, in this next great age of transformation, the images generated in that earlier period of crisis still are of use, and if so for whom, and why?

It was during the Basal Neolithic, Substage 2, in the phase now known as Ceramic Neolithic (identified at Çatal Hüyük c. 6500 B.C.), that the earliest of those neolithic mother-goddess figurines appear that mark, throughout the world, the dawn of an order of myths and rites relative specifically to the generative and nourishing, "female" powers of the tilled earth. But there is also a much earlier series of naked figurines, of the type of the paleolithic Venus of Willendorf, from the period of the art of the hunters of the great French and Spanish caves. And there is an extremely perplexing question connected with the history of that series; for it has been observed that, although their cult seems to have extended all the way from the Pyrenees to Lake Baikal in Siberia, the period of their florescence was comparatively brief. As the art of painting developed and the beautiful animal forms took possession of the walls of the great caves, the carving of the figurines was discontinued. Furthermore, whenever human forms do appear among the painted animals, they are of masculine shamans, the representation of the human female having practically ceased. And so we have to understand that there were two quite distinct orders of culture in which female figurines played a preponderant role in the symbolism of magic and religion, and that these now appear to have been separated by a span of at least ten thousand years.

We find certain symbols in the centers of the high neolithic mandalas, and these have remained characteristic of such organizations to the very present. In the Samarra ware, for example, we discover the earliest known association of the swastika with the mandala—in fact, there is only one earlier known occurrence of the swastika anywhere, and that is on

Figure 11. Swastika on late paleolithic bird figurine of mammoth ivory; earliest swastika known, Mezin, Ukraine, c. 10,000 B.C.

the wings of a flying bird, carved of mammoth ivory (Figure 11), found in a late paleolithic site, not far from Kiev.* Frequently, in the Samarra ware, the swastika appears in the sinister form, with the angled arms pointing leftward, and this may or may not be a significant fact. We also find the Maltese cross in the centers of these early mandalas—occasionally modified in such a way as to suggest stylized animal forms, as

* One of six figures of birds carved of mammoth ivory, unearthed near the village of Mezin, on the right bank of the river Desna, about halfway between Briansk and Kiev. As described by Dr. Fran Hančar ("Zum Problem der Venusstatuetten in eurasiatischen Jungpaläolithikum," *Prähistorische Zeitschrift*, XXX–XXXI Band, 1939–1940, 1/2 Heft, pp. 85–156): "A wedge-shaped projection suggests the head. The back runs on without interruption through the long tail, while the breast and belly swell out in an exaggerated bulge, cutting back sharply to the tail. The long tails spread a little toward the tip. An elaborate geometric pattern covering the flat surfaces removes the bird-likeness still further from its natural model. On the various separate areas of these curious bodies we find bands of angular and

though the beasts were emerging from the whirling arms (supra, p. 94, Figure 1). In several examples the stylized forms of women appear, with their feet or heads coming together in the middle of the mandala, to constellate a star. Such mandalas are usually fourfold in design, but occasionally fivefold, sixfold, or eightfold. Or again, the forms of four gazelles may circumambulate a tree. Some of the designs show lovely wading birds catching fish.[41]

The archaeological site after which this superb series of decorated vessels has been named—Samarra—is located in Iraq, on the river Tigris, some twenty miles above Baghdad; and the area over which the ware has been diffused extends northward to Nineveh, southward to the head of the Persian Gulf, and eastward, across Iran, as far as to the border of Afghanistan. The Halaf ware, on the other hand, is scattered through an area northwestward of this, with its chief center in northern Syria, just south of the so-called Taurus, or Bull, Mountains of Anatolia (neighboring Çatal Hüyük and Hacilar), whence the river Euphrates and its tributaries descend from the foothills to the plain. And what is most remarkable is the prominence in this beautifully decorated ware of the bull's head (the bucranium, as at Çatal Hüyük), viewed from before and with great curving horns. The form is depicted both naturalistically and in various stylized, very

---

zigzag forms in lively variation, parallel hatchings, triangles, and meanders. And especially worthy of remark is the appearance, first noted by the Russian V. A. Gorodcov, of a superbly rendered swastika on the lower surface of one of the little birds, composed of meander motifs joined together. . . .

"In this little bird-figurine from Mezin," Dr. Hančar continues, "we have the earliest known example of a swastika; and of the greatest interest is the fact that it should have appeared in association with the figure of a bird: a fact suggesting, in Gorodcov's view, a genetic connection between the symbol and its prototype, recalling the explanation developed by Karl von den Steinen ("Prähistorische Zeichen und Ornamente," in *Festschrift für Adolph Bastian zu seinem 70. Geburtstag* [Berlin: D. Reimer, 1896], pp. 247–88) and A. A. Bobrinskoi, of the swastika as a stylized picture of a bird in flight—in particular, of the stork, the killer of serpents—and thereby the victorious symbol of the Good, of Spring, and of Light."

graceful designs. Another prominent device in this series is the double ax, which in later Cretan art is the sign and weapon of the goddess. Once again we find the Maltese cross, as in Samarra, but—significantly, perhaps—no swastika, nor those graceful gazelle designs. Furthermore, in association with the female statuettes (which are numerous in this context) we find clay figures of the dove, as well as of the pig, cow, humped ox, sheep, and goat.[42] One charming pottery fragment represents the goddess standing between two goats rampant—that on her left, a male, the other, a female giving suck to a young kid.[43] And all these symbols are associated in this Halafian culture complex with the so-called beehive tomb.

Now this, precisely, is the complex that not only appeared a millennium later in Crete [44] but also was carried from there by sea, through the Gates of Hercules, north to the British Isles and south to the Gold Coast, Nigeria, and the Congo. It is, in fact, the basic complex, also, of the Mycenaean culture, from which the Greeks, and therewith ourselves, derived so many symbols. And when the cult of the dead and resurrected moon god was carried from Syria to the Nile Delta in the fourth or third millennium B.C., these symbols went with it. Indeed, I believe that we may claim, with a very high degree of certainty, that in this Halafian symbology of the bull and the goddess, the dove and the double ax, we have at once a continuation of the mythological tradition already announced, two thousand years before, in the chapels of Çatal Hüyük, and a halfway station of that continuing tradition toward its culmination in the great historical religions of Ishtar and Tammuz, Isis and Osiris, Venus and Adonis, Mary and Jesus. From the Taurus mountains, the mountains of the bull god, who must already have been identified with the horned moon, which dies and is resurrected, the cult was diffused with the art of cattle-breeding itself, practically to the ends of the earth; and we celebrate the mystery of that mythological death and resurrection to this day, as a promise of our own eternity. The immanence, then, of eternity in the passages of time would be the meaning, or reference, of this archaic mystery play. But what is eternity and what time? And why in the image of the bull, or of the moon?

[d] THE HIERATIC CITY STATE:
C. 3500–2500 B.C.

Stage Four in the development in the Near East of the agriculturally based civilization from which all the high cultures of the world have been derived took place about 3500 B.C. Half a millennium earlier, c. 4000 B.C. (the date assigned in the Book of Genesis to the creation of the world), a number of the neolithic villages had begun to assume the size and function of market towns and there had been, furthermore, an expansion of the chalcolithic culture area southward into the mud flats of riverine Mesopotamia. That was the period in which the really great and still mysterious race of the Sumerians first appeared on the scene, to establish in the torrid Tigris and Euphrates delta flats those sites that were to become, by c. 3500 B.C., the kingly cities of Ur, Kish, Lagash, Eridu, Sippar, Shuruppak, Nippur, and Erech. The only natural resources in that land were mud and reeds. Wood and stone had to be imported from the north. But the mud was fertile, and the fertility was annually refreshed. Furthermore, the mud could be fashioned into sun-dried bricks that could be used for the construction of temples—which now appear for the first time in the history of the world, their form being of the ziggurat in its earliest stage: a little height, artificially constructed, supporting a chapel for the ritual of the world-generating union of the earth goddess with a god of the sky. And if we may judge from the evidence of the following centuries, the queen or princess of each city was in these earliest days identified with the goddess, and the king, her spouse, with the god.

During the course of the fourth millennium B.C. the temples in these riverine towns increased in size and importance, becoming the economic as well as the religious and political centers of the growing communities. And then, at a date that can now be almost precisely fixed at 3200 B.C. (the period of the archaeological stratum known as Uruk B), there appeared in this little Sumerian mud-garden—as though the flowers of its tiny cities were suddenly bursting into bloom—the whole cultural syndrome that has, ever since, constituted the ground base of the high civilizations of the world. This, the fourth and culminating stage of the development that I am here tracing, we may term that of the *hieratic city state.*

But let us pause, to repeat: We have named the proto-neolithic period of the Natufians, c. 9000 B.C., where the first signs of an incipient grain agriculture appear; the basal neolithic of the aceramic, ceramic, and early chalcolithic villages, c. 7500–4500 B.C., when the mother goddess of an already well-established peasantry makes her first dramatic appearance; then the high neolithic (middle and late chalcolithic) of the Halaf and Samarra painted wares, c. 4500 B.C., when the abstract concept of a geometrically organized aesthetic field first appears and the late neolithic market towns begin to elevate temple towers; and now, finally, we have come to an epochal date c. 3200 B.C., when, suddenly, at precisely that geographical point where the rivers Tigris and Euphrates reach the Persian Gulf, the wonderful culture-flower comes to blossom of the hieratic city state.[45]

The whole city now (not simply the temple area) is conceived as an imitation on earth of the celestial order—a sociological middle cosmos, or mesocosm, between the macrocosm of the universe and the microcosm of the individual, making visible their essential form: with the king in the center (either as sun or as moon, according to the local cult) and an organization of the walled city, in the manner of a mandala, about the central sanctum of the palace and the ziggurat; * and with

---

* "The deification of kings and worship of them during their reigns were characteristic of Sumerian religion in the time of the last dynasty of Ur and the succeeding dynasties of Isin and Ellasar" (Stephen Herbert Langdon, *Semitic Mythology,* "Mythology of All Races," Vol. V [Boston: Marshall Jones Company; 1931], p. 326). It is not yet clear when the transition from this concept of the king as god to that of the king as merely the heaven-appointed high priest or "Tenant Farmer" of the god was made

a mathematically structured calendar, furthermore, to regu-
late the seasons of the city's life according to the passages of
the sun and moon among the stars; as well as a highly developed system of ritual arts, including an art of rendering audi-
ble to human ears the harmony of the visible celestial spheres.
It is at this moment that the art of writing first appears in the
world, and that literately documented history begins. It is at
this moment that the wheel appears. And we have also evidence that the two numerical systems that are still normally
employed throughout the civilized world had just been developed, namely, the decimal and the sexagesimal: the former
used for business acounts in the offices of the temple com-
pounds, where the grain was stored that had been collected in
taxes, and the latter used for the ritualistic measuring of space
and time: three hundred and sixty degrees still represent the

in Mesopotamia. The so-called "Royal Tombs" of Ur (which some author-
ities are now dating as late as 2500 B.C.; viz. H. Frankfort, *The Birth of
Civilization in the Near East*, p. 71, note 1) have greatly confused the issue.
"For me," wrote their discoverer, "the chamber tombs of Ur are those of
local kings who were vassals of the kings of the First Dynasty of Erech,
and their date is the second half of the fourth millennium B.C." (C. Leonard
Woolley, *The Chronology of the Early Graves at Ur*, "Proceedings of the
First International Congress of Prehistoric and Protohistoric Sciences [Lon-
don 1932; Oxford University Press, 1934], p. 164). For Frankfort, on the
other hand, the chief personages found in these tombs had never been kings
and queens but their male and female substitutes in a ritual drama of
death and resurrection. "The main actors would then be . . . the priest
who acted the god for the king in the fatal ritual, and the divine bride"
(Frankfort, "Gods and Myths on Sargonid Seals," *Iraq*, Vol. I, Part 1, 1934,
p. 12, note 3). In Egypt, India, China, and Japan, the concept of the king
as god, or as the son of god, survived into very late times.

For a description and discussion of the Mesopotamian idea of the cosmos
as a state and the city as the god's manor, supervised by his "tenant farmer,"
see Thorkild Jacobsen (with John A. Wilson, Henri and Mrs. Henri Frankfort), *Before Philosophy* (Penguin Books, 1949), pp. 137–216. See also,
Hugo Winckler, *Himmels und Weltenbild der Babylonier als Grundlage
der Weltanschauung und Mythologie aller Völker* (Leipzig: J. C. Hinrichs,
1901), and *Die babylonische Kultur in ihren Beziehungen zur unsrigen*,
(Leipzig: J. C. Hinrichs, 1902). And finally, for a prodigious mass of evidence attesting to a conception of the king as god in the archaic background of all high civilization, see James George Frazer, *The Golden
Bough* (London and New York: The Macmillan Company, one volume
edition, 1922), passim.

circumference of the circle—that is to say, the mandala of space; while three hundred and sixty days, plus five, mark the measurement of the mandala of time, the cycle of the year. And those five intercalated days—which represent the opening through which spiritual energy flows into the sphere of time from the pleroma of eternity, and which, consequently, are days of feast and festival—correspond in the temporal mandala to that mystical point in the center of the spatial mandala which is the sanctuary of the temple, where the earthly and heavenly powers join. The four sides of the temple tower, oriented to the four points of the compass, come together at this fifth point, where the energy of the pleroma enters time—and so once again we have the number five added to three hundred and sixty to symbolize the mystery of the immanence of eternity in time.

This temple tower, of course, and the hieratically organized little city surrounding it, where everyone plays his role according to a celestially inspired divine plan, is the model of paradise that we find not only in the Hindu-Buddhist imagery of Mount Sumeru, the Greek Olympus, and the Aztec Temples of the Sun, but also in Dante's Earthly Paradise, for which Columbus went in search, and in the Biblical image of Eden, from which the medieval concept was developed, and which—according to the date that you will find in the marginal notes of your Bible—would have been created just about at the time of the founding of the first Sumerian towns: 4004 B.C.

It appears, in short, to have been demonstrated in a manner hardly to be doubted, that the idea of the hieratic city state, conceived as a mesocosm, or sociological imitation of the celestial order, first emerged as a paradigm in the little cities of Sumer, c. 3200 B.C., and was then disseminated westward and eastward, along the ways already blazed by the earlier Neolithic. The wonderful, life-organizing assemblage of ideas and principles—including those of writing, mathematics, and calendrical astronomy—reached the Nile and inspired the civilization of the First Dynasty of Egypt, c. 2800 B.C.; reached

Crete, on one hand, and, on the other, the Indus Valley, c. 2600 B.C.; Shang China, c. 1500 B.C.; and finally, Peru and Middle America—from China, by way of the Pacific?— possibly as early as c. 1000 B.C.[46] We have, therefore, to recognize what now appears to be the demonstrated and documented fact that all of the high civilizations of the world are, finally, but so many variants and developments of a single marvelous monad of mythological inspiration—and that, whereas the history and prehistory of the human race covers some one million seven hundred and fifty thousand years, this monad was constellated and brought into a living form in the mud flats and among the reeds of Mesopotamia hardly more than five thousand years ago.

If we now should attempt to put into words the sense or meaning of this monad, the sense or character of the realization that appears to have precipitated with such force this image of man's destiny as an organ participating in the organism of the universe, we might say that the psychological requirement already noted for a coordinating principle, to bring the parts of a differentiated social body into an orderly relationship to each other and simultaneously to suggest the play through all of a higher, all-suffusing, all-informing principle or energy—this profoundly felt psychological as well as sociological requirement—must have been fulfilled with the recognition, some time in the fourth millennium B.C., of the orderly round-dance of the five visible planets and the sun and moon through the constellations of the zodiac. And this celestial order was to become for all the civilizations and philosophers of the world the model of the revelation of destiny. In the words of Plato: "The motions akin to the divine part in us are the thoughts and revolutions of the universe; these, therefore, every man should follow, and correcting those circuits in the head that were deranged at birth, by learning to know the harmonies and revolutions of the world, he should bring the intelligent part, according to its pristine nature, into the likeness of that which intelligence discerns, and thereby win the fulfillment of the best in life set by the gods before mankind both for this present time and for the life to come." [47] The Egyptian term for this order was Ma'at; in India it is Dharma, and in China Tao. And if we now should attempt to epitomize in a sentence the sense or meaning of all the myths and rituals that have sprung from this conception of a universal order, we might say that they are its structuring agents, functioning to bring the human order into accord with the celestial. "Thy will be done on earth, as it is in heaven." The myths and rites constellate a mesocosm—a mediating, middle cosmos, through which the microcosm of the individual is brought into relation to the macrocosm of the universe. And this mesocosm is the entire context of the body social, which is thus a kind of living poem, hymn, or icon, of mud and reeds, and of flesh and blood, and of dreams, fashioned into the art form of the hieratic city state. Life on earth is to mirror, as nearly perfectly as possible in human bodies, the almost hidden—yet now discovered—order of the pageant of the spheres. This pageant is what has shaped the mesocosm, the middle, sociological cosmos of the City; and the patterns of this mesocosm are what, then, have shaped the soul. Art and custom shape the soul: art lived—as ritual.

[3]

Problem of the New Symbol Emergent

But then the soul—this microcosm, made identical in form with a supposed order of the macrocosm, must be an engram, something impressed or engraved, and not congenital. As already noticed: man, at birth, is not yet fully man; nor does he become man through a merely physical, biological development.* The child, as already remarked, grows and develops for a length of years that in most mammals would constitute a lifetime, and during this period is shaped in its growth by the local social order. To repeat the words of Adolf Portmann: "Man is the incomplete creature, whose completion is effected by a historically determined tradition." [48] So that each of us

* Cf. supra, pp. 52-55.

is but a part, a fragment or inflection, of what he might have been. And we can understand, in the light of this truth, the command of the Zen master, addressed to the candidate who would obtain release from the system of engraved ideas that had become for him his soul: "Show me the face that you had before you were born!" [49] or the question of the Hindu guru: "Where are you between two thoughts? " [50]

C. G. Jung has pointed out, in one of his numerous discussions of modern mandalas, that whereas in the traditional but now archaic forms the central figure was a god, "now," as he declares, "the prisoner, or the well-protected dweller in the mandala, does not seem to be a god, in as much as the symbols used, stars, for instance, crosses, globes, and so on, do not mean a god, but rather an apparently most important part of the human personality. One might also say that man himself, or at least his innermost soul, was the prisoner of the protected inhabitant of the mandala. . . . It is evident," he then continues, "that in the modern mandala, man—the complete man—has replaced the deity." "This replacement," he declares again, "is a natural and spontaneous occurrence, and it is always essentially unconscious." [51] And once again: "A modern mandala is an involuntary confession of a peculiar mental condition. There is no deity in the mandala, and there is also no submission or reconciliation to a deity. The place of the deity seems to be taken by the wholeness of man." [52]

One cannot but think of the words of Paracelsus: "I under God in his office, God under me in mine." [53]

For the great word and theme of the Renaissance, *humanitas*, appears, at last, in our day, to have broken the celestial enchantment that enthralled mankind for six thousand years, and to be offering, now, a new Alpha and Omega: a new image, a new engram, for the center of our mandala. However, before committing ourselves abjectly to this image —as formerly to the image of God—let us pause to ask (at this precious moment between two engrams!) whether it is not possible to penetrate to that void "between two thoughts" from which the symbols come, and attain thereby to some sort of independence from the qualification of the current century. For we cannot forget the distinction between sign and symbol defined by Dr. Jung: the sign is a reference to something known; the symbol is a figure by which allusion is made to an unknown. It is, then, into the unknown, beyond both the image of god and the image of man, that we must venture to find the ultimate ground of all these guiding and protecting, edifying yet imprisoning, names and forms.

Let us now, therefore, dig below the geometrically composed floor of the neolithic walled town and search the mystery of the paleolithic cave—where man, if we may judge from the observation of Dr. Róheim, was free, untrammeled, truly self-reliant, and grown up.

PART II

[4]

The Shaman and the Priest

This challenge can be approached, I have found, through a legend from that part of the United States still called the "Indian country"; where it is still possible to visit hunting tribes only recently influenced by the neolithic maize culture stemming from Mexico and Central America.

Contrasting patterns appear in North America according to whether tribes are hunters or planters. The hunters emphasize in their religious life the individual fast, for the gaining of visions. The boy of twelve or thirteen is left by his father in some lonesome place, with a little fire to keep the beasts away, and there he fasts and prays, four days or more, until some spiritual visitant comes in dream, in human or animal form, to speak to him and give him power. His later career will be determined by this vision; for his familiar may confer the power to cure people, as a shaman, to attract and slaughter animals, or to become a warrior. And if the benefits gained are not sufficient for the young man's ambition, he may fast again, as often as he likes. An old Crow Indian, named One Blue Bead, told of such a fast. "When I was a boy," he said, "I was poor. I saw war parties come back with leaders in front and having a procession. I used to envy them and I made up my mind to fast and become like them. When I saw the vision I got what I had longed for. . . . I killed eight enemies." [54] If a man has bad luck, he knows that his gift of supernatural power simply is insufficient; while, on the other hand, the great shamans and war leaders have acquired power in abundance from their visionary fasts. Perhaps they have chopped off and offered their finger joints. Such offerings were common among the Indians of the plains, on some of whose old hands there remained only fingers and joints enough to enable them to notch an arrow and draw the bow.

Whereas, among the planting tribes—the Hopi, Zuni, and other pueblo dwellers—life is organized around the rich and complex ceremonies of their Masked Gods. These are elaborate rites in which the entire community participates, scheduled according to a religious calendar, and conducted by societies of trained priests. As Dr. Ruth Benedict observed in her *Patterns of Culture*: "No field of activity competes with ritual for foremost place in their attention. Probably most grown men among the western Pueblos give to it the greater part of their waking life. It requires the memorizing of an amount of word-perfect ritual that our less trained minds find staggering, and the performance of neatly dovetailed ceremonies that are chartered by the calendar and complexly interlock all the different cults and the governing body in endless formal procedure." [55] In such a society there is little room for individual play. There is a rigid relationship not only of the individual to his fellows but also of village life to the calendric cycle; for the planters are intensely aware of their dependency upon the gods of the elements. One short period of too much or too little rain, at the critical moment, and a whole year of labor results in famine. For the hunter—hunter's luck is a very different thing.

We may sharpen this contrast by comparing the priest and

the shaman. The priest is the socially initiated, ceremonially inducted member of a recognized religious organization, where he holds a certain rank and functions as the tenant of an office that was held by others before him, while the shaman is one who, as a consequence of a personal psychological crisis, has gained a certain power of his own. The spiritual visitants who came to him in vision had never been seen before by any other; they were his particular familiars and protectors. The Masked Gods of the Pueblos, on the other hand, the corn-gods and the cloud-gods, served by societies of strictly organized and very orderly priests, are the well-known patrons of the entire village, and have been prayed to and represented in the ceremonial dances since time out of mind.

The legend that I wish to recall is the origin legend of the Jicarilla Apache tribe of New Mexico. Originally a hunting people, they entered the area of the maize-growing Pueblos in the fourteenth century A.D. and assimilated the local neolithic ceremonial lore.[56] The legend is long, but I shall summarize and bring us quickly to the point.

"In the beginning," we are told,[57] "nothing was here where the world now stands: no earth—nothing but Darkness, Water, and Cyclone. There were no people living. Only the Hactcin existed. It was a lonely place."

The Hactcin—the Apache counterparts of the Masked Gods of the Pueblo villages—are personifications of the powers that support the spectacle of nature. They created, first the Earth Mother and Sky Father, then the animals and birds, and finally man and woman. Throughout the first ages it was dark, but presently the Hactcin produced the sun and moon, which then moved from north to south.

And so now, the legend goes on to say, "there were all kinds of shamans among the people—men and women who claimed to have power from all sorts of things. These shamans saw the sun going from north to south and began to talk. One said: 'I made the sun.' Another: 'No, I did.' They commenced quarreling, and the Hactcin ordered them not to talk like that.

But they kept making claims and fighting. One said: 'I think I'll make the sun stop overhead, so that there will be no night. But no, I guess I'll let it go. We need some time to rest and sleep.' Another said: 'Perhaps I'll get rid of the moon. We really don't require any light at night.' But the sun rose the second day and the birds and animals were happy. The next day it was the same. When noon of the fourth day came, however, and the shamans, in spite of what the Hactcin had told them, continued to talk, there was an eclipse. The sun went right up through a hole overhead and the moon followed, and that is why we have eclipses today.

"One of the Hactcin said: 'All right, you people; you say you have power. Now bring back the sun.'"

"So they all lined up: in one line were the shamans, and in another all the birds and animals. The shamans commenced to perform. They showed everything they knew. Some would sit singing and then disappear into the earth, leaving only their eyes sticking out; then return. But this did not bring back the sun. It was only to show that they had power. Some swallowed arrows, which came out of their flesh at their stomachs. Some swallowed feathers; some swallowed whole spruce trees and spat them up again. But they were still without the sun and the moon.

"The Hactcin said: 'All you people are doing pretty well, but I don't think you are bringing back the sun. Your time is up.' He turned to the birds and animals. 'All right,' he said, 'now it is your turn.'

"They all began to speak to each other politely, as though they were brothers-in-law; but the Hactcin said: 'You must do something more than speak to each other in that polite way. Get up and do something with your power and make the sun come back.'

"The grasshopper was the first to try. He stretched out his hand to the four directions, and when he brought it back he was holding bread. The deer stretched out his hand to the four directions, and when he brought it back he was holding yucca fruit. The bear produced choke-cherries in the same

way, and the ground hog, berries, the chipmunk, strawber-
ries, the turkey, maize, and so it went with all. But though the
Hactcin were pleased with these gifts, the people were still
without the sun and moon.

"Thereupon, the Hactcin themselves began to do something. They sent for Thunder of four colors from the four
directions, and these thunders brought clouds of four colors,
from which rain fell. Then sending for the Rainbow, to make
it beautiful while the seeds were planted that the people had
produced, the Hactcin made a sand painting with four little
colored mounds in a row, into which they put the seeds. The
birds and animals sang, and presently the little mounds began
to grow, the seeds began to sprout and the four mounds of
colored earth merged and became one mountain, which continued to rise.

"The Hactcin then selected twelve shamans who had been
particularly spectacular in their magical performances, and
painting six of them blue all over, to represent the summer
season, and six white, to represent the winter, called them
Tsanati: and that was the origin of the Tsanati dance society
of the Jicarilla Apache. After that the Hactcin made six
Clowns, painting them white with four black horizontal
bands, one across the face, one across the chest, one across the
upper leg and one across the lower. The Tsanati and the
Clowns then joined the people in their dance, to make the
mountain grow." [58]

Do you see what has happened to the shamans? They have
been discredited in their individualistic, paleolithic style of
magical practice and given a place in the social mandala of a
seed-planting, food-growing community, as one contributing
unit in a larger whole. The episode represents the victory of
the principle of a socially anointed priesthood over the highly
dangerous and unpredictable force of individual endowment.
And the teller of the Jicarilla Apache story himself explained
the necessity for incorporating the shamans in the ceremonial
system. "These people," he said, "had ceremonies of their
own which they derived from various sources, from animals,

from fire, from the turkey, from frogs, and from other things. They could not be left out. They had power, and they had to help too." [59]

I do not know of any myth that represents more clearly than this the crisis that must have faced the societies of the Old World when the neolithic order began to make its power felt in a gradual conquest of the most habitable portions of the earth. The situation in New Mexico and Arizona at the period of the discovery of America was, culturally, much like that which must have prevailed in the Near and Middle East, and in Europe, from the fourth to second millenniums B.C., when the rigid patterns proper to an orderly settlement were being imposed on peoples used to the freedom and vicissitudes of the hunt. And there is an important parallel to be noted between this contrast of the wild, quarrelsome, dangerous shamans and the people, who were so polite to each other that they were like brothers-in-law, and that of the titans and gods, devils and angels, asuras and devas, in the numerous agriculturally based traditions of Asia and Europe. In the Hindu Puranas there is a well-known myth of the gods and demons cooperating under the supervision of the two supreme deities, Vishnu and Shiva, to churn the Milky Ocean for its butter. They took the World Mountain as a churning-stick and the World Serpent as a twirling-rope, and wrapped the serpent around the mountain. Then, the gods taking hold of the head end of the snake and the demons of the tail, while Vishnu supported the World Mountain, they churned for a thousand years and produced in the end the Butter of Immortality.[60] It is almost impossible not to think of this myth when reading of the efforts of the quarrelsome shamans and orderly people, under the supervision of the Apache Hactcin, to make the World Mountain grow and carry them to the world of light.

The Tsanati and Clowns, we are told, joined the people in their dance, and the mountain grew, until its top nearly reached the hole through which the sun and moon had disappeared; and it remained, then, only to construct four ladders of light of the four colors, up which the people could ascend to the surface of this our present earth. The six Clowns went ahead with magical whips to chase disease away and were followed by the Hactcin, and then the Tsanati came, after whom, the people and animals. "And when they came up onto this earth," said the teller of the story, "it was just like a child being born from its mother. The place of emergence is the womb of the earth." [61]

[5]
The Wild Gander

The highest concern of all of the mythologies, ceremonials, ethical systems, and social organizations of the agriculturally based societies has ever been that of suppressing the manifestations of individualism; and this has been generally achieved by compelling or persuading people to identify themselves not with their own interests, intuitions, or modes of experience, but with archetypes of behavior and systems of sentiment developed and maintained in the public domain. For example, in India the ideal of Dharma is that of an unconditional submission to the archetypes of caste—these being functions of the social order, rationalized for the individual by way of a theory of graded incarnations, through many lifetimes, from caste to caste. The sternest expression of this ideal is implied in the word "suttee" (*satī*), which is the feminine form of the verbal root *sat*, "to be." A suttee is a woman who *is* something: namely, an archetypal wife. She has suppressed every impulse to become an autonomous individual, even to that final extent of throwing herself on her husband's funeral pyre. For in the archaic Orient, every act well performed is an act of suttee—a burning out, purging out, of ego.

In the Occident, too, ego has been regarded as the province of the devil. The Titans conquered by the Olympians were incarnations of this principle, just as the demons were in India —and we know how they were chained and imprisoned beneath mountains. A similar fate was accorded, in the Germanic tradition, to the giants and dwarfs, the Fenris Wolf, the Midgard Serpent, and the dog Garm. However, the day will come, we are warned, when their chains will drop away, and that day will be the Weird of the Gods, Ragnarök. Then shall nothing be without fear in heaven or on earth.[62]

But that day has already come—indeed, has been here since 1492, when the mandala broke that had been fashioned six thousand years before, in the period of the Halaf and Samarra bowls. Aeschylus, in *Prometheus Bound*, represented the spirit of the titan who is now loose:

> In one round sentence, every god I hate,
> That injures me who never injured him.
>
> Deem not that I, to win a smile from Jove,
> Will spread a maiden smoothness o'er my soul
> And importune the foe whom most I hate
> With womanish upliftings of the hands! [63]

It is not by accident that Prometheus became the hero of the humanistic enlightenment, or that, today, when the mythos of the mandala is in full dissolution, we find a symbol of the wholeness of man emerging from the dark abyss of the unconscious, where it has been chained for six thousand years. Will the mandala continue to contain this unbound Prometheus?

There have been collected from the American tribes hundreds of popular tales depicting, in various transformations, the fire-bringer, the titanic trickster-hero of the paleolithic hunters. Among the Plains Indians his form was that of a kind of jackal, Coyote; among the forest dwellers he was the Great Hare (some of whose adventures have been attributed by the Negroes of America to an African rabbit-hero, whom we meet in the tales of Br'er Rabbit); among the tribes of the Northwest Coast he was the Raven. The closest counterpart in the myths of Europe would be the mischief-maker Loki, who at the time of Ragnarök will be the leader of the hosts of Hel. Coyote, Raven, the Master Hare—or Old Man, as he is called when he appears in a fully human form—is a lecherous fool as well as an extremely clever and cruel deceiver; but he is also the creator of mankind and shaper of the world. It is hardly proper to call such a figure a god, or even to think of him as supernatural. He is a super-shaman. And we find his counterparts in myth and legend throughout the world, wherever shamanism has left its mark: in Oceania and Africa, as well as in Siberia and Europe.

Authorities differ as to the period of the first migrations of paleolithic man into North America. During the glacial ages a land bridge as wide as the nation of France stretched from Siberia to Alaska, and across this, grazing animals passed (herds of horses, cattle, elephants, camels), sometimes followed by hunters. As already noted,* tribes of men may have begun arriving as early as thirty or forty thousand B.C. However, the majority—if not all—of our present American Indian races represent much later periods of migration, extending even into the first millennium A.D.; and these were not purely paleolithic. They appear to have stemmed, largely, from a late paleo-mesolithic culture platform in Siberia, in the neighborhood of Lake Baikal, where the Yakuts and the Tungus, the Voguls and the Ostiak, live today.[64] In fact, it has been recognized that in physical race the Vogul and the Ostiak of the Yenisei river basin might be classified as Americanoid.[65]

I have already spoken briefly of the paleolithic caves. Early in the history of the art of these imposing underground temples there appeared the famous paleolithic female statuettes—a full twenty thousand years or so before their neolithic counterparts, in a date range at the close of the glacial era, not much earlier, if at all, than that of the first arrivals of hunters in the New World. No paleolithic statuettes have been found in Spain, or anywhere southward of the Pyrenees. All belong to the hunting plains that commenced north of the Pyrenees and stretched eastward, as far as to the borders of China. And in the neighborhood of Lake Baikal, at a site known as Mal'ta, some eighty-five kilometers northwestward of Irkutsk, there was a particularly important paleolithic hunting station where no less than twenty of these statuettes have been found, asso-

* Supra, pp. 98–99.

iated with a number of figures of flying geese—all carved in mammoth ivory (or, according to one authority, in bone).[66]

Thus it appears that in the last great period of the paleolithic hunt there was a cultural continuum extending from the Pyrenees to Lake Baikal, whence much of the culture, as well as some of the racial strains, of the hunting tribes of North America were derived during the millenniums following the close of the Paleolithic. A significant continuity, that is to say, appears to have been established, extending in time and space from the Upper Paleolithic of Europe to the final twilight of the Great Hunt in the North American Plains. In its various provinces this tradition absorbed influences both from the local landscape and from neighboring neolithic and post-neolithic cultures. Nevertheless, there is a persistent syndrome of motifs that can be readily identified throughout, which is clearly that of a hunting, and not of a settled, planting system of societies. And one of its most persistent features is the association of the shamanistic trance with the flight of a bird. The hawk and eagle, wild gander and duck, appear to be common throughout the range; but locally, other birds may appear: the owl and vulture, for example, the raven, magpie, or woodpecker—the last-named, because of the flash of red on its head, being frequently the chief hero of the fire-theft.

As Professor Mircea Eliade has shown in an exhaustive study of the subject,[67] the main talent of the shaman is that of throwing himself into a trance at will. The rhythms of the shaman's drum, like the rhythms of the Indo-Aryan Vedic hymns, are conceived as wings, the wings of spiritual transport: they simultaneously elevate the shaman's spirit and conjure his familiars. And it is while in this trance that he performs his miraculous deeds. While in this trance he is flying as a bird to the upper world, or descending as a reindeer, bull, or bear to the world beneath. Among the Buriat, the animal or bird that protects the shaman is called *khubilgan*, meaning "metamorphosis," from the verb *khubilku*, "to change oneself, to take another form." [68] The early Russian missionaries and voyagers in Siberia in the first part of the eighteenth century noted that the shamans spoke to their spirits in a strange, squeaky voice.[69] They also found among the tribes numerous images of geese with extended wings, sometimes of brass.[70] And here we are reminded that in Mal'ta, that paleolithic hunting station where no less than twenty female figurines have been discovered, a number of flying geese or ducks were also found, carved, like the figurines, in mammoth ivory. Flying birds, in fact, have been found in many paleolithic stations; and on the under-wings of one example, as I have already remarked, there appears the earliest swastika of which we have record.* Like the swastikas on the much later Samarra ware of the High Neolithic, this one is in the sinister form, whirling to the left—the form that Dr. Jung has suggested would normally symbolize a regressive process: such a process, perhaps, as the shaman flight. And we must remember, also, that in the paleolithic cavern of Lascaux, there is a shaman depicted, lying in trance, wearing a bird mask and with the figure of a bird perched on a staff beside him.† The shamans of Siberia wear such bird costumes to this day, and many are believed to have been conceived by their mothers from the descent of a bird.

In many lands the soul has been pictured as a bird, and birds commonly appear as spiritual messengers: angels are modified birds. But the bird of the shaman is one of particular character and power, endowing him with an ability to fly in trance beyond all bounds of life, and yet return. "Up above there is a certain tree," said a shaman of the Tungus, who was questioned at his home on the Lower Tunguska River in the spring of 1925. "There the souls of the shamans are reared before they attain their powers. On the boughs of this tree are nests in which the souls of the shamans lie and are attended. The name of the tree is 'Tuuru.' The higher the nest is placed in this tree, the stronger will the shaman be who is raised in it, the more will he know, and the farther will he see." [71] The shaman, then, is not only a familiar denizen, but even the fa-

* Supra, p. 147 and note.
† Supra, p. 101.

vored scion, of those realms of power that are invisible to our normal waking consciousness, which all may visit briefly in vision, but through which he roams, a master.

We have observed that the birds found at Mal'ta and in the other paleolithic stations are ducks and water birds, wild geese and ganders; and I have tried to suggest something, also, of the rich context of associations linking the figure of the bird to the spiritual flight of the shaman, as well as that linking the figure of the trickster-hero, the titan fire-bringer and demonic enemy of the gods, to the paleolithic context of shamanism. Let me now add that the Hindu master yogis, who in their trance states go beyond all the pales of thought, are known as *haṁsas* and *paramahaṁsas:* "wild ganders" and "supreme wild ganders." In the imagery of traditional Hinduism, the wild gander is symbolic of *brahman-ātman*, the ultimate, transcendent yet immanent ground of all being, with which the yogi succeeds in identifying his consciousness, thus passing from the sphere of waking consciousness, where A is not not-A, passing even beyond dream, where all things shine of their own light, to the nonconditioned, nondual state "between two thoughts," where the subject-object polarity is completely transcended and the distinction even between life and death dissolved.

But before pursuing this developing flight, we must pause for a moment to regard again our problem of the nature and function of the symbol.

[6]

Mythologies of Engagement and Disengagement

Two contrasting functions of the religious symbol can now be distinguished. The first is of reference and engagement; the second, disengagement, transport, and metamorphosis. The first is illustrated by the social mandala of the hieratic city state, which engages every member in a context of experienced significance, relating him as a part to a whole. An equivalent illustration would be the medieval mandala of the

Church Militant, Suffering, and Triumphant. The significance, or ultimate ground, of such a symbol is unquestioned. Like a successful work of art, it is an end in itself, communicating to the mind beholding it a sense of felicity, and to the life engaged in it a sense of meaning. As Dr. Jung has said, the symbol, in contrast to the sign, is "the best possible designation or formula for something relatively unknown, yet recognized to be present, or required." [72] When, then, the symbol is functioning for engagement, the cognitive faculties are held fascinated by and bound to the symbol itself, and are thus simultaneously informed by and protected from the unknown. But when the symbol is functioning for disengagement, transport, and metamorphosis, it becomes a catapult, to be left behind. There is an illuminating representation of the symbol functioning in this manner, in the Mundaka Upanishad:

The syllable AUM is the bow; the arrow is the soul:
  Brahman is said to be the target.
Undistractedly [meditating on AUM], one is to hit the mark.
One is to become joined to the target, like an arrow.[73]

The rhythm of the shaman's drum is the syllable AUM; his trance is the bird-flight of the feathered arrow. His mind, disengaged from the protection of the symbol, is to meet directly the *mysterium tremendum* of the unknown.

But the unknown is of two degrees. There are (1) the relatively unknown, and (2) the absolutely unknowable. The relatively unknown may be said to be represented, psychologically, by the contents of the unconscious; sociologically, by the dynamics of history; and cosmologically, by the forces of the universe. This is the unknown to which reference is made by the term *parokṣa*, discussed above,* meaning "beyond or higher than the reach of the eye." The references of a *parokṣa* vocabulary are not immediately perceptible to waking consciousness. They have been said to be *adhidaivata*, "angelic," or "divine." They are perceived by saints and sages in vision,

* Supra, pp. 127–28.

and so are said to pertain to the field of "dreaming." But in the modern world, we have come to talk and think about such things in a very different way from the sages of the past. Aquinas was correct when he maintained that the Scriptures should be found true on both the corporeal and the spiritual levels. At the time of their formulation they were thought to be corporeally true, and their spiritual truth inhered in the corporeal world of their depiction. Today that corporeal world has vanished and another has taken its place: correlatively, that spiritual world has vanished and another has taken, or is taking, its place. But no living system of symbols functioning for engagement can survive when it has lost contact with the actual conscious and unconscious worlds of its society—when its references to the field of waking consciousness have been refuted and its notices to the seats of motivation are no longer felt. Like the signs referring to the known, so the symbols referring to the relatively unknown are functions of the knowledge of the time.

But there is another degree or category of the unknown, which is that understood to lie beyond even the highest references of a *parokṣa*, mystical, esoteric, "spiritual" or "angelic" vocabulary. "The Tao that can be named is not the true Tao," wrote Lao-tzu at the opening of his *Tao Te Ching*.[74] "For then alone," wrote Aquinas, "then alone do we know God truly, when we believe that he is far above all that man can possibly think of God." [75] And we have heard the words of the Kena Upanishad:

> It is other, indeed, than the known
> And, moreover, above the unknown.[76]

This is the category or degree of the unknown to which all of the high mythologies and high religions are ultimately directed. It is recognized, however, to be absolutely ineffable, a plenum of unknowability, inexhaustible in its dark; and toward it two attitudes have been fostered. The first is that of absolute terror, submission, or, as we say, piety. One does not seek to penetrate, for that would be *hybris:* one remains with its symbol, as the only possible medium of relationship. This is the case of the Church Suffering, Militant, and Triumphant. But the second attitude is that of the mystic whose soul would become an arrow, and in this case the symbol functions only for disengagement. The Sanskrit term is *moksa*, "release." And whereas the symbol functioning for engagement had to remain convincing on the levels of both corporeal and spiritual reference, that functioning for disengagement need refer to neither. Its function is simply to propel the soul.

"Before the moment when I commenced to shamanize," said the old shaman of the Tungus whom I have already quoted, "I lay sick for an entire year. I became a shaman at the age of fifteen. The sickness that forced me to become a shaman showed itself in a swelling of my body and frequent fainting spells.* When I began to sing, the sickness usually disappeared." And then he told of the visions that he experienced in his period of sickness. "My ancestors appeared to me and began to shamanize. They stood me up like a block of wood and shot at me with their bows until I lost consciousness. They cut up my flesh, they separated my bones and counted them, and they ate my flesh raw. When they counted my bones they found that there was one too many. Had there not been enough I should not have been able to become a shaman. While they were accomplishing this rite, I, for a whole summer, ate and drank nothing. At the end the shaman priests drank the blood of a reindeer and gave some to me, also, to drink. After these events, a shaman has less blood and looks pale."

"The same thing happens to every Tungus shaman," the old man went on to say. "Only when his shaman ancestors have cut up his body in this manner and separated his bones can he begin to practice." [77]

The Tungus shaman's bow did not have the power of that of the Mundaka Upanishad, by any means; for it sent the

* Similar symptoms afflicted the American Indian boy Black Elk, before and during his experience of the "great vision." *Cf.* supra, p. 113. The symptoms are described in Neihardt, *op. cit.*, pp. 21–22.

arrow of his soul only as far as to the sphere of his ancestors in the unconscious, the *relatively* unknown. Worthy of note in this fantasy, however, is the paleolithic trait of not assigning any universal, cosmic significance to the individual vision. The spiritual powers encountered were the shaman's ancestors, merely, and the reference was to himself.

But, as we have seen in the Jicarilla Apache myth, this strongly individual orientation became archaic and disruptive, titanic and demonic, once the neolithic organization of the universe around one power center had been effected. We must now, therefore, attempt to develop our view of the symbol functioning for disengagement under the ban of this constraint—that is to say, within the pale of the mandala itself. And I propose to do this through a brief—necessarily schematic—sketch of the evolution of the ideals and attitudes toward society of the Asian yogi.

[7]

The Flight between Two Thoughts

This is not an arbitrary choice of illustration, but justified by a number of considerations. The first and most important, I should say, is that in the Orient there is a richly documented history of spiritual disengagement dating from the period of the earliest Indian Upanishads; which is to say, since the eighth century B.C. The second is that throughout that long history, the linkage of the techniques and experiences of yoga to their base in the shamanistic trance-tradition remained so firm that when Buddhism went northward into Tibet and Mongolia it readily fused with the local Bon religions in which shamanistic magic played a central role. In fact, the word *shaman* itself, which is from the language of the Siberian Tungus, has been thought by some to be derived from the Sanskrit *śramaṇa*, meaning "monk," "yogi," or "ascetic." [78] The legendary biography of the eleventh-century Tibetan sage Milarepa supplies evidence enough of the close connection; [79] while to this day, in certain Buddhist sects of Japan,

Figure 12. Swastika on Chest of Amida, "The Buddha of Immeasurable Light," in Posture of Meditation; Japan, 13th century.

shamanistic magic is still practiced as a department of religion. Let us not forget, furthermore, that, engraved on the chest of the meditating Buddha in the Far East, the counterclockwise swastika frequently appears (Figure 12), which, as we have seen, made its first appearance on the wings of a paleolithic flying bird (Figure 11, supra, p. 147).* And then, finally, my third reason for choosing this context to illustrate the reaction of the titan spirit to the restrictions and archetypes of the hieratic state is that in Asia these restrictions were never relaxed. The force of the ideals of the archaic caste system, for example, remains tremendous in India to the very present.

---

* I believe it safe to say that in a region as open as medieval China to influences from the classical centers of late paleolithic shamanism, the denotation of this sign cannot have been fundamentally altered.

And so here we still have before us, in full force, an unrelenting continuation of the vehement dialogue that has been carried on for millenniums between the priestly guardians of the social archetypology and the fearless masters of *mokṣa*, "release."

During the course of this grandiose dialogue, four distinct stages can be noted in the transformation of the character of the shamanistic titan. The first, as we have already seen, was that of the shaman as titan-demon, overthrower of the gods. The great Indian asuras are figures of this sort. They engage in austerities in the forest, but their aim is not to achieve illumination. It is to gain magical powers and then to apply these to the attainment of their own earthly ends. They are depicted in the mythological tales of India as subjecting themselves to the most rigorous ordeals possible, and through these compelling even the highest gods to submit to their will. But the highest gods, fortunately for the cosmic order, always have a trick or two in reserve, so that in the end the titans are deceived and overthrown.

It is clear that we have here, in a mythological rendition, essentially the same notion of the relationship of the individual will to the controls of the social and cosmic order that we find in the Greek tradition, where it is usually presented, however, in human terms. The idea of *hybris*, individual imprudence, and the necessity that fate or destiny imposes even on the gods, runs through the philosophical as well as religious thinking of all high civilizations. There is a moral law, and it must be obeyed. In the Far East the idea is represented by the Tao, the Way, the manifest course, sense, or meaning of the universe: that manifestation of inexorable laws through which all are bound together as the variously functioning organs of a single mighty organism. In India this binding principle is Dharma. The word is derived from the root *dhṛī*, meaning "to support"; for Dharma, the law, is the support of the universe, and one who knows and performs without resistance his own Dharma (*svadharma*), the duties imposed on him by the circumstances of his birth, becomes himself a support, a well-functioning organ, of the universal being. The Biblical legend of the Fall, too, is a tale of *hybris* and the fall of the titan, Man, who dared to follow his own will in contravention of the law, imposed in this case not by the universe, but by the maker of the universe, God the Father. Man is here a child, a naughty child, locked out of doors by a stormy parent, to freeze and blister. And we know that even as late as the period of the Renaissance, when Europe, having arrived at its age of adolescence and being ready to consign this nursery tale to the past, took to its heart the term *humanitas* and dared the high adventure of leaving Father behind—we know that in this great and bold age even such a stirring titan as Michelangelo quailed before the realization of what he was doing. Faced, in the end, with the reckoning of the Last Judgment, "the final reckoning of good and evil for eternity," as he called it, "Now," he wrote . . .

> Now know I well how that fond phantasy
> Which made my soul the worshiper and thrall
> Of earthly art, is vain. . . .[80]

And we know well, too, how those wild titans of Shakespeare's mighty visions shattered, one and all, on the rocks that ring the world.

The formula has been accepted throughout the civilized sphere of the agriculturally based neolithic mandala-psyche, ringed around by the cosmic serpent, who both tempts man to dare and crucifies him when he has done so. In this phase of his history the titan is completely prisoner of the mandala; its symbols operate upon him in their own terms, both within and without. Still having a meaning for him, they press upon him from all sides, until he breaks.

The second stage or phase in the transformation of the titan is one in which he dissipates and destroys this force for himself, but for no one else. This is the victory represented in India by the forest philosophers, who rejected and despised not only the pains and pleasures of earth but equally those of hell and heaven. "The first requisite of yoga," we read in one statement after another, "is the renunciation of the fruits of action, whether in this world or in the next." [81] And in the classical work on the subject, the Yoga Sutra of Patanjali, we read that when the yogi has begun to make progress in the course of his world-renouncing, world-transcending austerities, "those in high places" (namely, the gods) will seek to tempt him from his purpose by seducing him with the joys of heaven. "Sir," they will say, "will you not stay here? Will you not take rest here?"

"Thus addressed," warns the commentator, "let the yogi ponder upon the defects of pleasure: 'Broiled on the horrible coals of the round of rebirths and writhing in the darkness of birth and death, I have only this minute found the lamp of yoga, which makes an end of the obscurations of the 'impairments' (kleśa). The lust-born gusts of sensual things are the enemies of this lamp. How then should it be that I, who have seen its light, should be led astray by these phenomena of sense—this mere mirage—and make fuel of myself for that same old fire again of the round of rebirths, as it flares anew? Fare ye well, O ye sensual things, deceitful as dreams, to be desired only by the vile!' "

"Determined thus in purpose," the commentary continues, "let the yogi cultivate concentration. Giving up all attachments, let him not take pride even in thinking that it is he who is being thus urgently desired even by the gods. . . ." [82]

For those not yet ready for the high adventure, the gods surround the world and are its guardians. By those ripe, however, the same gods are experienced in dream and vision as mere names and forms (nāmarūpam), no more real, no less real, than the names and forms known to waking consciousness. But in deep sleep, both worlds—that of waking consciousness and that of dream and vision—are dissolved. Would it not be possible, then, to enter the sphere of deep sleep without losing consciousness and there to *see* the worlds dissolve—gods and dreams, and all? That is the victory of yoga. And one cannot gaze on the world, after that, with any of the fears and pieties of the virtuous citizen of the mandala, who has not yet watched God himself, together with his universe, evaporate like dew at dawn. As we read in a celebrated Buddhist text:

> Stars, darkness, a lamp, a phantom, dew, a bubble,
> A dream, a flash of lightning, or a cloud:
>   Thus should one look upon the world.[83]

Here is disengagement with a vengeance. The entire mandala of the meso-micro-macrocosm is dissolved, and the individual, having burned out of himself the so-called "impairments" (*kleśas*)—or, as we might say, the "engrams" of his culturally and biologically conditioned personal character—now experiences, through complete withdrawal, the wholeness of an absolutely uncommitted consciousness in the pristine state called *kaivalyam*, "isolation." The universe has been rejected as a meaningless delusion, referring to nothing beyond the mirage of its own horizon, and that transcendent state has been realized which Schopenhauer celebrated at the close of his *magnum opus*, when he wrote that "to those in whom the will has turned and denied itself, this our world, which is so real, with all its suns and milky ways—is nothing." [84]

According to the Mandukya Upanishad, the world of the state of waking consciousness is to be identified with the letter A of the syllable AUM; that of dream consciousness (heaven and hell, that is to say) with the letter U; and deep sleep (the state of the mystical union of the knower and the known, God and his world, brooding the seeds and energies of creation: which is the state symbolized in the center of the mandala) with M.[85] The soul is to be propelled both by and from this syllable AUM into the silence beyond and all around it: the silence out of which it rises and back into which it goes when pronounced—slowly and rhythmically pronounced, as AUM —AUM—AUM.

That silence is where we are between two thoughts.

The world, the entire universe, its god and all, has become a symbol—signifying nothing: a symbol without meaning. For to attribute meaning to any part of it would be to relax its force as a bow, and the arrow of the soul then would lodge only in the sphere of meaning—like the shaman's soul among his ancestors, or the Christian's among the saints and angels. The bow, in order to function as a bow and not as a snare, must have no meaning whatsoever in itself—or in any part of itself—beyond that of being an agent for disengagement— from itself: no more meaning than the impact of the doctor's little hammer when it hits your knee, to make it jerk.

A symbol—and here I want to propose a definition—is an energy-evoking and -directing agent. When given a meaning, either corporeal or spiritual, it serves for the engagement of the energy to itself—and this may be compared to the notch- ing of the arrow to the bowstring and drawing of the bow. When, however, all meaning is withdrawn, the symbol serves for disengagement, and the energy is dismissed—to its own end, which cannot be defined in terms of the parts of the bow. "There is no heaven, no hell, not even release," we read in one of the texts celebrating the yogic rapture. "In short," this text continues, "in the yogic vision there is nothing at all." [86]

It is impossible to say when this absolute dismissal of all that the universe, god, or man, might offer began first to enchant the Indian mind; but as early as the period of the Indus Valley civilization, between 2500 and 1500 B.C., we find the figure of a three-faced divine being sitting in yoga posture, surrounded by animals (Figure 13); and it has been suggested that this must have been an early form of Shiva in the role of Pashu- pati, the Lord of Animals, who is the archetype of the forest- dwelling yogi, smeared with ashes to indicate his death to the world and wearing living serpents for bracelets, to indicate his transcendence of the world-enveloping serpent: whereas others are bounded by it, he wears it simply as an ornament— or casts it off, at will. The ideal appears to have come to India, therefore, almost as soon as the mandala itself, and in its earli- est phases would appear to have been of such an absolutely ruthless character that the aim of the yogi was no less than

Figure 13. "Lord of the Animals"; Indus Valley civilization,
c. 2000 B.C.

physical death—which was to supervene at precisely that
moment when the complete extinction within the heart of all
fear and hope whatsoever had been accomplished. At that instant of the absolute stilling of the mind, the titan, perfectly
balanced in the stance known as that of dismissing the body—
dismissed the body; and with it the whole mandala, with all its
priestly kings and kingly priests, heavens and hells, virtues and
vices, devils and gods.

Something of this ideology can be felt in the Stoic philosophers of the Classical world, and in the Near East in the
various gnostic and apocalyptic movements of the time of
Christ. In fact, there is too much of the spirit of this same
world-disdain in the words and deeds of Christ himself to
allow us to think that he was untouched by a titanism of this
sort. "Let the dead bury their dead" is certainly a tidy summary of the yogi's typical judgment of the world. "Sell all
that you have . . . and follow me" is the first requirement
placed by the guru on the candidate for release. But there is a
quality, at least in the *legend* of Christ, that would seem to
imply something considerably more gentle than sheer titanic

disdain; and this brings us to the next transformation of the titan principle in the sphere of the agricultural civilizations.

In the period of the early Upanishads, the eighth and seventh centuries B.C., it began to appear to some of the Indian titans that what was being sought by their fellows in isolation is to be found everywhere; that the inward center of absolute repose, which the forest yogis were attaining by a removal of themselves from the world, actually inhabits the world as the ground of its reality. The silence is to be heard resounding even through and within the tones of AUM. A shift of perspective, therefore, is what is required; and this is not achieved by running away. Running away implies the recognition of two distinct states—that of bondage and that of release. What the yogi must realize, however, is that all distinctions whatsoever—even this one, which is a great favorite of yogis—belong to that sphere of rational logic wherein A is not not-A. The world, the gods, man, and all things, have only to be looked upon with a new eye—but *looked* upon; not shunned.

Though it is hidden in all things
That Self shines not forth.
Yet It is seen by subtle seers
With superior, subtle intellect.

As the one fire has entered the world
And become corresponding in form to every form,
So the one interior Self of all things
Corresponds in form to every form, and yet is beyond.

The inward Self of all things, the One Controller,
Who makes his one form manifold:
The wise who perceive Him as standing within themselves,
They and no others, know eternal bliss.[87]

The titanic aspect of *this* kind of knowledge becomes apparent the moment it is realized that since everything is to be experienced as an ephiphany of the One Holy Power, there can be no such fundamental distinction between good and evil, holiness and vice, God and the Devil, as the lords and guardians of the mandala would have us believe. In fact (and this, in time, was to become one of the principles of the so-called "left-hand path"), to give credence to such a belief is to remain locked in the fractional state characteristic of those caught in the great trap of Reason, Virtue, and the Law. Those Tantric disciplines of illumination, where the Five Forbidden Things become the Five Good Things, rungs on the ladder of illumination, as well as the wild images of erotic orgy that abound on many of the temples of the Indian middle ages, let us know that when all is divine, all is affirmed— and with a degree of emphasis that is no less appalling to the socially grounded, readily shocked, antimystical consciousness than the ruthless world-denial of the earlier dismissers of the body.

And so again we have a discipline of disengagement; now, however, not observed through a dismissal of the signs and symbols that for others imply engagement, but through a dismissal merely of their references. Throughout the period of one's life, throughout the period of one's residence in the sphere of time, one is to go on being continually released from the bowstring. "*Bhoga* is *yoga!*" became the great cry: "Delight is religion!" Or again: "It is here! It is here!" And whereas for the forest philosopher every thrill of the senses was a danger, a distraction of the mind from that point of concentration through which the unmoving state was to be attained, and the first exercise of all discipline was to be *dama*, "control," "the restraint of the external organs," now, on the contrary, the *identity* of temporal experience and eternal realization, *saṁsāra* and *nirvāṇa*, has become the first principle both of philosophy and of practice. Whether in the floods of passion or in the desert of boredom, the honey-doctrine of the universal presence is to be tested for its truth, and its truth experienced in act. "In the ocean of *brahman*," we read, "filled with the nectar of Absolute Bliss, what is to be shunned and what accepted, what is there that is not myself, and what is there that is different in kind?" [88]

In the West this brand of titanism may have had its day in

some of the early Gnostic cults, which apparently shocked the conventional Romans enough to give Christianity a very bad name. "Split the stick," runs a Gnostic aphorism, "and there is Jesus!" But the memories of such beliefs have been pretty well expunged from the Western record. In the period of the Renaissance, however, there was a fresh stir of such possibilities. The sense of the immanent presence of God in all things, which inspired much of the new life as well as the art that burgeoned in that period, conduced to a hardiness in experiment that tended to break the bounds not only of the astronomical and geographical orders but of the moral as well. "Sin bravely!" said Luther, *Fortiter pecca!* And he was not the only man of his age to have recognized the spiritual sense of such a command.

But we are still in a trap; for we are attached to something. We are attached to the idea of enlightenment, release from the bow, disengagement. According to these disciplines, full of striving, tumult, and ecstasy, it would still appear that there is a notable difference between the "subtle seers with subtle intellect," who "know," and those of us who are not so wise. The ultimate import of the principle of nonduality, the identity of A and not-A, that is to say, has still to be given its full due. And so, we are brought to a fourth and final stage in the development of the titan principle within the circle of the social mandala.

What is now to be realized simply carries one step further the principle just described as that of stage three. For if *bhoga* is *yoga*, if *saṁsāra* is *nirvāṇa*, then illusion is enlightenment, engagement disengagement, and bondage is freedom. There is nothing to be done, no effort to be made; for in our very bondage we are free, and in our very striving for release we are linking ourselves the more to bondage—which is already freedom.

We are here presented with what a modern physicist would call, I believe, a "pair of aspects" system, or a principle of complementarity. According to the one mode or aspect of our experience, all things—ourselves included—are implicated in a context of space-time determinants and are bound; and yet, simultaneously, according to the other mode of our experience (which is impossible to reconcile with the first), all things—ourselves included—are freely creating themselves all the time, spontaneously arising. Professor Max Knoll discussed this double-aspect predicament in his Eranos Lecture of 1951, when he contrasted the dynamic and the structural, the energetic and the space-time, modes of description in physics and psychology.[89] In the Buddhism known as the Mahayana, the Great Vehicle, this same realization is rendered in the concept and ideal of the Bodhisattva: that great Savior, the reality of whose being (*sattva*) is enlightenment (*bodhi*), and who, yet, has not vanished in *nirvāṇa* but has remained in the world—which is already *nirvāṇa*—out of love and compassion for the forms of the world. The great point of this profoundly paradoxical doctrine or ideal is that we are all that Bodhisattva, simultaneously bound and free, implicated in a context of space-time determinants, yet spontaneously arising; indeed, that all things are that Bodhisattva. Let me term this stage in the development of the titan principle, therefore, that of the Realization of Universal Saviorhood. "Consider the lilies of the fields, how they grow; they toil not, neither do they spin!"

The meaning of release, disengagement, freedom (*mokṣa*), is no longer "escape"; the term has become a reference, rather, to a mode or aspect of our present being and sense of being. Bodhisattvahood is precisely—and merely—that nonduality which is everywhere experienced through a "pair of aspects," and, though generally thought and said to be dual, is actually and immediately known to be not so. Let us for a moment contrast this ideal with that of Prometheus, defying Zeus, who suggests an irreconcilable dichotomy between the principle of the free individual and that of the social and cosmological order. The realization of the Bodhisattva recognizes that any such sense of a radical dichotomy is an effect, simply, of systematic thinking. In accord with the principle of complementarity, we should say, rather, Prometheus and Zeus, I and the Father, are one.

But how can we attain to this realization, which is already ours somewhere in our being?

There is a legend that tells of the Buddha, teaching, speaking to the minds of those with ears to hear; and as he taught, his hand lifted a lotus. The only one with eyes to see was the sage Kashyapa, who, being ripe for illumination, saw the lotus. In the way of a religious or doctrinal reference, the lotus lifted by the Buddha might have been interpreted allegorically, as signifying the lotus of the world, which is our vehicle of redemption. For, as we are taught by the well-known Buddhist prayer and aspiration, "The jewel in the lotus" (OM MAṆI PADME HUM), the jewel of *nirvāṇa* is in the lotus of life. Which is to say, that, since, according to the testimony of those illuminated ones who have transcended the dualistic deceptions of the senses and logical thought, bondage and freedom are the same, this world itself, with all its pains and imperfections, is to be known as the golden lotus world of perfect purity and joy. It could certainly have been supposed that the lotus lifted in the Buddha's hand might have been a reference to some such idea, and the reference, then, would have constituted the meaning of the symbol. But then, of course, we, as good modern logicians, ambitious for the precision of science, would have had to ask whether this proposition could be demonstrated, either by direct or by indirect verification. And failing verification, we should have had either to reject it, as representing a disproved hypothesis, or to consign it to the category of mere expression—like a poem, a cry, or a piece of music—as a pretty symptom of the Buddha's feeling about the world, his mood or character, his sense of affinity with the world of nature, his personal charm, or what not. However, with all these referential considerations, logical propositions, psychological intuitions, and fine notions about our own exactitude, we should not yet even have begun to try to see or imagine what it was that Kashyapa saw when he saw just—*that* lotus.

Aldous Huxley, in his little book *The Doors of Perception*, describes the impressions he received during the course of a day when he had swallowed four-tenths of a gram of mescalin dissolved in half a glass of water. He tells of a chair that he saw in a garden.

> For what seemed an immensely long time, I gazed without knowing, even without wishing to know, what it was that confronted me. At any other time I would have seen a chair barred with alternate light and shade. Today the percept had swallowed up the concept. I was so completely absorbed in looking, so thunderstruck by what I actually saw, that I could not be aware of anything else. Where the shadows fell on the canvas upholstery, stripes of a deep but glowing indigo alternated with stripes of an incandescence so intensely bright that it was hard to believe that they could be made of anything but blue fire. Garden furniture, laths, sunlight, shadow—these were no more than names and notions, mere verbalizations, for utilitarian purposes, after the event. The event was this succession of azure furnace doors separated by gulfs of unfathomable gentian. It was inexpressibly wonderful, wonderful to the point, almost, of being terrifying. And suddenly I had an inkling of what it must feel like to be mad.[90]

Thus it was, I imagine, that Kashyapa saw the lotus in the Buddha's hand—though without such emotional affect. It was not a reference to any teaching associated with the figure of the lotus, or an expression of the character, mood, sentiments, or emotions of the Buddha. Neither was it a reference to the botanical genus of the lotus. It was simply *that* lotus: that thing which it was and no other thing: a *mysterium tremendum*—as we all are. But we are all protected from each other by our references, the engrams of those cosmic systems to which we have been educated and to which our minds immediately refer the data of the senses. Following these references, we let the concept swallow up the percept, and so reverse the process of a revelation, thus defending ourselves from experience. And yet each thing, each person, all around us, all the time, each insisting on itself as being that thing which it is and no other thing, is striving with all its might to provide an experience of—itself.

Some minds require mescalin to dissolve in them their references; others may be quelled by the hypnotizing beat of a drum or the rhythmical organization of a work of art. (For example, which of us ever looked, really, at an old pair of shoes until they were shown to us by Van Gogh?) Certain religious exercises, involving the repetition of meaningless or almost meaningless syllables, the contemplation of some design or image, or the prolonged consideration of metaphysical riddles until the mind breaks, may be meant to effect a similar result: to lull, hypnotize, or dissolve the busy brain and release the senses. The phenomena of dream commonly impress us more strongly than those of waking life just because in sleep the brain is off guard. If it could be caught off guard when we were awake, this "directly obvious" (*pratyakṣa*) world, deprived of its varnish of meaning, would shine forth of itself. Our experience then would be *paramārtha pratyakṣa:* "in the highest manner before the eyes"; "immediate, unmitigated, perfectly direct."

This order of experience has been described for us by the Zen masters of China and Japan, in terms that may seem a little strange and puzzling, as "the doctrine of no-mind." However, I believe if expressed in terms more congenial to our own tradition, the experience would be recognized as one that we ourselves have had on occasion. In the simplest terms, I think we might say that when a situation or phenomenon evokes in us a *sense of existence* (instead of some reference to the possibility of an *assurance of meaning*) we have had an experience of this kind. The sense of existence evoked may be shallow or profound, more or less intense, according to our capacity or readiness; but even a brief shock (say, for example, when discovering the moon over city roofs or hearing a sharp bird cry at night) can yield an experience of the order of no-mind: that is to say, the poetical order, the order of art. When this occurs, our own reality-beyond-meaning is awakened (or perhaps better: *we* are awakened to our own reality-beyond-meaning), and we experience an affect that is neither thought nor feeling but an interior impact. The phenomenon, disengaged from cosmic references, has disengaged ourselves, by that principle, well known to magic, by which like conjures like. In fact, both the magic of art and the art of magic derive from and are addressed to experiences of this order. Hence the power of the meaningless syllables, the mumbo jumbo of magic, and the meaningless verbalizations of metaphysics, lyric poetry, and art interpretation. They function evocatively, not referentially; like the beat of a shaman's drum, not like a formula of Einstein. One moment later, and we have classified the experience and may be having utterable thoughts and describable feelings about it—thoughts and feelings that are in the public domain, and they will be either sentimental or profound, according to our education. But according to our life, we have had, for an instant, a sense of existence: a moment of unevaluated, unimpeded, lyric life—antecedent to both thought and feeling; such as can never be communicated by means of empirically verifiable propositions, but only suggested by art.

And now, I think, I am ready to formulate two or three final suggestions.

The first is that since what we are now discussing is an experience not of the relatively unknown but of the absolutely unknowable, it cannot be termed "knowledge," in the usual Occidental sense of this term. It is true that the Sanskrit terms *bodhi, vidyā,* and *prajñā,* which refer to this range of experience, are commonly translated with such words as "knowledge, supreme knowledge, illumination, enlightenment, or wisdom"; but the history of these words in our tradition makes it impossible for them to carry the meaning intended. According to the Oriental usage, everything to which these words of ours refer is to be known as *a-vidyā,* "non-knowledge, the lack of enlightenment, ignorance, folly, delusion." Let us accept this suggestion and recognize, then, that what is intended by art, metaphysics, magical hocus-pocus, and mystical religion, is not the knowledge of anything, not truth, or goodness, or beauty, but an evocation of a sense of the absolutely unknowable. Science, on the other hand, will take care of what can be known.

Art and science, then (and here, in line with the suggestion already quoted from Professor Rudolf Carnap, I am including under the term "art" the whole vocabulary of metaphysics and religion), art and science constitute a "pair of aspects" system. The function of art is to render a *sense of existence*, not an *assurance of some meaning:* so that those who require an assurance of meaning, or who feel unsure of themselves and unsettled when they learn that the system of meaning that would support them in their living has been shattered, must surely be those who have not yet experienced profoundly, continuously, or convincingly enough, that sense of existence—of spontaneous and willing arising—which is the first and deepest characteristic of being, and which it is the province of art to waken.

What—I ask—is the meaning of a flower? And having no meaning, should the flower, then, not be?

And so, with reference, now, to our problem of the symbol, we may say that a symbol, like everything else, shows a double aspect. We must distinguish, therefore, between the "sense" and the "meaning" of the symbol. It seems to me perfectly clear that all the great and little symbolical systems of the past functioned simultaneously on three levels: the corporeal of waking consciousness, the spiritual of dream, and the ineffable of the absolutely unknowable. The term "meaning" can refer only to the first two: but these, today, are in the charge of science—which is the province, as we have said, not of symbols but of signs. The ineffable, the absolutely unknowable, can be only sensed: and not more in the religious sanctuary, today, than elsewhere. It is of the province of art—which is not "expression" merely, or even primarily (as Pro-

fessor Carnap and the other logical positivists have supposed), but a quest for, and formulation of, experience-
evoking, energy-waking images: yielding what Sir Herbert
Read has aptly termed "a sensuous apprehension of being."

I will not dwell on this point any longer. I think it must be
clear by now that a certain relationship is indicated here between the courage of the paleolithic hunter in his individualism and his willingness to face unprotected the spiritual experiences available to our race. Personally—though I do not
wish to make a point of this—I believe that there is a precise
relationship between the format or stature of the psyche and
the quantum of immediate experience that one is capable of
sustaining and absorbing, and that the training and shaping of
the mandala-conditioned psyche of the incomplete man of the
agriculturally based societies has simply unfitted him for the
reception of the full impact of any *mysterium* whatsoever.
Aldous Huxley has noted that what he saw when, for once,
he really *saw* something, was "wonderful almost to the point
of being terrifying," so that suddenly he had an inkling of
what it must feel like to be mad. The mad are those who,
when they have broken contact with the mode of meaning,
with the integrating component of thinking consciousness,
cannot again restore it—whereas the great artist, like the
shaman, like the *paramahaṁsa*, the "supreme wild gander" of
the titanic yogic flight, can be carried away and return.

And so now, my second suggestion is that, today, when the
mandala itself, the whole structure of meaning to which society and its guardians would attach us, is dissolving, what is required of us all, spiritually as well as corporeally, is much
more the fearless self-sufficiency of our shamanistic inheritance than the timorous piety of the priest-guided Neolithic.
Those of us who never dared to be titans but only obedient
children, following as loyally as possible the commands of
Zeus, or Yahweh, or the State, now find that the commands
themselves are in a somewhat fluent condition, changing with
time. For the circle has been broken—the mandala of truth.
The circle is open, and we are sailing on a sea more vast than

that of Columbus. The propositions of science, which have broken the mandala, and to which we are referred for our morality, knowledge, and wisdom, do not pretend to be true in any final sense, do not pretend to be infallible, or even durable, but are merely working hypotheses, here today and gone tomorrow. There is no guiding bird, no landfall, no Hispaniola that is not soon dissolved in further revelations of outer and inner space.

"O ye," said Dante, at that point in his journey when, taking leave of the Earthly Paradise on the summit of the cosmic mountain in the southern ocean, he was about to set forth for the sphere of the Moon, "O ye who in a little bark, desirous to listen, have followed behind my craft which singing passes on, turn to see again your shore; put not out upon the deep; for haply losing me, ye would remain astray. The water which I take was never crossed. Minerva breathes, and Apollo guides me, and the nine Muses point out to me the Bears." [91] But Dante, through a series of theological propositions, reached in safety the term of his voyage: the Empyrean, the River of Light, and the Celestial Rose, beyond the sphere of the Fixed Stars. And there, as he declares, he found the ultimate image confirmed to the measure of the circle, and in this high vision his desire and his will were resolved, like a wheel which is moved evenly, by the love which moves the sun and the other stars.[92]

Our circle today, however, is rather that announced two centuries later by the genius of Nicholas Cusanus: whose circumference is nowhere and whose center is everywhere; the circle of infinite radius, which is also a straight line.* Or, to state the principle in other terms: our meaning is now the meaning that is no meaning; for no fixed term of reference can be drawn. And to support such a temporal situation, each must discover himself to be the titan—without fear of the open world.

As the researches and writings of Dr. Jung have shown us, the deep aim and problem of the maturing psyche today is to

* Compare supra, pp. 80 and 116 (Black Elk Speaks).

recover wholeness. But such a recovery will necessarily center us far deeper within ourselves and within the universe than any concept or image that we may hold of Man, or of *humanitas*, can possibly suggest. As the Californian poet Robinson Jeffers has declared:

> Humanity is the
> start of the race; I say
> Humanity is the mold to break away from, the crust to break
>   through, the coal to break into fire,
> The atom to be split.[93]

The first stage of the process of individuation, Jung has described as one of dissolving—not re-enforcing—the individual's identification of his personality with the claims of the collective archetypes. These, I have tried to show, are functions, not only of the psyche, but also of the history of society, and today are in full dissolution. The scientific method has released us, intellectually, from the absolutes of the mythological ages; the divine authority of the religiously founded state has been completely dissolved, at least in the Occident; and the power-driven machine is progressively releasing human energy from the onerous physical tasks that were formerly rationalized as valuable moral disciplines: thus released, these energies constitute what Jung has termed a quantum of disposable libido—now flowing from the corporeal to the spiritual task. And this spiritual task can now be only that which I have here termed the task of art.

The epoch of the Renaissance, to which we owe in large measure the scientific vision, was at its apogee in 1492—the year of the death of Lorenzo the Magnificent as well as that of the Fall of Granada and Discovery of the New World. Leonardo da Vinci that year was forty years old, Machiavelli twenty-three, Copernicus nineteen. Moreover, by another coincidence, precisely in the year of the first battle of the American Revolution, James Watt conceived the idea of the steam condenser, to which we owe the first successfully operated power-driven machine. And so, in a sense, it is true indeed, or at least true enough, that the world in which we are now living was not only created in 1492 but redeemed in 1776.

Within the time of our lives, it is highly improbable that any solid rock will be found to which Prometheus can again be durably shackled, or against which those who are not titans will be able to lean with confidence. The creative researches and wonderful daring of our scientists today partake far more of the lion spirit of shamanism than of the piety of priest and peasant. They have shed all fear of the bounding serpent king. And if we are to match their courage, and thus participate joyfully in their world without meaning, we must allow our own spirits to become, like theirs, wild ganders, and fly in timeless, spaceless flight—like the body of the Virgin Mary—not into any fixed heaven beyond the firmament (for there is no heaven out there), but to that seat of experience, simultaneously without and within, where Prometheus and Zeus, I and the Father, the meaninglessness of the sense of existence and the meaninglessness of the meanings of the world, are one.

[VI]

The Secularization of the Sacred

[1]

The Tree in the Garden

As I understand the phrase "the secularization of the sacred," it suggests an opening of the sense of religious awe to some sphere of secular experience, or more marvelously, to the wonder of this whole world and oneself within it.

"One day," said, for example, the Indian saint and sage Shri Ramakrishna, "it was suddenly revealed to me that everything is Pure Spirit. The utensils of worship, the altar, the door frame—all Pure Spirit. Men, animals, and other living beings—all Pure Spirit. Then like a madman I began to shower flowers in all directions. Whatever I saw I worshiped.

"One day, while worshiping Shiva, I was about to offer a bel-leaf on the head of the image, when it was revealed to me that this Virat, this Universe, itself is Shiva. . . . Another day I had been plucking flowers, when it was revealed to me that each plant was a bouquet adorning the universal form of God. That was the end of my plucking flowers. I look on man in just the same way. When I see a man, I see that it is God Himself who walks on earth, as it were, rocking to and fro, like a pillow floating on the waves." [1]

Another time, when he was approaching an image of the goddess Kali to pay it worship, someone said to him, "I have heard that it was made by the sculptor Nabin." "Yes, I know," he answered. "But to me She is the embodiment of Spirit." [2]

Actually, this order of experience is basic, not only to Indian religiosity, but to the entire range of the high religions of the Orient eastward of Iran. We have it in the Buddhist aspiration: OM MAṆI PADME HUM: "The Jewel in the Lotus": The Jewel of Absolute Reality (nirvāṇa) is in the Lotus of the Universe (in life); likewise in the Chinese concept of the Tao:

> The Valley Spirit never dies:
> It is the base from which heaven sprang and earth.
> It is here within us all the while.[3]

The ultimate goal of Oriental worship is, accordingly, the realization of one's own identity with this reality and a recognition of its presence in all things—not, as in our Western religions, to worship a god distinct from his creation, of a different order of being—apart—"out there." A telling statement to this point appears in the ancient Brihadaranyaka Upanishad (c. 700 B.C.?):

> This that people say: "Worship this god! Worship that god!"—one god after another—this whole universe itself is His creation! And he Himself is all the gods. . . .
>
> Whoever worships one or another of those, knows not: He is incomplete as worshiped in one or another. One should worship with the thought that He is one's own essential Self, for therein all these become one.
>
> Whoever thus knows, "I am brahman!" becomes this All; not even the gods have the power to prevent his becoming thus, for he then becomes their Self. So whoever worships a divinity other than this Self, thinking, "He is one and I another," knows not. He is like a sacrificial animal for the gods. And as many animals would be of service to a man, even so is each single person of service to the gods. But if even one animal is taken away it is not pleasant. What, then, if many? It is not pleasing to the gods, therefore, that people should know this.[4]

Compare with this, the Book of Genesis:

Then the Lord God said, "Behold, the man has become like one of us, knowing good and evil; and now, lest he put forth his hand and take also of the tree of life, and eat, and live for ever"—therefore the Lord God sent him forth from the garden of Eden, to till the ground from which he was taken. He drove out the man; and at the east of the garden of Eden he placed the cherubim, and a flaming sword which turned every way, to guard the way to the tree of life.[5]

But this Way to the Tree of Life is exactly the *mārga*, the "path," of the Indian disciplines, the *tao* of the Chinese, the "gateless gate" (*mumon*) of Zen. And the cherubim at the entrance to the Garden of the Knowledge of Immortality, guarding it with a flaming sword, correspond exactly to the temple guardians at the entrance to any Oriental sanctuary.

Never shall I forget a picture that I saw in a New York newspaper during our recent war with Japan. It showed one of the two giant temple guardians at the gate to the Todaiji temple in Nara: fierce figures with lifted swords. There was no picture of the temple itself, or of the Buddha within, beneath the Tree of Enlightenment, hand lifted in the "fear-not" gesture, but only that one threatening cherub in his frightening attitude and, beneath the picture, the legend: "The Japanese worship gods like this."

The only thought that crossed my mind, and it is with me still, was the obvious one: "Not they, but we!" For it is *we* whose god would keep men out of the Garden. The Oriental idea, on the contrary, is to go past the guardian cherubim and to pluck the fruit of the Tree of Immortal Life—ourselves—right now—while here on earth.

[2]

Religions of Identity

Such an aim and such a realization I am going to call "mythic identification." Briefly, the underlying idea is that the ultimate truth, substance, support, energy, or reality of the universe transcends all definition, all imaging, all categories, and all thought. It is beyond the reach of the mind, i.e., transcendent. Consequently, to ask, as our theologians do: "Is the Godhead just? merciful? wrathful?" "Does it favor this people or that: the Jew, the Christian, or Mohammedan?" is from this point of view absurd. To think thus is to project human sentiments and concerns beyond their temporal sphere, and so, to short-circuit the problem altogether. It is a kind of anthropomorphism, hardly more appropriate to a developed religion than the attribution of gender to the source-mystery of being—which is another of the absurdities of our bewildering religions. But now, on the other hand (and here is the great point): that which is thus ultimately transcendent of all definition, categories, names, and forms, is the very substance, energy, being, and support, of all things, including ourselves: the reality of each and all of us. Transcendent of definition, transcendent of enclosure, it is yet immanent in each:

OM MAṆI PADME HUM

Take, for example, a pencil, ashtray, anything, and, holding it before you in both hands, regard it for a while. Forgetting its use and name, yet continuing to regard it, ask yourself seriously, "What is it?" As James Joyce states in *Ulysses* (and here is the touchstone of his art): "Any object, intensely regarded, may be a gate of access to the incorruptible eon of the gods." [6] Cut off from use, relieved of nomenclature, its dimension of wonder opens; for the mystery of the *being* of that thing is identical with the mystery of the being of the universe—and of yourself. Schopenhauer, somewhere in his great work, *The World as Will and Representation*, has summarized the leading theme of his philosophy in a single memorable sentence: "Every thing is the entire world as Will in its own way." And in the Indian Chandogya Upanishad there is the famous phrase addressed by the charming sage Aruni to his son, Shvetaketu: *tat tvan asi:* "You are It!" "You, Shvetaketu, my son, are yourself that immortal Being of beings." [7]

The Oriental sages and their texts are unanimous in insisting, however, that the "you" referred to in teachings of this kind is not exactly the "you" that you think yourself to be, individuated in space and time, a temporary member of this world of passing forms, named, loved, and separate from your neighbor. *Neti neti,* "not this, not this," is the meditation properly applied to everything so known, so named and numbered: all those facets of the jewel of reality that present themselves to the mind. "I am not my body, my feelings, my thoughts, but the consciousness of which these are the manifestations." For we are all, in every particle of our being, precipitations of consciousness; as are, likewise, the animals and plants, metals cleaving to a magnet and waters tiding to the moon. And as the great physicist, Erwin Schrödinger, states in his book, *My View of the World:* "To divide or multiply consciousness is something meaningless. In all the world, there is no kind of framework within which we can find consciousness in the plural; this is simply something we construct because of the spatio-temporal plurality of individuals, but it is a false conception." [8] "What," he asks, "justifies you in obstinately discovering this difference—the difference between you and someone else—when objectively what is there is *the same?. . .* This life of yours which you are living is not merely a piece of the entire existence, but is in a certain sense the *whole;* only this whole is not so constituted that it can be surveyed in one single glance. And this, as we know, is what the Brahmins express in that sacred, mystic formula which is really so simple and so clear: *Tat tvam asi,* this is you. Or, again, in such words as 'I am in the east and in the west, I am below and above, I am this whole world.' " [9]

Letting *a* signify oneself, and *x*, ultimate reality, we might represent this manner of self-identification, as follows:

$$a \neq\, =\, x$$

As known phenomenologically, *a* is not *x;* yet, in truth, is indeed *x*.

The oxymoron, self-contradictory, the paradox, the transcendent symbol, pointing beyond itself, is the gateless gate, the sun-door, the passage beyond categories. Gods and Bud-

dhas in the Orient are, accordingly, not final terms—like
Yahweh, the Trinity, or Allah, in the West—but point beyond themselves to that ineffable being, consciousness, and
rapture that is the All in all of us. And in their worship, the
ultimate aim is to effect in the devotee a psychological trans-
figuration through a shift of his plane of vision from the passing to the enduring, through which he may come finally to
realize in experience (not simply as an article of faith) that he
is identical with that before which he bows. These are, then,
religions of identity. Their mythologies and associated rites,
philosophies, sciences, and arts, are addressed, in the end, not
to the honor of any god "out there" but to the recognition of
divinity within.

Returning to our text, "The Great Forest Book" or Brihadaranyaka Upanishad:

> He has entered into all this, even to the fingernail tips,
> like a razor in the razor case, like fire in firewood. Him
> they see not; for as seen, he is incomplete.
>
> When breathing, He is named breath, when speaking
> voice, when seeing the eye, when hearing the ear, when
> thinking mind: these are just the names of His acts. Who-
> ever worships one or another of these, knows not; for He
> is incomplete in one or another of these. One should wor-
> ship with the idea that He is just one's self (*ātman*), for
> therein all these become one.
>
> That same thing, namely, this Self, is the footprint of
> this All, for just as one finds cattle by a footprint, so one
> finds this All by its footprint, the Self.[10]

Something similar appears to have been implied in the following quotations from the earliest religious writings known:
the *Pyramid Texts* of the Fifth and Sixth Dynasties of Old
Kingdom Egypt (c. 2350–2175 B.C.), where the spirit of the
deceased takes back into itself the manifold powers of the
various gods that during his lifetime had been regarded as
without.

"It is he [the deceased] who eats their magic and swallows
their spirits. Their Great Ones are for his morning meal, their

middle-sized ones are for his evening meal, their little ones are for his night meal, their old men and old women are for his fire." [11]

"Behold, their soul is in his belly. . . . Their shadows are taken away from the hand of those to whom they belong. He is as that which dawns, which endures." [12]

And again, a millennium or so later, more explicitly, from *The Book of the Dead*, where the deceased himself is supposed to be speaking:

"My hair is the hair of Nu. My face is the face of the Disk. My eyes are the eyes of Hathor. My ears are the ears of Ap-uat. . . . My feet are the feet of Ptah. There is no member of my body that is not the member of some god. . . .

"I am Yesterday, Today, and Tomorrow, and I have the power to be born a second time. I am the divine hidden Soul who creates the gods. . . .

"Hail, lord of the shrine that stands in the middle of the earth. He is I and I am he, and Ptah has covered his sky with crystal.[13]

Essentially the same, or at least a like, idea is suggested in certain early Mesopotamian seals, some of which are of about the date of the Pyramid Texts. Figure 14, for instance, shows a devotee approaching the altar of the Lord of the Tree of Life, with his right hand lifted in worship and on his left arm a goat, his offering. The gracious god, in return, proffers the cup of ambrosial drink, drawn from the fruit or sap of the tree, which bestows that gift of immortality which, centuries later, was to be denied to Adam and Eve. The god is horned, like the moon above his cup; for the moon is the sign celestial of the ever-enduring resurrection. As Lord of the Tides of the Womb, forever waxing and waning, it carries—like life—its own death within it; yet, also, its victory over death. In Figure 15 we see its crescent again. However, the tree, this time, is attended by the dual apparition of a goddess known as Gula-Bau, whose later, Classical counterparts, Demeter and Persephone, were the goddesses, without peer, of both the Orphic and the Eleusinian mysteries. In this ancient Baby-

Figure 14. "Lord of the Tree of Life"; Sumer, c. 2500 B.C.

Figure 15. "The Garden of Immortality"; Babylonia, c. 1750–1550 B.C.

Figure 16. "The Lord and Lady of the Tree"; Sumer, c. 2500 B.C.

lonian seal of c. 1750–1550 B.C. (approximately one millen-nium earlier than the Garden text of the Bible), the dual goddess of the plains of life and of death is passing the fruit of deathlessness to a mortal woman approaching from the left. Figure 16, from an early Sumerian seal, c. 2500 B.C., shows the god and goddess together, Lord and Lady of the Tree, in the company, however, of the Serpent, not the moon: for as the moon sheds death in the figure of its shadow, so the ser-pent its slough, to be born again of itself. These are equivalent symbols, heavenly and earthly, of the ever-dying, ever-living Being of beings that is Life in the garden of this world.[14]

In India, Shiva is the counterpart—worshiped to this hour —of the god at the foot of the Tree, dispensing the moon-elixir of life; and in the sixth century B.C., when the prince Siddhartha, in his meditations, arrived at the foot of that same World Tree, he there achieved the boon of Illumination, which he then dispensed to the world, himself in the place and role of the god. Likewise, in the classical mystery cults, the aim of the quest of the initiate was to realize in himself divinity. "Happy and Blessed One," we read on a golden Orphic tablet of c. 300 B.C., "thou shalt be God instead of mortal." [15] And Apuleius, second century A.D., at the end of the ordeal of *The Golden Ass*, was, through the bounty of the goddess Isis, transformed into the likeness of a god. "In my right hand I carried a lighted torch and a garland of flowers was on my head, with white palm leaves sprouting out on every side like rays. Thus I was adorned, like to the sun and made in fashion of an image, when the curtains were drawn aside and all the people crowded to behold me." [16]

Among the North European Celts and Germans, also, the wonderful drink of "Deathlessness" (Sanskrit *amṛta*, Greek αμβροσία) was known under many guises. Odin (Wotan) gave an eye for a sip from the Well of Wisdom at the foot of the World Ash, Yggdrasil, where it was guarded by Mimir, the dwarf; and aloft in Valhall, his hero-hall, the warrior dead drank of a mead, served by the Valkyries, that restored them to life and joy. Similarly, the Celtic sea god Manannan served in his dwelling under waves an ale that bestowed immortality on his guests; and, for a taste of the sort of knowledge once gained from such ambrosial fare by initiates of the Celtic race, we have the famous charm of Amairgen the magician, from the Irish *Lebor Gabala* ("Book of Invasions").

> I am the wind that blows o'er the sea;
> I am the wave of the deep;
> I am the bull of seven battles;
> I am the eagle on the rock;
> I am a tear of the sun;
> I am the fairest of plants;

I am a boar for courage;
I am a salmon in the water;
I am a lake on the plain;
I am the word of knowledge;
I am the head of the battle-dealing spear;
I am the god who fashions thought in the mind.[17]

[3]
Religions of Relationship

But now, in irreconcilable contrast to this ancient, practically universal mode of experience of the world's and one's own dimension of divinity, which I have termed "mythic identification," there is the order of beliefs derived from the biblical tradition, where Yahweh, as we know (arriving very late on the scene), cursed the serpent of the Garden (Figure 16, supra, p. 200), and with it the whole earth, which he seems to have thought he had created. Here God creates the World and the two are *not* the same: Creator and Creature, ontologically distinct, are *not* to be identified with each other in any way. In fact, an experience of identity is the prime heresy of these systems and punishable by death. Their formula, therefore, is not, as in the earlier and more general order, $a \neq = x$, but a is related to x:

$$a \, R \, x$$

And what is the medium of relationship? The local social group.

For example, in the Hebrew context: God has ordained a Covenant with a certain Semitic people. Birth as a member of that holy race, and observance of its rituals of the Covenant, are the means of achieving a relationship with God. No other means are known or admitted to exist.

Comparably, in the Christian view: Christ, the only son of God, is at once True God and True Man. This, throughout the Christian world, is regarded as a miracle, whereas, in keeping with the earlier formula of $a \neq = x$, we are *all* true god and true man: "All things are Buddha things"; "Brahman sleeps in the stone": what is required is only that one should waken to that truth and thereafter live "illuminated" (*buddha*, from the root *budh*, to know, to notice, to wake, to revive, to come to one's senses). According to the Christian view, no one except Christ can declare, "I and the Father are one" (John 10:30); hence, also, "No one comes to the Father, but by me" (John 14:6). Through Christ's humanity, we are related to him; through his Godhood, he relates us to divinity. Thus he, and he alone, is the pivot. Apart from him, we are apart from God, who, though just and merciful, is wrathful too, and was sorely offended by Adam's sin, the guilt of which we have all, somehow, inherited. God, in Christ, became Man. Accepting death on the Cross, he atoned mankind with the Father. No individual, however, can participate in that reconciliation but by membership in his Church, which he founded on the Rock of Peter, some time around 30 A.D.

Mythologized, the Cross of Christ was equated early in the Middle Ages with the Tree of Immortal Life, the tree forbidden in the Garden, and Christ crucified was its fruit; his blood, the ambrosial drink. The sacrifice of the Mass, furthermore, was interpreted as "a renewal of the Sacrifice on Calvary," through which the Redeemer imparts to the faithful of his Church the grace gained for them on the Cross. In terms of the imagery of the closed garden gate with the cherubim and the turning sword, Christ, as a kind of Prometheus, had broken past the frightening guard and gained access for mankind to immortal life, as proclaimed in the hymn, *O Salutaris Hostia*, sung at the Benediction of the Blessed Sacrament:

> *O Salutaris Hostia,*
> *Quae caeli pandis ostium. . . .*
>
> O saving Victim,
> Who hast opened wide heaven's gates. . . .

However, in contrast to the Oriental, Buddhist and Vedantic, ways of interpreting the symbolism of the guarded gate and passage to the tree—as referring, namely, to an inward, psychological barrier and crisis of transcendence—the authorized Christian reading has been of an actual, concrete, historic event of atonement with an angry god, who for centuries had withheld his boon of paradise from mankind, until strangely reconciled by this curious self-giving of his only son to a criminal's death on the Cross. The fact of the crucifixion was read as the central fact of all history, and along with it certain other associated "facts" were accepted, such as in other mythological traditions would be interpreted psychologically (or, as theologians say, "spiritually") as symbols; such as (1) the Virgin Birth, (2) the Resurrection, (3) the Ascension, (4) the existence of a heaven to which a physical body might ascend, and, of course, (5) that Fall in the garden of Eden, c. 4004 B.C., from the guilt of which the Crucifixion has redeemed us.

God in this system is a kind of fact somewhere, an actual personality to whom prayers can be addressed with expectation of a result. He is apart from and different from the world: in no sense *identical* with it, but *related*, as cause to effect. I call this kind of religious thinking "mythic dissociation." The sense of an experience of the sacred is dissociated from life, from nature, from the world, and transferred or projected somewhere else—an imagined somewhere else—while man, mere man, is accursed. "In the sweat of your face you shall eat bread till you return to the ground, for out of it you were taken; you are dust, and to dust you shall return" (Genesis 3:19).

The sacred is now not secular, of this world of mere dead dust, but canonical, supernaturally revealed and authoritatively preserved; that is to say: God, from "out there," has condescended graciously to accord special revelations: (1) to the Hebrews, historically, on Sinai, via Moses; (2) to mankind, historically, in Bethlehem, via Jesus; but then also, apparently, (3) to mankind, once again, historically, in a cave near Mecca, via Mohammed. All, it will be noted, Semites! No other revelations of this desert god are admitted to exist, and *Extra ecclesiam nulla salus.*

To the formula of mythic dissociation, therefore, there must now be added that of "social identification": identification with Israel, with the Church as the Living Body of Christ, or with the Sunna of Islam—each body overinterpreted by its membership as the one and only holy thing in this world. And the focal center and source of all this holiness is concentrated in each case in a completely unique and special fetish—not a symbol, but a fetish: (1) the Ark of the Covenant in the Temple; (2) the Torah in the synagogue; (3) the Transubstantiated Host of the Roman Catholic Church; (4) the Bible of the Reformation; (5) the Koran, as well as (6) the Ka'aba, of Islam.

In India and the Far East such revered supports of the religious life would be known, finally, to point beyond themselves and their anthropomorphic god: beyond names, forms and all scriptural personification, to that immanent transcendent mystery of being which defies thought, feeling, and figuration. For, whereas the attitude of focused piety is there recognized as appropriate for those not yet able to live in the realization of their own identity with "That" (*tat tvam asi*), for anyone ready for an actual religious experience of his own, such canonized props are impediments. "Where is Self-knowledge for him whose knowledge depends on the object?" we read in a Vedantic text. "The wise do not see a this and a that, but the Self (*ātman*) Immutable." [18] "You have your own treasure house," said the eighth-century Chinese sage Ma-tsu; "why do you search outside?" [19]

However, as another sage, Wei-kuan, once declared to a monk in quest of enlightenment: "As long as there is 'I and thou,' this complicates the situation and there is no seeing Tao."

"When there is neither 'I' nor 'thou,' is it seen?" the monk then asked.

"When there is neither 'I' nor 'thou,'" came the paradoxical answer, "who is here to see it?" [20] (I.e., $a \neq = x$.)

Or, to quote, again, Ramakrishna: "The essence of Vedanta is: *brahman* alone is real and the world illusory; I have no separate existence; I am that *brahman* alone. . . . But for those who lead a worldly life, and for those who identify themselves with the body, this attitude of 'I am He' is not good. It is not good for householders to read the Vedanta. It is very harmful for them to read these books. Householders should look on God as Master and on themselves as His servants. They should think, 'O God, You are the Master and the Lord, and I am Your servant.' People who identify themselves with the body should not have the attitude of 'I am He.' " [21]

The point is simply that the meditation "Not this, not this" (*neti neti*) must be accomplished before "I am *brahman*" (*brahmāsmi*) and "it is here, it is here" (*iti iti*). However, when the latter is begun, the fetish, the idol, is left behind, as it was when Ramakrishna flung his flowers all about. And there is a parallel here to Socrates' doctrine of Beauty in the *Symposium*, when he states (quoting the wise woman Diotima) that when the lover has learned to appreciate the beauty of one individual body, "he must consider how nearly related the beauty of any one body is to the beauty of any other, when he will see that if he is to devote himself to loveliness of form, it will be absurd to deny that the beauty of each and every body is the same. Having reached this point, he must set himself to be the lover of every lovely body, and bring his passion for the one into due proportion by deeming it of little or of no importance." [22]

No such whoring after alien gods, however, for the lover of that jealous god in the Bible! Nor is there any allowance, there, for the following of one's own light: the leadership and guidance of one's own expanding, deepening, enriched experience of the nature of the world and oneself. All life, all thought, all meditation, is to be governed by the authority of the shepherds of the group; and there can be no doubt, from what we know of the history of this tradition, that this authority was imposed and maintained by force.

But any religious symbol, so interpreted that it refers not to a thought-transcending mystery but to a thought-enveloping social order, misappropriates to the lower principle the values of the higher and so (to use a theological turn of phrase) sets Satan in the seat of God.

[4]

The European Graft

And is it not one of the strangest anomalies of history that a religion of this overbearing kind—exclusive, authoritative, collective, and fanatic—should have been carried intact from its Levantine hearth to be grafted onto the living stock of Europe? In the light of what can be seen today in the so-called Christian world, the graft would appear not to have taken hold. And in earlier centuries, also: the outstanding characteristic of the history of the Church in Europe has been its agony in a constant battle against heresies of all kinds, on every side, in every age—and heresy now has won. Already in the fifth century, the Irish heresy of Pelagius posed a challenge that the African Augustine was supposed to have put down. But Pelagianism today is the only brand of Christianity with any possibility of an Occidental future. For who, outside of a convent, actually believes today, in his heart, that every child born of woman, throughout the world, will be sent to an everlasting hell, unless somebody of Christian faith splashes water on its head, to the accompaniment of a prayer in the name of the Father, Son, and Holy Ghost? Furthermore, since there was no garden of Eden c. 4004 B.C.—nor even c. 1,800,000 B.C. in the period of Zinjanthropus—no Adam and no Eve back there, no serpent speaking Hebrew and, consequently, no Fall—no guilt—then what is all this talk about a general atonement? Unless Fall and Redemption, Disobedience and Atonement, are poetic names for the same psychological states of Ignorance and Illumination that the Hindus and the Buddhists also are talking about! In which case, what happens to the doctrine of the unique historical importance of the Incarnation and Crucifixion of Christ?

Meister Eckhart surely understood this when he preached

to his congregation: "It is more worth to God his being brought forth spiritually in the individual good soul than that he was born of Mary bodily." [23] And again: "God is in all things as being, as activity, as power." [24] Such teachings were condemned by John XXII; and Eckhart fortunately died before responding to the summons to Rome—or the Church would now have him on its record as well.

The great period of the breakthrough of the native European spirit against the imposed authority of decisions made by a lot of Levantine bishops at the Councils of Nicaea, Constantinople, Ephesus, and Chalcedon (fourth to eighth centuries A.D.), occurred in the twelfth and thirteenth centuries, in the period, precisely, of the rise of the great cathedrals: the period marked by Henry Adams as that of the greatest Christian unity—whereas actually it was a period of heresy bursting everywhere: Waldensians, Albigensians, and multitudes of others, the establishment of the Inquisition, and the Albigensian crusade.

As I see it, this breakthrough followed as the consequence of the courage of an increasing number of people of great stature to credit their own experience and to live by it against the dictates of authority. And I see the evidences of this courage in the spheres, successively, of feeling, thinking, and observation: love, philosophy, and science. I shall here deal only with the first, which marked the dawn, the first fair light, of the world we know today. It was eloquently and bravely announced at the very start of the twelfth century in the life and letters of Abelard's Heloise; defined psychologically in the poetry of the Troubadours and Minnesingers; celebrated with exquisite art in the Tristan romance of the great German poet Gottfried von Strassburg; and brought to its culminating statement in the unsurpassed Grail romance of the greatest poet of the Middle Ages, Wolfram von Eschenbach.

The beautiful though ugly story of Heloise and Abelard is known to all: of how he, in his middle thirties, the most brilliant intellectual of the schools of Paris, deliberately seduced her, a girl of seventeen; and, when she was about to bear their child, sent her for protection to his sister in Brittany, then, conscience-stricken, urged her to a secret marriage. She argued strongly against this, declaring, firstly, that domestic life would be beneath his dignity as a philosopher and, secondly, that she would rather be his mistress than bind him with a matrimonial chain. But he insisted, and, as the world knows, following the marriage, her uncle, the brutal canon Fulbert, sent a gang of thugs who castrated him, and he, in turn, sent Heloise to a convent. Then, after years of silence, not another word from him to her, she wrote to him:

"When little more than a girl, I took the hard vows of a nun, not from piety but at your command. If I now merit nothing from you, how vain I deem my labor! I can expect no reward from God, as I have done nothing from love of him. . . . God knows, at your command I would have followed or preceded you to fiery places. For my heart is not with me but with thee. . . . " [25]

Essentially the same sentiment is expressed in Gottfried's poem, a century later, in the words of his hero Tristan, where he states that for Isolt's love he would accept an "eternal death" in hell.[26] And again, seven centuries later—today, in the twentieth century—James Joyce's hero, Stephen Dedalus, in *A Portrait of the Artist as a Young Man*, declares to a Catholic schoolmate: "I will not serve that in which I no longer believe whether it call itself my home, my fatherland, or my church. . . . And I am not afraid to make a mistake, even a great mistake, a lifelong mistake, and perhaps as long as eternity too." [27]

[5]

Eros, Agape, Amor

In theological sermons we are used to hearing of a great distinction between fleshly and spiritual love, *eros* and *agapē*. The contrast and conflict were already recognized and argued by the early Christian Fathers and have been argued ever

since. An important point to be recognized, however, is that
the ideal of love, *amor*, of the lovers and poets of the Middle
Ages corresponded to neither of these. In the words, for example, of the troubadour Giraut de Borneil, "Love is born of
the eyes and the heart" (*Tam cum los oills el cor ama
parvenza*): the eyes recommend a specific image to the heart,
and the heart, "the noble heart," responds.[28] That is to say,
this love is specific, discriminative, personal, and elite. *Eros*,
on the other hand, is indiscriminate, biological: the urge, one
might say, of the organs. And *agapē*, too, is indiscriminate:
Love thy neighbor (whoever he may be) as thyself. Whereas,
here, in the sentiment and experience of *amor*, we have something altogether new—European—individual. And I know of
nothing like it, earlier, anywhere in the world.

In Sufism and the Indian "left-hand path," with which this
concept and experience of *amor* has often been compared, the
woman is treated rather as a vessel or symbol of divine import
than as a person, individual in character and charm. She is
commonly of lower caste, and the consortium is undertaken
as a programmed spiritual discipline. Whereas here, on the
contrary, the woman was almost always of equal or superior
rank and honored for and as herself. In an essay in *The Dance
of Shiva* on the discipline of a Hindu-Buddhist "left-hand"
cult called "Sahaja" (root meaning "cognate, innate," hence,
"spontaneous"), the late Dr. Ananda K. Coomaraswamy has
described their aim as a mystic realization of "the self-oblivion
of earthly lovers locked in each other's arms, where 'each is
both.'" "Each as individual," he explains, "has now no more
significance for the other than the gates of heaven for one
who stands within. . . . The beloved may be in every ethical
sense of the word unworthy. . . . The eye of love perceives
her divine perfection and infinity, and is not deceived. . . .
The same perfection and infinity are present in every grain of
sand and in the raindrop as much as in the sea."[29] In the Oriental literature, the great principle of this erotic discipline is
described as the transformation of *kāma* into *prema* through
"self-elimination." *Kāma*, "desire, lust," is exactly *eros*.

Prema, "divine love," which is described as "the fulfillment of divine desires in and through our whole being," [30] may not correspond to *agapē*, as today understood in the Christian fold; however, in the orgiastic "love feast" (*agapē*) of such early Gnostic sects as the Alexandrian-Syrian Phibionites of the first five Christian centuries—described with horror, yet in detail, by the renegade eye-witness Saint Epiphanius (c. 315–402 A.D.) [31]—essentially the same ideal may be recognized of a conscientiously amoral, depersonalized "love-in." And there can be no doubt that in twelfth- and thirteenth-century Europe, the period of the Troubadours, there developed in certain quarters of the rampant Albigensian heresy a formidable resurgence of this type of religious thought and practice. Denis de Rougemont, in his learned volume *Love in the Western World*,[32] has even argued that the cult and poetry of *amor* was a by-product of this "Church of Love."

It seems to me essential to remark, however, that the aim in the European "cult" (if we may call it that) of *amor* was not in any sense ego-extinction in a realization of nonduality, but the opposite: ego-ennoblement and -enrichment through an altogether personal experience of love's poignant pain— "love's sweet bitterness and bitter sweetness," to quote Gottfried—in willing affirmation of the irremediable yearning that animates all relationships in this passing world of ephemeral individuation. It is true that in the doctrine of love represented by the Troubadours marriage was not only of no interest but actually contrary to the whole feeling, and that likewise in India, the highest type of love, from the point of view of the Sahajiya cult, was not of husband and wife, but (to quote one authority), "the love that exists most privately between couples, who are absolutely free in their love from any consideration of loss and gain, who defy society and transgress the law and make love the be-all of life." [33] It is almost certainly not by mere coincidence that the greatest Indian poetic celebration of this ideal of adulterous (*parakīya*) love—namely the Gita Govinda ("Song of the Cowherd") of the young poet Jayadeva—is of a date exactly contemporary with the flowering in Europe of the Tristan romance (c. 1175-A.D.).[34] A moment's comparison of the two romances, however, immediately sets apart the two worlds of spiritual life. The Indian lover, Krishna, is a god; the European, Tristan, a man. The Indian work is allegorical of the yearning of flesh (symbolized in Radha) for the spirit and of spirit (symbolized in Krishna) for the flesh, or, in Coomaraswamy's terms, symbolic of "the 'mystic union' of the finite with its infinite ambient"; [35] whereas the European poets, Thomas of Britain (c. 1185), Eilhart von Oberge (c. 1190), Béroul (c. 1200), and Gottfried von Strassburg (c. 1210), the four leading masters of the Tristan cycle, have represented the lovers as human, all too human—overwhelmed by a daemonic power greater than themselves. In the poems of the first three, the power of the potion, the releaser of the passion, is treated simply as of magic. In Gottfried's work, on the other hand, a religious dimension opens—heretical and dangerous—when he states, and states again, that the power is of the goddess Minne (Love). And then, moreover, to ensure his point, when the lovers flee to the forest, he brings them to a secret grotto of the goddess, described explicitly as an ancient heathen chapel of love's purity, and with a bed—a wondrous crystalline bed—in the place of the Christian altar.

Now Saint Augustine had already compared Christ's death on the Cross to a marriage: "Like a bridegroom," he wrote, "Christ went forth from his chamber, he went out with a presage of his nuptials into the field of the world. He ran like a giant exulting on his way and came to the marriage bed of the cross, and there in mounting it he consummated his marriage. And when he perceived the sighs of the creature, he lovingly gave himself up to the torment in place of his bride, and he joined himself to the woman forever." [36]

Saint Bernard (1091–1153) in his passionate "Sermons on the Song of Songs" had provided further inspiration for Gottfried's radical secularization of the sacred in an area of life utterly rejected and condemned by the authorities of Rome, whose very name, ROMA, was the contrary, the reverse spelling, of AMOR. Marriage in the Middle Ages was little better (from the point of view of the Troubadours) than sacramentalized rape: an affair exclusively of family, political, and social concerns, whereby the woman (or rather, teen-age girl) was used for the ends of others, and into which the accident of love could fall only as a calamity, perilous to the social order as well as to the lives—both eternal and earthly—of its victims. Woman, with her power both to experience and to inspire love, was—like Eve, her prototype— the "Door of the Devil" (*janua diaboli*). And Bernard, in his sermons on the Song of Songs, assigning to the passion of love a yonder-worldly, virginal, nonexistent object, had striven with every ounce of his zeal to turn this energy of the glory of life to the ends ordained by the Church.

"I think," he preached, "that the chief reason why the Invisible God wished to become visible in the flesh, and to live as a Man among men, was manifestly this—that He might first win back the affections of fleshly creatures who could not love otherwise than in the flesh, to the salutary love of Himself in the Flesh, and thus step by step lead them finally to a love that is purely spiritual. Was it not, ultimately, in this degree of love that they were standing who said: *Behold, we have left all things, and have followed Thee* [Matthew 19:27] [37]

"By desire, not by reason, am I impelled," he exclaimed before his congregation. "A sense of modesty protests, it is true: love, however, conquers. . . .

"I am not unmindful of the fact that the *king's honor loveth judgment* [Psalm 99:4]. It is not restrained by counsel; it is not checked by a sense of false modesty; it is not subject to reason.—I ask, I implore, I entreat with all my heart: *Let him kiss me with the kiss of his mouth* [Canticles 1:2]." [38]

"Thus, therefore, even in this body of ours the joy of the Bridegroom's presence is frequently felt, but not the fullness of it; for although His visitation gladdens the heart, the alternation of His absence makes it sad. And this the beloved must of necessity endure until she has once laid down the burden of the body of flesh, when she too will fly aloft borne up on the wings of her desires, freely making her way through the realms of contemplation and with unimpeded mind following her Beloved *withersoever He goeth* [Apocalypse 14:4]." [39]

Essentially, Bernard was doing with the name and figure of Christ exactly what the Indian Jayadeva, half a century later, was to do with the name and figure of Krishna, the Incarnation of Vishnu, lover and seducer of the buxom matron Radha and the other married Gopis, luring them with his flute from their husbands' earthly beds to the rapture of divine love in the forest of Vrindavan. But the Hebrew Song of Songs itself—a composite of scraps of erotic Levantine poetry, such as abounds, for example, throughout the *Arabian Nights*— had already been reinterpreted, before admission to the Canon, as metaphoric of this same way of the love between Yahweh and Israel.

> How graceful are your feet in sandals,
>   O queenly maiden!
> Your rounded thighs are like jewels,
>   the work of a master hand.
> Your navel is a rounded bowl
>   that never lacks mixed wine.
> Your belly is a heap of wheat
>   encircled with lilies. [40]

Whether as Krishna, Yahweh, or Christ—and the bride as Radha, the Holy Jewish Race, Holy Mother Church, or the individual soul: the lover in all these devotional traditions is an agent of spiritual transformation, converting *eros* into *agapē*, *kāma* into *prema*; whereas in the Tristan legend the two lovers are equally of this world. In India the ultimate union is registered as the realization of *identity*, an experience of non-duality, where "each is both." In Israel and the Catholic Church, the union is a *relationship*, where the two terms, God and Creature, though united, remain distinct. Yet in both contexts, the tide of thought is away from the marriages of *this* world to *that*. Saint Paul's announcement that "the desires of the flesh are against the Spirit, and the desires of the Spirit are against the flesh" (Galatians 5:17), and Coomaraswamy's statement that when "lovers locked in each others arms" realize self-oblivion, "each as individual has now no more significance for the other than the gates of heaven for one who stands within," amount, in the end, to much the same: namely, a spitting out of this world. That is not the mood of the Tristan romance, or of anything that has ever been really great and typical of Europe, from the period of Homer to *Finnegans Wake.*

If $a \neq\, = x$ be taken as the formula of the Oriental, Buddhist-Vedantic order of experience, and $a\,R\,x$ the Levantine, Hebrew-Christian-Islamic, then $a\,R\,b$ will represent the European, where b is not an assumed being or personality transcendent of temporality, but another phenomenal entity, like a: as were both Tristan and Isolt. The Greeks and Romans, the Celtic and Germanic peoples have generally tended to maintain a decent respect for the interests and value judgments of the empirical sphere of experience. And yet their perceptions have not been confined to this foreground view. There is more to $a\,R\,b$ than meets the eye.

In Gottfried's representation, for example, of the mystery of love, as symbolized particularly in the grotto chapel of the goddess Minne, something not a little like the Indian *sahaja* concept appears, when he writes that the young lovers, when they had drunk of the potion, "realized that there was between them just one mind, one heart, and one will. . . . The sense of a difference between them was gone." [41] Through the influence of the potion of love, that is to say, a dimension had opened beyond the plane of time and space, wherein the two experienced themselves as one, though in the field of space and time they remained two—and not only two, but each as an individual irreplaceable, not at all (as in Coomaraswamy's formula) of no more significance for each other "than the gates of heaven for one who stands within." For according to the principle of *amor*, as opposed to both *agapē* and *eros*, the particular person, the form and character of the individuation of perfection, continues to be of great moment, even of central concern, and "in every ethical sense" respected. An appropriate formula for *this* mode of experience of the Love dimension, then, would be, where *a* is Tristan and *b* Isolt:

$$a \neq \, = x = \, \neq b$$

while in the field of space and time, which is where that dimension is experienced:

$$a \, \mathrm{R} \, b$$

the experience of the *x* dimension being a function of R.

In Gottfried's poem, tragedy follows the inability of the characters to reconcile love (*minne*), on one hand, and honor (*ere*), on the other. Gottfried himself and his century were torn between the two.[42] The Love Grotto in the dangerous forest represents the dimension of the depth experience(*x*) and King Mark's court, the world in which that experience has to be borne. Holiness, the ideal, and intimations of eternity are focused in the cave, which, though described as if in Cornwall, is not a historical place but a shared psychological condition: "I have known that cave," states the poet, "since I was eleven years old, yet have never set foot in Cornwall." *[43] Though himself probably a cleric, and certainly learned in theology, Gottfried is openly disdainful of current Christian doctrines.[44] (See especially the poet's comment on the surprising outcome of Isolt's dishonesty in her trial by ordeal for adultery: "There it was revealed and confirmed for all the world that the very virtuous Christ is as yielding as a wind-blown sleeve: he adapts himself and goes along whatever way he is pressed, as readily and easily as anyone could ask.") He prays for inspiration not to the Trinity and saints but to Apollo and the Muses; shows the destiny of his characters to have been governed neither by their own free will nor by God but by the goddess of the Grotto, Minne, "Love," and employs the very language of Saint Bernard in celebration of the eucharist to recommend to his readers the lovers in adultery on their blessed crystalline bed.

* Compare Cusanus, supra, p. 190, and Black Elk, supra pp. 80 and 116.

We read their life, we read their death,
And to us it is sweet as bread.
Their life, their death, are our bread.
So lives their life, so lives their death,
So live they still and yet are dead
And their death is the bread of the living.[45]

Chiefly, Gottfried's inspiration had sprung from his recognition in the Celtic legend, compounded of Pictish, Irish, Welsh, Cornish, and Breton elements, an order of poetic imagery congenial to his own mode of experience. It was a legend rooted, like all Arthurian romance, in the most ancient native European mythological tradition—that of the old megalithic, bronze-age goddess of many names, mother of the gods and the immanent power of all nature: the earth, not as dust (Genesis 3:19) but as the source, the living body out of which all things proceed and to which they return at peace. Moreover, that Gottfried knew of whom he was speaking when he wrote of the goddess Minne is evident in his statement (among others) that her chapel, the grotto, *la fossiure a la gent amant*,[46] had been designed and built for lovers by giants in pre-Christian times. The Grail legend, also, had sprung from that pagan base. However, whereas in the Tristan legend the tragical theme is of a dissociation between the spheres of nature and society, sincerity and religion, the timeless forest and the time-bound court, love and life, in the Grail legend the leading theme is of the healing of that breach: a renewal of the Waste Land of the Christian social order through a miracle of uncorrupted nature, the integrity of a noble, resolute heart.

The earliest extant version of this most profound European legend is the *Perceval, Li Contes del Graal* (c. 1181–1191) of Chrétien de Troyes, the court poet of the Countess Marie de Champagne. Chrétien was apparently a clergyman, a canon of the Abbey of Saint-Loup.[47] The story had been assigned to him, he declares, by Count Philip of Flanders, who had presented him with a "book" in which the legend was contained.[48] But he left his poem unfinished. Like all his work, it is fluent and charming. However he here shows little sense for the import of the symbols and may have felt that they went against his grain.

The best-known version of the Grail legend is the one that inspired Tennyson—a late version translated by Malory from the work of a Cistercian monk, *La Queste del Saint Graal* (c. 1215–1230)—in which the Grail is identified with the chalice of the Last Supper, and its quest is achieved by the saintly youth Galahad, who is not, like Perceval, a married man, but a knightly monk, absolutely chaste, whose achievement consists not in service to this world but in leaving it for heaven together with the Grail.[49]

The primary source of the Grail symbol, on the other hand, was the vessel of ambrosial drink of the Celtic sea-god, Manannan (compare supra, p. 201, and the cup in Figure 10).[50] A second sphere of association was with the sacramental bowls of the late Classical Orphic sects that were brought into northern Europe during the Gallo-Roman period[51] and which, though indeed equivalent in a way to the Christian chalice of the Redeemer's blood, referred to a mystery rather of inward illumination than of reconciliation with an angry god. And one of the most impressive things about the great *Parzival* of the master poet Wolfram von Eschenbach (an exact contemporary of Gottfried) is the way in which the author linked his central symbol to both of these early contexts, the Celtic and the Classical, while at the same time suggesting the relevance of its legend to the cure of the malaise of his time. In his work, the Grail is not a vessel at all but a stone, "The Wish of Paradise," named "lapsit exillis" (*lapis exilis*, "little, feeble, or uncomely stone"), which, as we read in a late alchemical work, the *Rosarium philosophorum*, was a name of the Philosopher's Stone.[52] This alchemical Grail, Wolfram declares, was carried from heaven to earth by the angels who had remained neutral when Satan turned against God and the war in heaven ensued. They had been those, so to say, "in the middle," " 'twixt black and white." But such a stone, brought down by angels, suggests the Ka'aba of Islam. Thus Wolfram makes an explicit effort to assimilate to his symbol Islamic as well as Christian themes. The Grail, for him, was a cult-transcending talisman of cross-cultural associations, pointing to an image of man ("The Wish of Paradise") released from ecclesiastical authority, perfected in his nature through his own personal adventure, serving the world not through servitude but through mastery, and through love fulfilled, not ravaged and destroyed.

For, in connection with the Grail Quest, the obvious question arises as to why anyone in the Middle Ages should have thought it necessary to embark on such a lonely, dangerous enterprise when the Holy Mass, with Christ himself on the altar, was being celebrated, right next door, every day. The answer—simply and plainly—is that the Mass was an ecclesiastical sacrament associated with a doctrine of vicarious salvation, administered in those centuries, furthermore, by a clergy notoriously corrupt and protected by Augustine's antidonatist argument, the dogma, namely, of the incorruptibility of the sacrament on which salvation hung, no matter what the moral character of the clergy by which it was administered. In contrast: the Grail is housed not in a church but in a castle; its guardian is not a priest but a king. It is carried not by an assortment of questionable males but by twenty-five young women, whose virtue must be unsullied, and the knight who achieves the quest, and so restores the Waste Land to bounty, succeeds through integrity of character, in the service of a singly focused love, *amor*.

In Wolfram's work, furthermore, a number of additional points are made, among which, the following:

(1) The knight, on his first visit to the Castle of the Grail, fails to achieve the aim of the quest because he acts as he has been taught to act, not on the impulse of his nature.

(2) He is told, subsequently, that no one who has failed on the first visit will ever have a second chance, yet he resolves to succeed notwithstanding, and, when he has done so, is told

that he has accomplished a miracle, since, through his integrity of character and persistence in resolve, he has caused the Trinity to change its rules.

(3) Following his first failure and the shame that falls upon him as a consequence, he renounces God and wanders for some five years in a Waste Land. And when he finally returns in his heart to God, it is *not* to the churchly sacramental theology of his mother and her clergy but to a view of God as a cosmic principle corresponding and responding to the movements—whether of love or of hate—of the individual heart.

(4) Parzival is striving to repair his failure through holding one-pointedly to this quest; yet what gains for him his victory is *not* directly his quest but the fervor and loyalty of his love —not for God but for a woman, whose very name, Condwiramurs (*Conduire amour*—in Old French, the nominative singular ends in -*s*), reveals her role as the guide and vessel of the energy of his life.

(5) Wolfram's ideal of love is neither that of the Church nor exactly that of the Troubadours' *amor*. The idea of marriage without love (the Church's view) he rejects, but he rejects also love in adultery. Love, for him, is absolute, singlefold, and for life. It makes no difference, furthermore, whether it is ritually sacramentalized. It is fulfilled in a union that amounts, in effect, to the only type of marriage worthy of the name.

(6) Parzival's half-brother is a Moslem, as noble as himself. "One might speak of them as two," states the author when they come together on a battlefield, "but they are actually one: the one substance, through loyalty doing itself much harm."

(7) Man's life is neither all black nor all white, nor can it ever be: but through integrity to oneself, to one's nature, the poet states, one trends toward the white, whereas irresolution augments the black. His hero's name he interprets, through the French, as *per-ce-val*, "through the middle."

(8) And finally, when the hero arrives the second time at

the Castle of the Grail, he is accompanied by his Moslem brother, Feirefiz; so that, in Wolfram's view, a noble heathen might attain to this goal inaccessible to most Christians. However, an amusing and most remarkable scene then takes place. For, when the Grail is brought in, the Moslem prince cannot see it. All he can see are the beautiful form and eyes of the lovely maiden queen, Repanse de Schoye (*Repense de Joie*), by whom it is carried. The Grail company becomes gradually aware of this alarming fact, and presently word arrives from the ancient, ageless Grail King Titurel, reposing on a couch in the next hall (an Arthurian counterpart, he was, of the old sea god, Manannan), that the reason the heathen cannot see the Grail is that he has not yet been baptized. An old priest thereupon enters who has baptized many heathen and he instructs Feirefiz in the doctrine of the Trinity. "Is that her god?" the Moslem asks. "If I accept that god, can I marry her?" Told "Yes!" he consents willingly, and the sacrament is administered. But what a strange baptism it is! For the empty font is first tilted toward the Grail, whereupon it fills with water from the boon-bestowing stone; so that, although the form of the rite is ecclesiastical, its content is of another order, namely, of the so-called *aqua permanens*, the water of life of the alchemists and of the ancient pre-Christian world (see, again, Figure 10).

Moreover, when the heathen, so baptized, beholds the Grail with his own eyes, there appears written upon it the following statement—which, I believe, is for the date 1210 A.D., unprecedented; to wit, as Feirefiz reads: IF ANY MEMBER OF THE GRAIL COMPANY SHOULD, BY THE GRACE OF GOD, BE GIVEN MASTERY OVER A FOREIGN FOLK, HE MUST NOT SPEAK TO THEM OF HIS RACE OR OF HIS NAME, AND MUST SEE TO IT THAT THEY GAIN THEIR RIGHTS.

It is my belief and argument, in conclusion, then, that:

(A) In these twelfth- and thirteenth-century works and words of Heloise, the Troubadours, Gottfried, and Wolfram, a noble, serious, profoundly significant secularization of the sense of the sacred is to be recognized, wherein the courage of love is the revealing power, opening, as it were, a dimension of union, wonder, and sweet mystery in the world of separate beings, not quenching all thereby in a yonder sea, but augmenting each in its own form and right to regard;

(B) that in rejecting absolutely the authority of the Church, these lovers and poets returned consciously and conscientiously to an earlier, pre-Christian, native European order of conscience, wherein the immanence of divinity was recognized in nature and its productions;

(C) but, then, also that, in this return, there was nevertheless a new factor, namely, a dissociation of the individual from the body of the group, as one unique in himself, who, if he is to realize his own potentialities, *must not* follow the paths or ways of any other but must discover himself his own. In fact, even in the strictly monastic Cistercian version of the legend, the *Queste del Saint Graal*, it is declared that when the knights of Arthur's court rode forth to adventure, they thought it would be disgraceful to start out in a group, but each entered the forest alone at a point that he had chosen, "there where he saw it most dark, and he found no way or path." [53]

[6]

The Western Individual

It is my thought, that the wealth and glory of the Western world, and of the modern world as well (in so far as it is still in spirit Western), is a function of this respect for the individual, not as a member of some sanctified consensus through which he is given worth,

$$a \, R \, x$$

nor as an indifferent name and form of that "same perfection and infinity . . . present in every grain of sand, and in the raindrop as much as in the sea,"

$$a \neq \, = x$$

but as an end and value in himself, unique in his *im*perfection, i.e., in his yearning, in his process of becoming not what he "ought" to be but what he is, actually and potentially: such a one as was never seen before.

This way of appreciating life was known already to the Greeks, in the Homeric epics, in Aeschylus, and in Pindar. Nietzsche, in *The Birth of Tragedy*, writes of the perfect union in Classical art of the Apollonian and Dionysian principles: delight in the dreamlike wonder of individuated forms together with a poignant—even rapturous—recognition of their impermanence, not as a refutation but as a heightening of the wonder of their moment in the sun. "Short," wrote Pindar, in celebration of the young winner of a wrestling match, "short is the space of time in which the happiness of mortal men groweth up, and even so, doth it fall to the ground when stricken down by adverse doom. Creatures of a day, what is any one? what is he not? Man is but a dream of a shadow; yet, when a gleam of sunshine cometh as a gift of heaven, a radiant light resteth on men, aye and a gentle life." [54] It was in this mode that Greek science developed, Greek science as well as Greek art: through a recognition and search for general archetypes or principles in individual instances, yet with a recognition also of the value of the instance in itself, and particularly of the exception as revelatory of principles and powers yet unknown, which is precisely the opposite view to that of archaic, Oriental, and Orthodox life, where anyone who picked up sticks on the sabbath was to be "stoned to death with stones by the congregation" (Numbers 15:32-36).

The coming of the Church to Europe reversed, for a time, the order of precedence in native European thought, placing the group before the individual, its fetishes above the quest for truth, and idiocy above genius (see I Corinthians 1:21: "For since, in the wisdom of God, the world did not know God through wisdom, it pleased God through the folly of what we preach to save those who believe"). The confessional, the heretic's death, and eternal hell were established, like the cherubim and turning sword at the gate of Paradise, to keep men *out* of the garden of an individual life. However, as the poet Blake found when he was walking, as he declares, "among the fires of hell, delighted with the enjoyments of Genius, which to Angels look like torment and insanity":

"A fool sees not the same tree that a wise man sees." And again:

"The apple tree never asks the beech how he shall grow; nor the lion, the horse, how he shall take his prey." [55]

If it was in the kingdom of the courageous heart, as in that of Heloise, that the first portents appeared of the new age dawning for the West, it was through those of the mind and the observant eye (philosophy and science) that the promise was fulfilled. Heloise in her life was mangled and the country of the Troubadours turned into an eloquent waste; yet the ideal of heterosexual love that prevails in the world today was originally hers and theirs. Moreover, the history of the poetry and song of the modern West commences with the works of the Troubadours.

And likewise, in philosophy: though the bold Scholastic effort to bring reason to bear on religion was summarily crushed with the publication of the authoritative Condemnations of 1277—where a catalogue of two hundred and nineteen philosophical propositions was condemned as contrary to Faith—what has triumphed in the modern world has been, obviously, not canonical but individual thought; so that, although as late as 1864, Pope Pius IX could state in a Syllabus of Errors, condemning rationalism, socialism, communism, naturalism, the separation of Church and State, freedom of the press and of religion, that "the Roman pontiff cannot and should not be reconciled and come to terms with progress, liberalism, and modern civilization," a century later John XXIII found it prudent, rather, to relent and to do just that—with what result, however, the Church itself is yet to learn. The Protestant theologian Rudolf Bultmann, who has been suggesting, meanwhile, what he calls a "demythologization," or rationalization, of the Christian religion, has found it necessary to hold—if there is to be any specifically "Christian" religion at all—to the Resurrection of Jesus from the grave, not as a mythic image, but as a fact—which is, of course, what has been the problem here, all along: the concretization of myth. Compare the so-called Second Letter of Peter (which is actually not of Peter but of some later hand): "For we did not follow cleverly devised myths when we made known to you the power and coming of our Lord Jesus Christ, but we were eye-witnesses of his majesty" (II Peter 1:16).

One can only suggest to these stubborn gentlemen that if, instead of insisting that their own mythology is history, they would work the other way and dehistoricize their mythology, they might recover contact with the spiritual possibilities of this century and salvage from what must otherwise be inevitable discard whatever may still be of truth to life in their religion.

For it is simply an incontrovertible fact that, with the rise of modern science, the entire cosmological structure of the Bible and the Church has been destroyed and not the cosmological only but the historical as well. The gradual, irresistible, steady development of this new realization of the wonder of the world and of man's place and possibilities within it, against every instrument of resistance of the Church—resistance even to the present hour—has been, and continues to be, the fruit of the labors of a remarkably small number of men with the wit and courage to oppose authority with accurate observation. Their work began inconspicuously in the period of Adelard of Bath (a contemporary of Heloise and Abelard), coming to two great moments of climax, first with the publication of Copernicus' *De revolutionibus orbium coelestium* (1543), and then of Darwin's *Origin of Species* (1859). The number of creative minds was few; yet the magnitude of the crisis brought about for the entire world by their probings of the wells of truth can hardly be overstated. For in the broadest view of the history of mankind, it can be said without exaggeration that, with the rise of the modern scientific method of research in the sixteenth and seventeenth centuries, and development in the eighteenth, nineteenth, and twentieth of the power-driven machine, the human race was brought across a

culture threshold of no less magnitude and import than that
of the invention of agriculture in the ninth or eighth millennium B.C. and the rise of the earliest cities and city states in the
fourth. Furthermore, just as the mythologies and rituals of the
primitive hunting and root-gathering tribes of the earlier
million-or-so years of human life had then to give place to
those that arose of the high bronze and iron age civilizations,
so also, now, must those of our outdated bronze and iron age
heritages give place to forms not yet imagined. And that they
are already giving place surely is clear. For, firstly, in so far as
the Waste Land condition recognized by the poets of the
Middle Ages persists within the Christian fold—where the
sense of the sacred is still officially dissociated from this earth
and its life (*mythic dissociation*) and the possibility of estab-
lishing a *relationship* with ultimate ends is still supposed to be
achievable only through participation in the faith and rites of
Christ's church (*social identification*)—the situation has
worsened, not improved, since, for many, not only is the
earth (as taught) mere dust, but the claims of the Church and
its book to supernatural authorship have been destroyed absolutely and forever. And the resultant sense of alienation from
value (variously interpreted in Marxian, Freudian, and Ex-
istentialist terms) is one of the most-discussed spiritual phenomena of our time. "Man is condemned," as Sartre says, "to
be free." [56] However, not all, even today, are of that supine
sort that must have their life values given them, cried at them
from the pulpits and other mass media of the day. For there
is, in fact, in quiet places, a great deal of deep spiritual quest
and finding now in progress in this world, outside the sanctified social centers, beyond their purview and control: in small
groups, here and there, and more often, more typically (as
anyone who looks about may learn), by ones and twos, there
entering the forest at those points which they themselves have
chosen, where they see it to be most dark, and there is no
beaten way or path.

Reference Notes

INTRODUCTION

1. Sigmund Freud, *The Interpretation of Dreams*, translated and edited by A. A. Brill, *The Basic Writings of Sigmund Freud* (New York: Random House, The Modern Library, 1938), p. 480.
2. C. G. Jung, "General Aspects of Dream Psychology," in *The Structure and Dynamics of the Psyche*, translated by R. F. C. Hull, Bollingen Series XX Vol. 8 (New York: Pantheon Books, 1960), pp. 277–78.
3. *Ibid.*, p. 253.
4. *Chāndogya Upaniṣad* 8.3.2.
5. *Kena Upaniṣad* 1:3 and 2:3.
6. *Tao Te Ching* 56.

I: THE FAIRY TALE

1. Johannes Bolte and Georg Polívka, *Anmerkungen zu den Kinder- und Hausmärchen der Brüder Grimm* (Leipzig: Dieterich'sche Verlagsbuchhandlung, 1915–1937), Vol. IV, pp. 443-44. To this "story-wife of Niederzwehren" we owe nineteen of the finest tales of the Grimm collection, namely numbers: 6, 9, 22, 29, 34, 58, 59, 61, 63, 71, 76, 89, 94, 98, 100, 102, 106, 108, 111.
2. Frau Wild gave stories 18, 30; Lisette gave variants of 41, 55, 105; Gretchen gave 2, 3, 154; Dortchen 13, 15, 24, 39, 46, 49, 56, 65, 88, 103, 105, parts of 52, 55, 60, and a variant of 34. *Die alte Marie* herself supplied 11, 26, 31, 44, 50, and a variant of 53.
3. Ludwig Hassenpflug's sisters, Jeanette and Amalie, gave stories 13, 14, 17, 20, 29, 41, 42, 53, part of 26, and variants of 61, 67, 76.
4. A family of eight sons and six daughters. Their contributions began only after publication of the first edition of Volume One (1812), but in the later editions some of their tales replaced earlier numbers. From their village of Bökendorf, near Brakel, come stories 7, 10, 16, 27, 60, 70, 72, 86, 91, 99, 101, 112, 113, 121, 123, 126, 129, 131, 134, 135, 139, and parts of 52, 97. The von Haxthausens gave also 133 and 143, from Münsterland, as well as some half dozen others from various parts of the country. (*Cf.* Bolte and Polívka, *op. cit.*, Vol. IV, pp. 437 ff.)
5. Richard Cleasby, *An Icelandic-English Dictionary*, (Oxford: Clarendon Press, 1874), Introduction, p. lxix.
6. This volume underwent revision for its final edition in 1856. It has recently been wholly reno-

vated, and increased to five sturdy volumes, under the editorship of Professors Johannes Bolte and Georg Polívka (*cf. op. cit.*).

7. From Bolte and Polívka, *op. cit.*, Vol. IV, p. 34.

8. Antti Aarne, *Verzeichnis der Märchentypen*, Folklore Fellows Communications, (Helsinki, 1911), Vol. I, No. 3. Johannes Bolte notes that the following are missing from Aarne's listing: *Animal tales*, 30, 80, 173, 190; *Ordinary folk tales*, 39, 43, 78, 109, 117, 137, 150, 154, 175, 177, 180, 182, 184, 196, 201–205, 208–210; *Jokes and anecdotes*, 77, 95, 119, 131, 162, 170, 200. (Bolte and Polívka, *op. cit.*, Vol. IV, pp. 467–70).

9. A review by Dr. Ruth Benedict will be found in *The Encyclopedia of the Social Sciences*, article, "Folklore"; one by Professor William H. Halliday, under the same heading in *The Encyclopedia Britannica*. A more detailed account with complete bibliography appears in Bolte and Polívka, *op. cit.*, Vol. V, pp. 239–64.

10. Theodor Benfey, *Pantschatantra: Fünf Bücher indischer Fabeln, Märchen und Erzählungen. Aus dem Sanskrit übersetzt mit Einleitung und Anmerkungen* (Leipzig: F. A. Brockhaus, 1859).

11. Benfey, *op. cit.*, p. xxvi.

12. Friedrich von der Leyen, *Das Märchen* (Leipzig, 3rd ed., 1925), pp. 147–48.

13. Archer Taylor, *The Black Ox*, Folklore Fellows Communications (Helsinki: 1927), Vol. XXIII, No. 70, p. 4.

14. Adapted from Antti Aarne, *Leitfaden der vergleichenden Märchenforschung*, Folklore Fellows Communications (Helsinki, 1913), Vol. II, No. 13, pp. 23–29. Cf. also, Taylor, *op. cit.*, p. 9, for a translation of the original list as given by Kaarle Krohn in *Mann und Fuchs* (Helsingfors, 1891), pp. 8–9.

15. Kaarle Krohn, *Die folkloristische Arbeitsmethode* (Oslo: Instituttet for Semmenlignende Kulturforskning, 1926), pp. 13–14.

16. *Ibid.*, p. 13.

17. Cf. Kaarle Krohn, *Bär (Wolf) und Fuchs* (Helsingfors, 1888); also, *Mann und Fuchs*.

18. Antti Aarne, *Verzeichnis der Märchentypen*, Folklore Fellows Communications (Helsingfors, 1910), Vol. I, No. 3. This work was re-edited and brought up to date in 1928 by the American folklorist Stith Thompson (Aarne and Thompson, *The Types of Folk-Tale*, Folklore Fellows Communications [Helsinki, second edition, 1964]) and in 1929 by the Russian N. P. Andrejev (*Ukazateli skazochnych syuzhetov po system Aarne* [Leningrad: 1929]). Professor Thompson has since prepared a gigantic index of motifs, *Motif-Index of Folk-Literature*, Indiana University Studies (Bloomington, Ind., second edition, 1955–1958).

19. Walter Anderson, in Lutz Mackensen, *Handwörterbuch des deutschen Märchens* (Berlin and Leipzig, 1934 ff.), Vol. II, article: "Geographisch-historische Methode." A good example of such a monograph is the above-noticed work of Archer Taylor, *The Black Ox*.

20. Friedrich von der Leyen, *op. cit.*, p. 36.

21. Müller always stressed descriptions of the sunset and sunrise. Other scholars, following his lead, cogitated on the lunar phases and the interplay of sun and moon. (E. Siecke, *Die Liebesgeschichte des Himmels*, 1892; *Die Urreligion der Indogermanen*, 1897), or on the terror of storms and winds (A. Kuhn, *Die Herabkunft des Feu-*

ers und des Göttertranks, 1859, 1886; W. Schwarz, *Die poetischen Naturerscheinungen der Griechen, Römer und Deutschen*, 1864–1879), or on the wonder of the stars (E. Stucken, *Astralmythen der Hebräer, Babylonier und Aegypter*, 1896–1907). For Müller's celebrated interpretation of "The Frog-King" (Grimm I) as a sun personification, see *Chips from a German Workshop* (London: Longmans, Green, and Co., 1880), Vol. II, pp. 249–52.

22. F. Max Müller, *op. cit.*, Vol. II, pp. 1–146 ("Comparative Mythology," 1856).

23. Cf. Edward B. Tylor, *Primitive Culture* (London: John Murray, 1871), Chapters VIII–X.

24. Cf. Jane Ellen Harrison, *Prolegomena to the Study of Greek Religion* (Cambridge: Cambridge University Press, 3rd ed., 1922).

25. Émile Durkheim, *Les Formes élémentaires de la vie religieuse* (Paris, 1912; 2nd ed., 1925); English translation (London: George Allen and Unwin, Ltd.; New York: The Macmillan Company, 1915), Book I, Chapter 1; Book II, Chapters 5–6.

26. Hugo Winckler, *Himmels- und Weltenbild der Babylonier, als Grundlage der Weltanschauung und Mythologie aller Völker* (Leipzig: J. C. Hinrichs, 1903), p. 49.

27. Ananda K. Coomaraswamy, "De la 'Mentalité Primitive,'" *Études traditionnelles*, 44e Année, Nos. 236, 237, 238 (Paris, 1939), p. 278.

28. Cf. Jacques Maritain, *Art and Scholasticism* (New York, Charles Scribner's Sons, 1930); Ananda K. Coomaraswamy, *The Transformation of Nature in Art* (Cambridge, Mass.: Harvard University Press, 1934); Heinrich Zimmer, *Kunstform und Yoga* (Berlin: Frankfurter Verlags-Anstalt, 1936).

II: BIOS AND MYTHOS

1. Fray Pedro Simon, *Noticias historiales de las conquistas de Tierra Firme en las Indias Occidentales* (Cuenca, 1627), published in Lord Kingsborough's *Antiquities of Mexico* (London: R. Havell, 1830–1848), Vol. VIII, pp. 263–64.

2. Adolf Bastian, *Ethnische Elementargedanken in der Lehre vom Menschen* (Berlin: Weidmannsche Buchhandlung, 1895), p. ix.

3. Adolf Bastian, *Das Beständige in den Menschenrassen und die Spielweite ihrer Veränderlichkeit* (Berlin: Dietrich Reimer, 1868), p. 88.

4. Franz Boas, *The Mind of Primitive Man* (New York: The Macmillan Company, 1911), p. 104.

5. *Ibid.*, p. 228.

6. Franz Boas, *The Mind of Primitive Man* (New York: The Macmillan Company, 1938).

7. Durkheim, *Les Formes élémentaires de la vie religieuse*, pp. 15–21. Contrast Immanuel Kant, *Kritik der reinen Vernunft*, Einleitung and I. "Transzendentale Elementarlehre."

8. See Géza Róheim's analysis of Malinowski's fallacy, "The Oedipus Complex, Magic and Culture," *Psychoanalysis and the Social Sciences*, (New York: International Universities Press, 1950), Vol. II, pp. 173–228.

9. Winckler, *op. cit.*; also, same author, *Die babylonische Geisteskultur in ihrer Beziehung zur Kulturentwicklung der Menschheit* (Leipzig: Quelle und Meyer, 1907).

10. James H. Breasted, *The Conquest of Civilization* (New York:

Harper and Brothers, 1926); G. Elliot Smith, *Human History* (New York: W. W. Norton and Company, 1929); W. J. Perry, *The Children of the Sun, A Study in the Early History of Civilization* (New York: E. P. Dutton and Company, n.d.).

11. Harold Peake and Herbert John Fleure, *Peasants and Potters* (New Haven, Conn.: Yale University Press, 1927).

12. V. Gordon Childe, *New Light on the Most Ancient East* (New York, 1934); *What Happened in History* (New York: D. Appleton-Century, 1934).

13. Sylvanus G. Morley, *The Ancient Maya* (Stanford, Calif.: Stanford University Press; London: Oxford University Press, 1946).

14. Leo Frobenius, *Geographische Kulturkunde* (Leipzig: Friedrich Brandstetter, 1904), pp. 443–664.

15. Adolf E. Jensen, *Das religiöse Weltbild einer frühen Kultur* (Stuttgart: August Schröder Verlag, 2nd ed., 1949).

16. G. F. Scott Elliot, *Prehistoric Man and His Story* (London: Seeley, Service, 1920), pp. 255–271.

17. Twenty-ninth International Congress of Americanists, Museum of Natural History, New York City, September 7, 1949, joint paper by Dr. Robert von Heine-Geldern and Dr. Gordon F. Ekholm, "Significant Parallels in the Symbolic Arts of Southern Asia and Middle America." This paper was supported by the evidence of a temporary exhibit housed in the Museum, as well as by a paper read in the same session by Dr. Carl Schuster, "The Circum-Pacific and Oceanic Distribution of Some Body-Markings and Petroglyphic Designs."

18. Betty J. Meggers, Clifford Evans, and Emilio Estrada, *Early Formative Period of Coastal Ecuador: The Valdivia and Machalilla Phases* (Washington, D.C.: Smithsonian Institution, 1965).

19. Peter H. Buck (Te Rangi Hiroa), *Vikings of the Sunrise* (New York: Frederick A. Stokes, 1938), p. 314.

20. Carl O. Sauer, *Agricultural Origins and Dispersals* (New York: The American Geographical Society, 1952); see also his article, "Cultivated Plants of South and Central America," in Julian H. Steward (ed.), *Handbook of South American Indians* (Washington, D.C.: Smithsonian Institution, Bureau of American Ethnology, Bulletin 143, 1950), Vol. 6, pp. 487–543.

21. C. C. Uhlenbeck, "The Indo-Germanic Mother Language and Mother Tribes Complex," *American Anthropologist*, 1937, XXXIX, 385–93.

22. J. Vendryes, *Le langage* (Paris: La Renaissance du livre, 1921), pp. 356–57.

23. See, for example, Leo Frobenius, *Kulturgeschichte Afrikas* (Zurich: Phaidon Verlag), and Jensen, *op. cit.*

24. For a review of the universal archetypes of the "adventure of the hero" and "cosmogonic cycle," see Joseph Campbell, *The Hero with a Thousand Faces*, The Bollingen Series XVII (New York: Pantheon Books, 1949).

25. Géza Róheim, "Dream Analysis and Field Work in Anthropology," *Psychoanalysis and the Social Sciences* (New York: International Universities Press, 1947), Vol. I, p. 90.

26. A. R. Radcliffe-Brown, *The Andaman Islanders* (Cambridge: Cambridge University Press, 1933), pp. 177–79.

27. Géza Róheim, *The Origin and Function of Culture* (New York:

Nervous and Mental Disease Monographs, 1943), p. 51.

28. Ananda K. Coomaraswamy, *Recollection, Indian and Platonic*, Supplement to the Journal of the American Oriental Society, Number 3, April–June 1944, p. 18.

29. Ananda K. Coomaraswamy, *Hinduism and Buddhism* (New York: Philosophical Library, n.d.), p. 6.

30. Géza Róheim, *The Origin and Function of Culture*, p. 17.

31. Adolf Portmann, "Das Ursprungsproblem," *Eranos-Jahrbuch 1947* (Zurich: Rhein-Verlag, 1948), p. 27.

32. Róheim, *The Origin and Function of Culture*, p. 100.

33. William King Gregory, "Marsupialia," *Encyclopaedia Britannica*, 14th edition, XIV: 975–76.

34. George Bernard Shaw, *Back to Methuselah* (New York: Brentano's, 1921), pp. 235 ff.

35. Róheim, *The Origin and Function of Culture*, p. 17.

36. *Ibid.*, p. 81.

37. *Ibid.*

38. *Ibid.*, p. 82.

39. James Joyce, *A Portrait of the Artist as a Young Man* (New York: The Viking Press, 1964 ed.), p. 204.

40. *Muṇḍaka Upaniṣad* 1.1. 4–6. Translation by Robert Ernest Hume, *The Thirteen Principal Upanishads* (London: Oxford University Press, 1921), pp. 366–67.

41. *Ibid.*, 1.2. 8–11, in Hume, *op. cit.*, pp. 368–69.

42. John 3:5–6.

43. Géza Róheim, *The Eternal Ones of the Dream* (New York: International Universities Press, 1945), p. 116.

44. Richard Thurnwald, "Primitive Initiations- und Wiedergeburtsriten," *Eranos-Jahrbuch 1939* (Zurich: Rhein-Verlag, 1940), pp. 364–66. This entire volume, by the way, should be consulted by anyone doubting the universality of the rebirth idea.

45. *Ibid.*, p. 369.

46. Alice C. Fletcher, *The Hako: A Pawnee Ceremony*, Twenty-second Annual Report, Bureau of American Ethnology (Washington, D.C., 1904), Part 2, p. 27.

47. *Cf.* Jeff King, Maud Oakes, and Joseph Campbell, *Where the Two Came to Their Father: A Navaho War Ceremonial*, The Bollingen Series I (New York: Pantheon Books, 1943).

48. Ananda K. Coomaraswamy, "Primitive Mentality," *Figures of Speech or Figures of Thought* (London: Luzac, 1946), p. 220. The italics are Dr. Coomaraswamy's.

49. Róheim, *The Origin and Function of Culture*, p. 93.

III: PRIMITIVE MAN AS METAPHYSICIAN

1. Boas, *The Mind of Primitive Man*, p. 156.

2. A. L. Kroeber (ed.), *Anthropology Today* (Chicago: University of Chicago Press, 1953).

3. William James, *Pragmatism* (New York: Longmans, Green and Company, 1907), Lecture I, "The Present Dilemma in Philosophy."

4. Franz Boas, *Race, Language and Culture* (New York: The Macmillan Company, 1940): "The Ethnological Significance of Esoteric Doctrines" (1902), p. 314.

5. Paul Radin, *Primitive Man as Philosopher* (New York and London: D. Appleton and Company, 1927), pp. 247–52.

6. Boas, *Race, Language and Culture*, p. 156.

7. *Ibid.*, p. 157.

8. Natalie Curtis, *The Indians' Book* (New York: Harper and Brothers, 1907), pp. 315–16.
9. *Bṛhadāraṇyaka Upaniṣad* I. iv. 1–5.
10. See also Heinrich Zimmer, *The King and the Corpse*, The Bollingen Series XI (New York: Pantheon Books, 1948; 2nd ed., with index, 1956), pp. 239 ff.
11. *The Prose Edda*, Gylfaginning IV–VIII.
12. Ovid, *Metamorphoses* I, 21.
13. Cf. Henri Frankfort, *Kingship and the Gods* (Chicago: University of Chicago Press, 1948), p. 25 and *passim;* see Index under "Ptah."
14. *Vedāntasāra*, 55–56.
15. Immanuel Kant, *Prolegomena zu einer jeden künftigen Metaphysik, die als Wissenschaft wird auftreten können*, paragraphs 57–58.
16. *Bhagavad Gītā*, chapter 10, abridged.

17. Morris Edward Opler, *Myths and Tales of the Jicarilla Apache Indians*, Memoirs of the American Folklore Society, XXXI (New York: G. E. Stechert and Co., 1938), pp. 133–34.
18. Aeschylus, *Heliades*, frag. 70.
19. Foreword to Joseph Epes Brown, *The Sacred Pipe: Black Elk's Account of the Seven Rites of the Oglala Sioux* (Norman, Okla.: University of Oklahoma Press, 1953), p. xx.
20. Sri Ramakrishna Centenary Committee, *The Cultural Heritage of India* (Mayavati, India: Advaita Ashrama, 1936), Vol. II, pp. 518–19.
21. Boas, *Race, Language and Culture*, pp. 314–15.
22. Radin, *Primitive Man as Philosopher*, pp. 211–12.
23. *Ibid.*, p. 386.
24. Curtis, *The Indians' Book*, p. 314.

IV: MYTHOGENESIS

1. Joseph Epes Brown, *op. cit.*, pp. 3–4 and 80.
2. *Ibid.*, p. 4, note 2.
3. Ovid, *Metamorphoses*, III, 143–252.
4. Brown, *op. cit.*, p. 5, note 4.
5. *Ibid.*, pp. x–xii.
6. See George E. Hyde, *Red Cloud's Folk: A History of the Oglala Sioux* (Norman, Okla.: University of Oklahoma Press, 1937), p. 3.
7. Brown, *op. cit.*, p. 108.
8. *Liber XXIV philosophorum*, Proposition II; Clemens Bäumker, "Das pseudo-hermetische 'Buch der vierundzwanzig Meister' (Liber XXIV philosophorum)," in *Abhandlungen aus dem Gebiete der Philosophie und ihrer Geschichte. Festgabe zum 70. Geburtstag Georg Freiherrn von Hertling* (Freiburg im Breisgau: Herdersche Verlagshand-

lung, 1913), p. 31; as cited in Joseph Campbell, *The Masks of God*, Vol. III, *Occidental Mythology*, p. 522, and Vol. IV, *Creative Mythology*, pp. 31, 36, and 135.
9. James G. Frazer, *The Golden Bough*, one-volume edition (New York and London: The Macmillan Company, 1922), p. 386.
10. Brown, *op. cit.*, pp. 3–7.
11. *Ibid.*, p. 23.
12. *Ibid.*, p. 25.
13. Francis La Flesche, *War Ceremony and Peace Ceremony of the Osage Indians*, Bulletin No. 101, Bureau of American Ethnology (Washington, D.C., 1939), pp. 62–63; cited by Brown, *op. cit.*, p. 21.
14. *Maitri Upaniṣad* 7.7, in Hume, *op. cit.*, p. 454.
15. *Chāndogya Upaniṣad* 3.13.7, in Hume, *op. cit.*, p. 209.

16. *Ibid.*, 3.18.1–2, in Hume, *op. cit.*, pp. 213–14.

17. Brown, *op. cit.*, p. 6, note 9.

18. C. G. Jung, *The Integration of the Personality* (New York and Toronto: Farrar & Reinhart, 1939), p. 189.

19. Brown, *op. cit.*, pp. 5–6, notes 6 and 7.

20. Rudolf Otto, *The Idea of the Holy* (London: Oxford University Press, 3rd printing, revised and enlarged, 1925), pp. 1–4.

21. Brown, *op. cit.*, p. 7, note 10.

22. *Ibid.*, pp. 7–9.

23. Hyde, *op. cit.*, p. 3.

24. Gordon R. Willey and Philip Phillips, *Method and Theory in American Archaeology* (Chicago: University of Chicago Press, 1958), pp. 158–66.

25. Carl O. Sauer, "Cultivated Plants in South and Central America," in Julian H. Steward (ed.), *Handbook of South American Indians*, Bulletin 143, Bureau of American Ethnology (Washington, D.C., 1944–1957), Vol. VI (1950), pp. 487–543.

26. My authorities for this summary are Richard S. MacNeish, "The Food-gathering and Incipient Agricultural Stage of Prehistoric Middle America," in Robert Wauchope (ed.), *Handbook of Middle American Indians* (Austin: University of Texas Press, 1964–1967), Vol. I, pp. 413–26; Paul C. Mangelsdorf, Richard S. MacNeish, and Gordon R. Willey, "Origins of Agriculture in Middle America," *ibid.*, Vol. I, pp. 427–45; Philip Phillips, "The Role of Transpacific Contacts in the Development of New World Pre-Columbian Civilizations," *ibid.*, Vol. IV, pp. 296–315; and Daniel Del Solar, "Interrelations of Mesoamerica and the Peru-Ecuador Area," *Kroeber Anthropological Society Papers*, No. 34, Spring 1966.

27. Joseph Campbell, *The Masks of God*, Vol. I, *Primitive Mythology* (New York: The Viking Press, 1959), pp. 205–15.

28. Pilot Chart of the North Pacific Ocean, No. 1401, Hydrographic Office, Navy Department, Washington, D.C., as cited in Betty J. Meggars, Clifford Evans, and Emilio Estrada, *op. cit.*, Figure 103, facing p. 168.

29. *Ibid.*, p. 160.

30. *Ibid.*, Plates 160–91; see especially, Plate 184, Figures C and D.

31. Leo Frobenius, *Geographische Kulturkunde* (Leipzig: Friedrich Brandstetter, 1904), p. 450; cited in Campbell, *The Masks of God*, Vol. I, *Primitive Mythology*, p. 205.

32. Adolf E. Jensen, *Das Weltbild einer frühen Kultur* (Stuttgart: August Schröder, 2nd ed., 1949); *Mythos und Kult bei Naturvölkern* (Wiesbaden: Franz Steiner Verlag, 1960).

33. For examples, see *The Masks of God*, Vol. I, *Primitive Mythology*, pp. 151–225.

34. Henry Schoolcraft, *Algic Researches* (New York: Harper and Brothers, 1839); reprinted in Mentor L. Williams, *Schoolcraft's Indian Legends* (East Lansing, Mich.: Michigan State University Press, 1956), pp. 58–61; "Mon-daw-min, or The Origin of Indian Corn, An Odjibwa Tale."

35. Willey and Phillips, *op. cit.*, pp. 163–70.

36. Gordon F. Eckholm, "A Possible Focus of Asiatic Influence in the Late Classic Cultures of Mesoamerica," *Memoirs of the Society of American Archaeology*, Vol. XVIII, No. 3, Part 2 (January 1953), pp. 72–89; also *ibid.*, "The New Orientation toward Problems of Asiatic-American Relationships," in *New Interpretations of Aboriginal*

American Culture History, 75th Anniversary Volume of the Anthropological Society of Washington (Washington, D.C., 1955), pp. 59–109. Likewise, Robert Heine-Geldern, "The Origin of Ancient Civilizations and Toynbee's Theories," *Diogenes*, No. 13 (Spring, 1956), pp. 93–96; *ibid.*, "Theoretical Considerations Concerning the Problem of Pre-Columbian Contacts between the Old World and the New," *Selected Papers of the Fifth International Congress of Anthropological Sciences*, September 1956 (Philadelphia: University of Pennsylvania Press, 1960), pp. 277–81; and *ibid.*, "The Problem of Transpacific Influences in Mesoamerica," in Wauchope (ed.), *op. cit.*, Vol. IV, pp. 277–295. A clumsy reply to all this by Philip Phillips immediately follows the last of the above-named Heine-Geldern papers, in Wauchope (ed.), *op. cit.*, Vol. IV, pp. 296–315.

37. *The Masks of God*, Vol. I, *Primitive Mythology*, pp. 283–86.

38. *Time*, August 6, 1956, p. 42, reporting a test made on charcoal from a Texas site at Louisville, near Dallas.

39. *The New York Times*, June 1, 1968.

40. Abbé H. Breuil, *Four Hundred Centuries of Cave Art* (Montignac, Dordogne: Centre d'Études et de Documentation Préhistoriques, n.d.), p. 234.

41. See *The Masks of God*, Vol. I, *Primitive Mythology*, p. 199, citing Ananda K. Coomaraswamy, *The Rg-Veda as Land-náma-bok* (London: Luzac and Company, 1935).

42. See Mircea Eliade, "Dimensions religieuses du renouvellement cosmique," *Eranos-Jahrbuch 1959* (Zurich: Rhein-Verlag, 1960), pp. 241–75, where a full bibliography is given in Footnote 5, p. 245.

43. Brown, *op. cit.*, p. 6, note 8, and p. 9, note 15; also, George A. Dorsey, *The Pawnee: Mythology*, Part I (Washington, D.C.: The Carnegie Institution of Washington, 1906), p. 134.

44. Heinrich Zimmer, *Myths and Symbols in Indian Art and Civilization*, ed. by Joseph Campbell, The Bollingen Series VI (New York: Pantheon Books, 1946), pp. 3–11.

45. See my larger discussion of the points here briefly viewed in *The Masks of God*, Vol. I, *Primitive Mythology*, pp. 30–131.

46. Nora Barlow (ed.), *The Autobiography of Charles Darwin* (London: Collins, 1958), p. 92; as cited by Ernst Benz, "Der dreifache Aspekt des Übermenschen," *Eranos-Jahrbuch 1959*, pp. 147–48.

47. James Joyce, *Finnegans Wake* (New York: The Viking Press, 1939), p. 115.

48. A. R. Radcliffe-Brown, *op. cit.*, pp. 233–34; as cited in *The Masks of God*, Vol. I, *Primitive Mythology*, pp. 33–34, and Vol. IV, *Creative Mythology*, p. 48.

49. John G. Neihardt, *Black Elk Speaks* (Lincoln, Neb.: University of Nebraska Press, 1961), pp. 192–93.

50. *Ibid.*

51. Thomas Mann, *Betrachtungen eines Unpolitischen* (Berlin: S. Fischer Verlag, 1922), p. 227.

52. Neihardt, *op. cit.*, p. 254.

53. Radcliffe-Brown, *op. cit.*, p. 186.

54. *Ibid.*, pp. 176–77.

55. Neihardt, *op. cit.*, pp. 1–2.

56. *Ibid.*, p. 39.

57. *Ibid.*, p. 43, note 8.

58. *Ibid.*, pp. 20–47.

59. *Ibid.*, p. 208.

60. *Ibid.*, p. 49.

V: THE SYMBOL WITHOUT MEANING

1. St. Thomas Aquinas, *Summa Theologica*, Part I, Question 102, Article 1, Reply 3.
2. Bede, *Glossa ordin.*, super Genesis 2:8 (I, 36F).
3. St. Augustine, *De Genesi ad Litt.* VIII, I (PL 34, 371); also *De Civit. Dei* XIII, 21 (PL 41, 395).
4. St. Thomas Aquinas, *Summa Theologica* I, 102, 1.
5. *The Voyages of Christopher Columbus; being the Journals of his First and Third, and the Letters concerning his First and Last Voyages, to which is added the Account of his Second Voyage written by Andreas Bernaldez* (London: The Argonaut Press, 1930), p. 36.
6. *Loc. cit.*
7. J. J. Fahie, *Galileo, His Life and Work* (London: John Murray, 1903), pp. 313 ff.; cited by Bertrand Russell, *The Scientific Outlook* (New York: W. W. Norton and Company, 1931), pp. 24–32.
8. Rudolf Carnap, *Philosophy and Logical Syntax* (London: K. Paul, Trench, Trubner and Co., 1935), pp. 30–31.
9. C. G. Jung, *Psychologische Typen* (Zurich: Rascher and Cie., 1921), pp. 674–85.
10. *Cf.* Ananda K. Coomaraswamy, *The Transformation of Nature in Art*, Chapter V, "Paroksa," p. 129; from which I have adopted this interpretation of the Indian terms, as well as their equation with the terms "sign" and "symbol" of C. G. Jung.
11. D. A. E. Garrod and D. M. A. Bate, *The Stone Age of Mount Carmel* (London: Oxford University Press, 1937).
12. Contrast, for example, James Mellaart, *Çatal Hüyük: A Neolithic Town in Anatolia* (New York: McGraw-Hill Book Company, 1967), pp. 17–26, and the earlier guess by Robert J. Braidwood, *Prehistoric Man* (Chicago: Chicago Natural History Museum Press, 1948, 3rd ed., 1957), p. 113.
13. Kathleen M. Kenyon, *Archaeology in the Holy Land* (New York: Frederick A. Praeger, 1960), p. 46.
14. *Ibid.*, p. 48.
15. James Mellaart, "Hacilar: A Neolithic Village Site," *Scientific American*, Vol. 205, No. 2 (August 1961), p. 90.
16. *Ibid.*, p. 89.
17. Kenyon, *op. cit.*, pp. 51–54.
18. Mellaart, *Çatal Hüyük: A Neolithic Town in Anatolia*, p. 22.
19. *Ibid.*, p. 184, Figure 52.
20. *Ibid.*, p. 124, Figure 37.
21. *The Masks of God*, Vol. II, *Oriental Mythology*, p. 53.
22. Mellaart, *Çatal Hüyük*, Caption to Plate 83.
23. *Ibid.*, Plate 83.
24. *Ibid.*, pp. 82–83, Figures 14, 15.
25. *Ibid.*, pp. 106–107.
26. *Ibid.*, Plate 27.
27. *Ibid.*, Plate 28.
28. *Ibid.*, Caption to Plates 27 and 28.
29. *Ibid.*, pp. 217–18.
30. Mellaart, "Hacilar: A Neolithic Village Site," pp. 94–95.
31. *Ibid.*, p. 92.
32. Kenyon, *op. cit.*, pp. 68–69.
33. *Ibid.*, p. 46.
34. André Leroi-Gourhan, *Les Religions de la préhistoire* (Paris: Presses Universitaires de France, 1964), pp. 84–90.
35. *Ibid.*, p. 103.
36. *Cf.* Abbé H. Breuil, *Four Hundred Centuries of Cave Art* (Montignac, Dordogne: Centre d'Études et de Documentation

Préhistoriques, n.d.), pp. 66, 160–165, 168–75, 154–57, 300–301, 320, 324–25, 389.

37. Henry Fairfield Osborn, *Men of the Old Stone Age* (New York: Charles Scribner's Sons, 3rd ed., 1925), p. 464.

38. For examples of Halaf ware see the beautiful series from "the potter's shop," published by M. E. L. Mallowan and J. Cruikshank Rose, Excavations at Tall Arpachiyah, "Iraq" (British School of Archaeology in Iraq), Vol. II, Part I (1935); and for a summary survey of Samarran motifs, Robert J. and Linda S. Braidwood, Edna Tulane, and Ann L. Perkins, "New Chalcolithic Material of Samarran Type and Its Implications," *Journal of Near Eastern Studies*, Vol. III, No. 1 (January 1944), appendix.

39. Géza Róheim, *Magic and Schizophrenia* (New York: International Universities Press, 1955), pp. 50–51.

40. Cf. Lidio Cipriani, "Excavations in Andamanese Kitchen Middens," *Acts of IVth International Congress of Anthropological and Ethnological Sciences* (Vienna, 1952), Vol. II, pp. 250–53.

41. Cf. Braidwood and Braidwood, Tulane and Perkins, *loc. cit.*

42. Cf. Mallowan and Rose, *loc. cit.*

43. V. Gordon Childe, *New Light on the Most Ancient East* (New York: D. Appleton-Century Company, 1934), p. 160, Fig. 59.

44. Mallowan and Rose, *op. cit.*, pp. 177–78.

45. The first three of these periods are described by Robert J. Braidwood as, respectively, the Era of Incipient Agriculture and Animal Domestication, the Era of Primary Village-Farming Efficiency, and the Era of Peasant Efficiency, with Market-sized Towns and Temples (*cf.* Robert J. and Linda Braidwood, *op. cit.*, pp. 282–87, 287–309, and 288,

note 19). The crisis of transition from Uruk A to Uruk B (Era of Peasant Efficiency, with Market-sized Towns with Temples, to Era of Cosmological Organization of the City State—my "High Neolithic" to "Hieratic State," c. 3200 B.C.) will be found discussed by Speiser, *op. cit.*, pp. 24–31; Childe, *op. cit.*, Chapter VI; and von Heine-Geldern, *op. cit.*, pp. 86–87.

46. In the dating of this diffusion I am following, in the main, von Heine-Geldern, "Theoretical Considerations Concerning the Problem of Pre-Columbian Contacts between the Old and New World," paper read at *Vth International Congress of Anthropological and Ethnological Sciences*, Philadelphia, September 1956, the chief points of which are summarized in the article already cited, "The Origin of Ancient Civilizations," *Diogenes* 13, pp. 81–99. An earlier diffusion across the Pacific of elements of the horticultural complex (*cf. supra*, p. 14, note 2) also is probable: see, for example, Adolf E. Jensen, *Das religiöse Weltbild einer frühen Kultur*, pp. 93–125. For a general discussion of the Asiatic-American cultural continuity, *cf.* Gordon F. Ekholm, "The New Orientation toward Problems of Asiatic-American Relationships," *New Interpretations of Aboriginal American Culture History*, 75th Anniversary Volume of the Anthropological Society of Washington (Washington, D.C., 1955), pp. 95–109.

47. *Timaeus*, 90C–D; translated by Francis MacDonald Cornford, *Plato's Cosmology* (New York: The Humanities Press, 1952), p. 354.

48. Adolf Portmann, "Das Ursprungsproblem," *Eranos-Jahrbuch 1947*, p. 27.

49. D. T. Suzuki, *Essays in Zen Buddhism*, First Series, p. 224.
50. Cf. Sri Krishna Menon, *Atmanirvriti* (Trivandrum: Vedanta Publishers, 1952), p. 18, Par. I.
51. C. G. Jung, *Psychology and Religion* (New Haven, Conn.: Yale University Press, 1938), pp. 105–106.
52. *Ibid.*, p. 99.
53. Paracelsus, *Selected Writings*, ed. by Jolande Jacobi (New York: Pantheon Books, 1951); cited by Giorgio De Santillana, *The Age of Adventure* (New York: George Braziller, Inc., 1956), p. 194.
54. Robert H. Lowie, *Primitive Religion* (New York: Boni and Liveright, 1924), p. 7.
55. Ruth Benedict, *Patterns of Culture* (Boston: Houghton Mifflin Company, 1934), p. 54.
56. Alex D. Krieger, "New World Culture History: Anglo-America," article in A. L. Kroeber (ed.), *Anthropology Today* (Chicago: University of Chicago Press, 1953), p. 251.
57. Opler, *op. cit.*, p. 1.
58. *Ibid.*, pp. 1–18, greatly abridged.
59. *Ibid.*, p. 17.
60. *Rāmāyaṇa* 1.45; 7.1.
61. Opler, *op. cit.*, p. 26.
62. *Vǒluspá*, 45 ff.
63. Aeschylus, *Prometheus Bound*, lines 975–76, 1003–1006; translation by John Stuart Blackie, *The Lyrical Dramas of Aeschylus*, Everyman's Library, No. 62 (New York: E. P. Dutton and Co.; London: J. M. Dent and Son, 1906).
64. Herbert J. Spinden, "First Peopling of America as a Chronological Problem," in George Grant MacCurdy, ed., *Early Man* (Philadelphia and New York: J. B. Lippincott Company, 1937), pp. 106–10. Spinden's rejection of the early dating was based on the evidence then available; for the later view, *cf.*

F. H. H. Roberts, "Earliest Men in America. Their Arrival and Spread in Late Pleistocene and Post Pleistocene Times," *Cahiers d'histoire mondiale*, Vol. I, No. 2, October 1953, pp. 255 ff.
65. N. N. Cheboksarov and T. A. Trofimova, "Antropologicheskoe inzushemie Mansi," *Kratie soobshchenia* II, M.K. 9, as reported by H. Field and E. Prostov, "Results of Soviet Investigations in Siberia," *American Anthropologist*, Vol. 44, 1942, p. 403 n.
66. Franz Hančar, *op. cit.*, pp. 106–121, and Alfred Salmony, "Kunst des Aurignacien in Malta," *Ipek* (Berlin, 1931), pp. 1–6.
67. Mircea Eliade, *Le Chamanisme et les techniques archaïques de l'éxtase* (Paris: Payot, 1951); English translation by Willard R. Trask, *Shamanism: Archaic Techniques of Ecstasy*, The Bollingen Series LXXVI (New York: Pantheon Books, 1964).
68. Uno Holmberg (Harva), *Finno-Ugric, Siberian Mythology*, "The Mythology of All Races" (Boston: Marshall Jones Company, 1927), Vol. IV, p. 499.
69. B. Munkacsi, *Vogul Népköltesi Gyüjtemény*, Vol. III, Budapest, 1893, p. 7; cited by Géza Róheim, *Hungarian and Vogul Mythology* (New York: J. J. Augustin, 1954), p. 22.
70. Munkacsi, *op. cit.*, Vol. II, Part 1, 1910–1921, p. 066; cited by Róheim, *Hungarian and Vogul Mythology*, p. 30.
71. From G. V. Kenofontov, *Legendy i rasskazy o shamanach u. yakutov, buryat i tungusov* (Moscow, 1930), translated by Adolf Friedrich and Georg Buddruss, *Schamanengeschichten aus Sibirien* (Munich: Otto-Wilhelm-Barth-Verlag, 1955), p. 213.
72. Jung, *Psychologische Typen*, p. 675.

73. *Muṇḍaka Upaniṣad*, 2.2.4.

74. *Tao Te Ching*, 1.

75. St. Thomas Aquinas, *Summa contra Gentiles*, Chapter V.

76. *Kena Upaniṣad*, 1.3.

77. Kenofontov, *op. cit.*, German translation of Friedrich and Buddruss, pp. 211–12.

78. *Cf.* W. Schott, "Über den Doppelsinn des Wortes Schamane und über den tungusischen Schamanencultus am Hofe des Mendju-Kaisers," *Abhandlungen der Berliner Akademie der Wissenschaften*, 1842, pp. 461–68. The derivation is rejected for lack of evidence by Professor J. A. MacCulloch (*Encyclopaedia of Religion and Ethics*, ed. James Hastings, Vol. XI, p. 441, article "Shamanism") and the editors of *The Oxford English Dictionary*, Vol. IX, p. 616, but accepted by the editors of *Webster's New International Dictionary of the English Language*, 2nd ed., 1937, article "shaman." The hypothetical derivation is from the Pāli *Samana* (Sanskrit *śramaṇa*) by way of the Chinese *sha mên*.

79. See W. Y. Evans-Wentz, *Tibet's Great Yogi Milarepa* (London: Oxford University Press, 1928).

80. Translation by John Addington Symonds, *The Sonnets of Michael Angelo Buonarroti and Tommaso Campanella* (London: Smith, Elder & Co., 1878), p. 102, Sonnet LXV, "On the Brink of Death" (to Giorgio Vasari, *Giunto è già . . .*).

81. *Vedāntasāra* 17.

82. *Yoga Sūtra* 3.51, Commentary. Translation by James Houghton Woods, *The Yoga-system of Patañjali* (Cambridge, Mass.: Harvard University Press, 1927), pp. 285–86.

83. *Vajracchedika* 32.

84. Arthur Schopenhauer, *Die Welt als Wille und Vorstellung*, Book IV, conclusion.

85. *Māṇḍūkya Upaniṣad* 9–11.

86. *Aṣṭavakra Saṁhitā* 80.

87. *Katha Upaniṣad* 3.12; 5.9 and 12.

88. *Vivekacūḍāmaṇi* 484.

89. Max Knoll, "Wandlungen der Wissenschaft in unserer Zeit," *Eranos-Jahrbuch 1951* (Zurich: Rhein-Verlag, 1952), pp. 387 ff.

90. Aldous Huxley, *The Doors of Perception* (New York: Harper and Brothers, 1954), pp. 53–54.

91. *Paradiso* II, 1 ff.

92. *Ibid.*, XXXIII, conclusion.

93. Robinson Jeffers, "Roan Stallion," in *Roan Stallion, Tamar, and Other Poems* (New York: Horace Liveright, 1925), pp. 19–20.

VI: THE SECULARIZATION OF THE SACRED

1. Swami Nikhilananda (transl.), *The Gospel of Śri Ramakrishna* (New York: Ramakrishna-Vivekananda Center, 1942), p. 396.

2. *Ibid.*, p. 487.

3. *Tao Te Ching* 6.

4. *Bṛhadāraṇyaka Upaniṣad* 1.4.6.

5. Genesis 3:22–24.

6. James Joyce, *Ulysses* (Paris: Shakespeare and Company, 9th printing, 1927), p. 396 (New York: Random House, 1934), p. 409.

7. *Chāndogya Upaniṣad*, 6.9.4.

8. Erwin Schrödinger, *My View of the World*, translation by Cecily Hastings (Cambridge: Cambridge University Press, 1964), p. 31.

9. *Ibid.*, pp. 21–22.

10. *Bṛhadāraṇyaka Upaniṣad*, 4.1.7.

11. Samuel A. B. Mercer, *The Pyramid Texts* (New York: Longmans, Green and Co., 1952), Vol. I, pp. 93–94. Text 404.

12. *Ibid.*, p. 95, Text 413.

13. Translation from E. A. W.

Budge, *The Papyrus of Ani,* as reprinted in Charles F. Horne (ed.), *The Sacred Books and Early Literature of the East* (New York and London: Parlee Austin, and Lipscomb, 1917), Vol. II, pp. 190–91 and 196–97: Chapters of "Abolishing the Slaughterings" and "On Coming Forth by Day in the Underworld."

14. These three cuts of seals are from W. H. Ward, *The Seal Cylinders of Western Asia,* Publication No. 100 (Washington, D.C., Carnegie Institution of Washington, 1910), respectively, Figures 302, 389, and 388.

15. Compagno Tablet (c. 4th or 3rd century B.C.), translation by Jane Harrison, *Prolegomena to the Study of Greek Religion* (Cambridge: Cambridge University Press, 3rd ed., 1922), p. 585.

16. Lucius Apuleius, *The Golden Ass,* translation by W. Adlington (1566), Modern Library edition (1928), p. 294.

17. Translation from Alfred Nutt, *The Voyage of Bran, The Celtic Doctrine of Rebirth,* Grimm Library No. 4 (London: David Nutt, 1897), Vol. II, pp. 91–92.

18. *Aṣṭavakrasaṁhitā* 18:38. Translation by Swami Nityaswarupananda (Mayavati: Advaita Ashrama, 1940), p. 175.

19. "101 Zen Stories," No. 28; from Paul Reps, *Zen Flesh, Zen Bones* (New York: Doubleday and Co., Anchor Books, 1961), p. 30.

20. From Daisetz Teitaro Suzuki, *The Zen Doctrine of No-Mind* (London: Rider and Company, 1949), pp. 90–91.

21. Nikhilananda, *op. cit.,* p. 593.

22. Plato, *Symposium* 210 b; translation by Michael Joyce in Edith Hamilton and Huntington Cairns (eds.), *The Collected Dialogues of Plato,* The Bollingen Series LXXI (New York: Pantheon Books, 1961), pp. 561–62.

23. Franz Pfeiffer (ed.), *Meister Eckhart,* translation by C. de. B. Evans (London: John M. Watson, 1947), Vol. I, "Sermons and Collations," No. LXXXVIII, p. 221.

24. *Ibid.,* No. II, p. 10.

25. The entire story is well retold by Henry Osborn Taylor, *The Mediaeval Mind* (Cambridge, Mass.: Harvard University Press, 4th ed., 1925), Vol. II, pp. 29–54. The source texts are in Migne, PL clxxviii.

26. Gottfried von Strassburg, *Tristan und Isold,* ed. by Friedrich Ranke (Berlin: Weidmannsche Verlagsbuchhandlung, 1959), p. 157, lines 12499–12502.

27. James Joyce, *A Portrait of the Artist as a Young Man,* p. 247.

28. Giraut de Borneil, *Tam cum los oills el cor ama parvenza. . . .* See John Rutherford, *The Troubadours* (London: Smith, Elder, and Co., 1873), p. 34.

29. Ananda K. Coomaraswamy, *The Dance of Shiva* (New York: The Sunwise Turn, 1918), p. 103.

30. Shashibhusan Dasgupta, *Obscure Religious Cults as Background of Bengali Literature* (Calcutta: University of Calcutta, 1946), p. 145.

31. Epiphanius, *Panarion* 26.4.1; cited in *The Masks of God,* Vol. IV, *Creative Mythology,* Chapter 3, Section V, "The Gnostics."

32. Denis de Rougemont, *Love in the Western World,* translation by Montgomery Belgion (New York: Pantheon Books, revised and augmented edition, 1956).

33. Dasgupta, *op. cit.,* p. 144.

34. An abridged rendition of Jayadeva's poem will be found in *The Masks of God,* Vol. II, *Oriental Mythology,* pp. 352–58. I am not aware of any adequate translation into English.

35. Coomaraswamy, *The Dance of Shiva,* p. 103.

36. St. Augustine, *Natali Domini* IV, *Sermo suppositus* 120:8. Translation from Marie-Louise von Franz, *Aurora Consurgens*, The Bollingen Series LXXVII (New York: Pantheon Books, 1966), p. 428.

37. Bernard of Clairvaux, *Sermones in Canta Canticorum* XX.6. Translation by Terence L. Connolly, S.J., *Saint Bernard on the Love of God* (New York: Spiritual Book Associates, 1937), p. 113.

38. *Ibid.*, IX. 2, in Connolly, *op. cit.*, pp. 82–83.

39. *Ibid.*, XXXII. 2, in Connolly, *op. cit.*, p. 141.

40. Canticles 7:1–2. Revised Standard Version (New York: Thomas Nelson and Sons, 1953).

41. Gottfried, *op. cit.*, 12029–12037 (Ranke edition, p. 151).

42. See the elegant study of this problem in Gottfried Weber's two-volume work, *Gottfrieds von Strassburg Tristan und die Krise des hochmittelalterlichen Weltbildes um 1200* (Stuttgart: J. B. Metzlersche Verlagsbuchhandlung, 1953).

43. Gottfried, *op. cit.*, lines 17136–17138 (Ranke edition, p. 215).

44. *Ibid.*, lines 15733–15740 (Ranke edition, p. 197).

45. *Ibid.*, lines 235–240 (Ranke edition, p. 3).

46. *Ibid.*, line 16700 (Ranke edition, p. 209).

47. See William A. Nitze, "Perceval and the Holy Grail," *University of California Publications in Modern Philology*, Vol. 28, No. 5 (1949), p. 282.

48. Chrétien de Troyes, *Perceval* (*Li Contes del Graal*), ed. by A. Hilke (Halle: Max Niemeyer, 1932), lines 63 ff.

49. For the Old French text, see Albert Pauphilet (ed.), *La Queste del Saint Graal* (Paris: Édouard Champion, 1949). Malory, *Le Morte Darthur*, renders an English translation in Books XIII–XVIII. An excellent analysis and exposition will be found in Frederick W. Locke, *The Quest for the Holy Grail* (Stanford: Stanford University Press, 1960).

50. See Roger Sherman Loomis, *The Grail, from Celtic Myth to Christian Symbol* (New York: Columbia University Press, 1963).

51. See Hans Leisegang, "The Mystery of the Serpent," in Joseph Campbell (ed.), *The Mysteries*, The Bollingen Series XXX, Vol. 2 (New York: Pantheon Books, 1955), pp. 194–260, and Campbell, *The Masks of God*, Vol. IV, *Creative Mythology*, Chapters VII and VIII.

52. *Artis Auriferae* (Basel, 1593), Vol. I, p. 210; as cited by C. G. Jung, *Psychology and Alchemy*, The Bollingen Series XX, Vol. 12 (New York: Pantheon Books, 1953), p. 171, note 117.

53. *La Queste del Saint Graal*, ed. by Pauphilet, *op. cit.*, p. 26, lines 7–19.

54. Pindar, Pythian Ode VIII, lines 92–97: for Aristomenes of Aegina, winner of the wrestling match, 446 B.C. Translation by Sir John Sandys *The Odes of Pindar*, Loeb Classical Library (London: William Heinemann, Ltd.; Cambridge, Mass.: Harvard University Press, 1915).

55. William Blake, *The Marriage of Heaven and Hell* (1793): "A Memorable Fancy," and "Proverbs of Hell."

56. Jean Paul Sartre, *Existentialism*, translation by Walter Kaufman, *Existentialism from Dostoyevski to Sartre* (New York: Meridian Books, 1957), p. 295.

Index

Aarne, Antti, 20, 28
Abelard, 208-209
Abraham, 118
acculturation, 102-103
Achim von Arnim, Ludwig, 11, 13, 14
Actaeon, 79
Adams, Henry, 208
Adelard of Bath, 225
adhidaivata, 127, 169
Aeschylus, 73, 164, 223
Aesop, 19
agapē, 209-22
Akhnaton, 50
Alan de Lille, 80
Albigensians, 208, 211
alchemy, 86-87, 218
al-Ghazali, 33
Algic Researches (Schoolcraft), 95
Allah, 73, 198
Amairgen, 201
American Anthropological Society, 46
American Revolution, 191
amor, 209-22
Anatolian plain, 132-38, 148
Andaman Islands, pigmies of, 109, 112, 144-45
anecdote, 19
Anthropology Today (Kroeber, ed.), 61
anthropomorphism, 25
Apuleius, Lucius, 201
Aquinas, St. Thomas, 33, 120, 170
Arabian Nights, see *Thousand Nights and One Night*
archaic civilizations, mythic forms of, 129-55; Proto-Neolithic stage (from c. 9000 B.C.), 130-31; Basal

Neolithic stage (c. 7500-4500 B.C.), 131-38; High Neolithic stage (c. 4500-3500 B.C.), 138-50; Hieratic City State stage (c. 3500-2500 B.C.), 150-55
Arthurian romance, 21; *see also* Grail legend; Tristan romance
Assumption of the Blessed Virgin Mary, 124
asuras, 174
Aucassin et Nicolette, 18
Augustine, Saint, 33, 120, 125, 207, 212, 219
AUM, 169, 177, 180; *see also* OM
Aurignacian caves, 55, 58
Australia, hunting peoples of, 142-144
avidyā, 67, 187

Babylonian astrological mythology, 33 *n.*
Babylonian seal, 199-200
Back to Methuselah (Shaw), 54
ballads, folk, 18-19, 26
baptism, 56, 221
bardic lays, 18
Basal Neolithic stage of archaic civilizations, 132-38; Aceramic Neolithic, substage 1 (from c. 7500 B.C.), 132-34; Ceramic Neolithic, substage 2 (from c. 6500 B.C.), 134-37; Early Chalcolithic, substage 3 (from c. 5500 B.C.), 137-38
Bastian, Adolf, 44, 47, 49, 81
Bede, Venerable, 120
Before Philosophy (Jacobsen, *et al.*), 152 *n.*
Benedict, Ruth, 158